PENGUIN ENGLISH LIBRARY

HOME AT GRASMERE

PACIFIC UNIVERSITY LIBRARY
FOREST GROVE, OREGON

Pacific
WITHDRAWN
University

D0036567

PR
5849
.A84
1978

HOME AT GRASMERE

*

Extracts from the Journal of
DOROTHY WORDSWORTH
(written between 1800 and 1803)
and from the Poems of
WILLIAM WORDSWORTH

*

EDITED BY
COLETTE CLARK

PACIFIC UNIVERSITY LIBRARY
FOREST GROVE, OREGON

Pacific
WITHDRAWN
University

PENGUIN BOOKS

Penguin Books Ltd, Harmondsworth, Middlesex, England
Penguin Books, 625 Madison Avenue, New York, New York 10022, U.S.A.
Penguin Books Australia Ltd, Ringwood, Victoria, Australia
Penguin Books Canada Ltd, 2801 John Street, Markham, Ontario, Canada L3R 1B4
Penguin Books (N.Z.) Ltd, 182–190 Wairau Road, Auckland 10, New Zealand

—

First published in Pelican Books 1960
Reissued in Penguin English Library 1978

—

Introduction and editorial material copyright © Colette Clark, 1960
All rights reserved

—

Made and printed in Great Britain
by C. Nicholls & Company Ltd, The Philips Park Press,
Manchester M11 4AU
Set in Linotype Juliana

Except in the United States of America,
this book is sold subject to the condition
that it shall not, by way of trade or otherwise,
be lent, re-sold, hired out, or otherwise circulated
without the publisher's prior consent in any form of
binding or cover other than that in which it is
published and without a similar condition
including this condition being imposed
on the subsequent purchaser

CONTENTS

To my Father

PREFACE

This little book makes no claim whatever to be a work of scholarship or original research. Any scholarship it contains I owe entirely to Mr Ernest de Selincourt and Miss Helen Darbishire. Their edition of Wordsworth's poetry published by the Oxford University Press in five volumes between 1940 and 1952 has been so exhaustively and imaginatively carried out that, for the time being at least, all further research on the subject would be quite fruitless. It was de Selincourt who first published the complete version of the Journals from the original manuscripts, and his two-volume edition printed by Macmillan in 1941 is again the most comprehensive we are likely to obtain. It is these two texts of the poems and Journal together with their notes and data which I am using here to form the basis of my book. I cannot hope to add anything to the deep learning they contain. I can only acknowledge my debt to Mr de Selincourt and Miss Darbishire and hope they would not disapprove of the use I have made of their work.

The only value of this book lies in its arrangement and presentation. So often the poetry, letters, and writings which surround a poet and his work are kept apart and the link between them is ignored. The ordinary reader of Wordsworth may hardly realize that not only the inspiration but even the source of much of his best poetry is so close at hand. De Selincourt, of course, never lost sight of this for a moment and is constantly referring from one Wordsworth to the other. But there is so much to be learnt from this relationship that I wanted to present his work in a more accessible form. I have even tried to carry it a stage further. By placing William's poems in the middle of Dorothy's Journal beside the very day on which they were written, I hope to make the unity between them more vivid and more credible to the general reader.

This is a purely personal selection from both the Journal and the Poems. I have tried to cut no more of the Journal than was strictly necessary in the interests of space and have included all poems written at the time. But with the poems to which Dorothy only refers or from which she quotes a single line, I have been more arbitrary. Some are printed in their entirety, but others such as 'Peter Bell', 'The Idiot Boy', or the 'The Old Cumberland Beggar' I thought too long or too remote from life at Grasmere and omitted altogether. So much is Grasmere the theme of the book that at one time I thought of ending with that lovely last day before they set off for France; but the opportunity to put in the sonnets was too tempting to be missed.

I have assumed some biographical knowledge of the period on the part of the reader. My comments and notes are only to underline all that the Journal gradually reveals of the unique 'oneness' of the Wordsworths in their writings and in their lives.

Finally I would like to acknowledge the enormous debt I owe to my father who first suggested the idea to me, and to Sir William Emrys Williams without whose constant encouragement the book would never have been finished.

INTRODUCTION

Dorothy Wordsworth was one of those sweet characters whose only life lies in their complete dedication to a man of genius. Without self-consciousness or self-congratulation she absorbed herself in her brother's life and work and starts the Journal 'because I shall give William pleasure by it'. This was the only way in which she could fulfil herself, and through it she became an artist in her own right. She is to us, as she was to William, 'a breath of fragrance independent of the wind'. From the austerity of her brother and the uncertainty of Coleridge we turn to the Journal, as they did, for her unfailing delight in the world around her. We too are refreshed by her sensitive eye and lively spontaneous style and come to realize why Wordsworth depended on her to preserve his own freshness of vision and daily contact with Nature. This interdependence of brother and sister was something that each valued more than anything else in their lives. It shines through such poems as 'The Glow-worm' or 'To a Butterfly', and every page of the Journal reflects it. It is the very essence of both.

All Wordsworthian scholars have, of course, studied Dorothy's Journal and used it as a commentary and guide to his works. Many of the poet's admirers enjoy it for its own sake and even the general reader is acquainted with certain passages such as the first sight of the daffodils or the description of the leech-gatherer. But there is still more to discover from Dorothy and her Journals. At first, perhaps, they are a little disillusioning. They contain no intimate glimpses of Wordsworth and Coleridge about the house, no reports of their literary discussions through the night. Dorothy never records a single conversation verbatim and only here and there jots down a remark her brother has made. Readers may be disappointed that she says so little of William's immediate responses to nature. She herself notes down the sights they have enjoyed and describes them minutely, but of William's reaction she says no more than that he is writing a poem on the subject. Above all, anyone who expects startling revelations of emotion will be put to shame. Dorothy gives no account of her feelings towards Coleridge, nor of his to her. She says nothing of William's sentiments over his marriage or of his love for his future wife. During this, the greatest emotional crisis of her life, she records only that it happened. Yet the elusive phrases, the broken asides which are found throughout the Journal, become more poignant in isolation. At moments they seem almost to be torn from her against her will, and they tell us all we need know of the deep emotional undercurrent beneath the surface of the book.

It is essential to remember the harmony of spirit which existed between the Wordsworths when we begin to question the source of their inspiration. Was it Dorothy or William who first spoke the phrases which seem so spontaneous in the Journal and then reappear in the poems? Sometimes we know it to be Dorothy. It was she who first saw the tall beggar woman and the two wild little boys in their flower-decked hats and set down the story in detail for William's pleasure. When two years later he came to write the poem, the poor man found he could not stop himself using her very words. Such a lively chronicle close at hand would have been irresistible to any poet, and William seems to have used it again and again. It was not until two years after that heavenly walk from Eusemere that he wrote 'The Daffodils', but there is no doubt that he first re-read Dorothy's account and tried to recapture the joy and delight of her description in his own poem. Even when he wrote a poem on the spot like 'Lines written in March' he was certainly aware of how much he owed to his sister's rapturous observation of the scene. But in most cases the problem of whose was the original invention remains unsolved. An example of this is Wordsworth's sonnet 'Composed after a Journey across the Hambleton Hills'. He had clearly watched the scene it describes with the same eyes as Dorothy and transformed it in the same spirit, but which piece was written first? In this case the vision seems Dorothy's while the moralizing at the end 'they are of the sky and from our earthly memory fade away' is typically William. Perhaps for once he did write his poem *ex tempore* (though Dorothy never mentions him doing so) and she only wrote up her Journal a day or two later. But once our speculations reach this stage we can only think of them as a game or literary exercise.

It was not only for her powers of descriptive detail, however, that Wordsworth valued Dorothy. It was, as he says in passages too well known to need repeating here, for her whole self. She had that boundless child-like delight in nature which the poet treasured above everything else. Every evening she walks out to see the failing light over Rydale and Grasmere and each time finds it more beautiful. She never wearies of describing the scene.

October 19th, 1800. Rydale was very very beautiful. The surface of the water quite still, like a dim mirror. The colours of the large island exquisitely beautiful, and the trees still fresh and green were magnified by the mists.

October 20th, 1800. The lights were very grand upon the woody Rydale hills. The two lakes divinely beautiful. Grasmere excessively solemn and the whole lake was calm and dappled with soft grey ripples.

October 24th, 1800. After dinner we walked round Rydale lake, rich calm, streaked, very beautiful.

She happily goes for the same walks every day, along their favourite path past John's Grove, over White Moss Common or up to Easedale Tarn. And as she leans over Sara's Gate, she is always enchanted by the view.

December 26th, 1801. Grasmere Lake a beautiful image of stillness, clear as glass, reflecting all things, the wind up and the waters sounding. The lake of a rich purple, the fields a soft yellow, the island yellowish-green, the copses red-brown, the mountains purple. The Church and buildings how quiet they were.

Another evening when William was away she finds consolation in her beloved vale.

Grasmere was very solemn in the last glimpse of twilight; it calls home the heart to quietness.

It would be a mistake to think of all this as a sentimental paradise where it was easy to find peace of heart. As a way of life it was lonely, remote, and intense beyond what most people can bear. Scarcely a day goes past wthout either Dorothy or William

11

complaining of feeling unwell. They suffer from the headaches, bad nights, and all the other complaints which seem to be an inseparable part of the creative life, and Dorothy never fails to record them. Only one thing gives her as much concern, and that is the troubles and disorders of their friend Coleridge. Coleridge emerges from the Journal as a shadowy and melancholy figure. Though he and Dorothy correspond daily, she says nothing of the cause of his unhappiness or of his love for Sara Hutchinson. She only records each evening 'A heart-rending letter from Coleridge – we were as sad as we could be', or another time, 'It was a sad melancholy letter and prevented us all from sleeping'. In the end his constant complaints of ill-health and depression grow a little wearisome. We begin to dread the arrival of his letters and resent their depressing effect on poor Dorothy. Once or twice, however, a glimpse of his personality filters through, and we are rewarded. He finds a bower among the rocks or dams a stream or reads poems on the water and lets the boat take its own course, and has a magical effect on them all.

William and C. read and repeated verses. I drank a little brandy and water and was in heaven.

Strangely enough whenever he visits them with his family or they go over to Keswick Hall, the Journal breaks off abruptly. Whether because Dorothy is then too busy to write or because it would not interest William is not made clear, but for whatever reason intimate details of Coleridge's life and household never make an appearance.

Of the literary circles of the time there is little to be learnt from the Journal. Dorothy seldom mentions the works of her contemporaries, although she does once comment on a play by Charles Lamb. Coleridge is the only poet whose work is discussed, and then she says no more than 'Exceedingly delighted with the second part of Christobel'. But we are always told what books they are reading and these make an absorbing study. Many of them were 'Lives', and the works of poets which have long been forgotten. They had more taste for the Elizabethans than we today, and both adored Ben Jonson. We find them reading unlikely plays of Shakespeare, such as *The Winter's Tale* and *Henry V* as well as *A Midsummer Night's Dream* and *As You Like It*. But

12

more interesting still are the references to poets William admires when they coincide with new phases in his own work. Scholars use the Journal to help trace these developments in his style, but even the lay reader will find it a rich source for discoveries. The poem 'A Farewell', for instance, which he wrote before going to Mary has always been considered one of his most Spenserian. The Journal shows that he was indeed absorbed in Spenser at the time and had been reading the exquisite 'Prothalamium' a short while before he began composition. It was his reading of Chaucer with his sister which fired him to translate the *Canterbury Tales* in the winter of 1801. In the following months when he was working on 'The Pedlar' Dorothy would read to him from *Paradise Lost*.

After tea I read aloud the eleventh book of Paradise Lost. We were much impressed and also melted into tears.

In 1802 another significant line appears in the Journal.

William wrote 2 sonnets on Buonaparte, after I had read Milton's sonnets to him.

These were the first of the great sonnets which Wordsworth was to compose with such ease and profusion at the end of the period.

In this Grasmere life the two Hutchinson sisters play a large part. William and Dorothy wrote to them every day, and at different times they both visited Dove Cottage. Dorothy is constantly referring to them, and always in the tenderest terms. They shared her passionate love for the flowers and mosses they used to find on their walks, her fear of cows, and her patience with William. On a particularly heavenly walk, she and Coleridge would often wish for Mary and Sara, and when they come to stay they are immediately led off by Dorothy to visit her favourite new sight. Yet neither of them ever really comes to life. Mary was more than a friend – she was to become William's wife, but the strange lack of emotion which surrounds the sisters persists in her relationship with him. On the day of their marriage, Dorothy almost breaks down. But as soon as they are back on the road to Grasmere, Mary retreats into the background once again. Throughout the journey home William and Dorothy only reminisced on the other happy times when they had gone along that way. They look out for the familiar landmarks and revisit the remembered sights. On one occasion Dorothy cannot prevent a note of anguish from creeping in.

> When we passed through the village of Wensley my heart was melted away with dear recollections – the bridge, the little water-spout, the steep hill, the church ... for they were the first objects that I saw after we were left to ourselves and had turned our whole hearts to Grasmere ...

Twice they set off exploring and leave Mary behind, and one evening when the carriage breaks down it is on Dorothy's breast that William falls asleep. Altogether a strange bridal home-coming following the most pathetic of weddings. Yet it is hard to say which of the two ladies is to be pitied most. We know that Dorothy first heard of William's engagement on 12 April 1802 when 'every question was like the snapping of a little thread about my heart'. But de Selincourt has pointed out that at that very hour William was riding home from Middleham and writing 'Among all lovely things my love had been'. How it must have consoled Dorothy, he says, that at such a time he should have composed for her alone one of his most affectionate and lovely poems. A comfort to Dorothy perhaps, but we cannot help feeling a pang of sympathy for Mary.

We can truly say that the Journal would be an enchanting and valuable book even supposing Wordsworth had been a bad poet. Dorothy never thought of it like this, of course, and was sadly conscious of shortcomings as a writer. One evening after a part-icularly lonely walk among the hills and stars of Grasmere, she cried out 'It made me more than half a poet', and when she arrived home she 'tried to write verses, but alas!' Was she not aware of the beauty and vividness of her own description of the scene which comes over to us today as fresh and alive as it was the night she wrote it? Yet she is more to us than just a fine writer of natural description. Nor is it only for her prose that we enjoy her. She takes the liveliest interest in all the neighbouring char-acters and listens with relish to the stories of her servant Molly. When she visits Mrs Clarkson at Eusemere she is delighted to find she shares her love of odd local gossip and sets down all she can remember. She is equally fascinated by the endless stream of beggars which pass the house or whom she meets out walking. She asks their history and describes them in extraordinarily vivid detail. The strange tales she records give us a good idea of the poverty and hardship of the time. Nothing is too trivial for Dorothy's attention.

I found a strawberry flower in a rock. I uprooted it rashly and I felt as if I had been committing an outrage, so I planted it again. It will have but a stormy life of it, but let it live if it can.

Her love of wild flowers lights up every page of the Journal. Even on the coldest days she finds one to console her.

We stopped to look at the stone seat at the top of the hill. There was a white cushion upon it, round at the edge like a cushion, and the rock behind looked soft as velvet, of a vivid green, and so tempting! The snow too looked as soft as a down cushion. A young foxglove like a star, in the centre.

Her human sympathy and love of natural beauty are boundless, but it is revealing to see how she breaks down over man-made works of art. When she visits Rievaulx Abbey on her way to France, it is of 'the grovelets of wild roses and other shrubs' that she writes. And on reaching Canterbury, 'the City and Cathedral disappointed me'.

But although we may delight in the Journal without William, for Dorothy it would have been empty; her love for him was its dynamo. Once he is married she never quite regains the rapturous spirit of their first two years alone at Grasmere. At first she tries to keep up her writing in the old enthusiastic way. But quite soon the entries start to dwindle, and often she only records the day, or makes desperate resolutions not to neglect her Journal. The rare beautiful passages which we still find, have a melancholy character which seems to reflect her mood.

It is a breathless, grey day, that leaves the golden woods of autumn quiet in their own tranquillity, stately and beautiful in their decaying.

Finally on a particularly cold January day, the Journal breaks off altogether. It is not, of course, the last she writes, but there is nothing else which contains quite the same degree of intimacy and freedom. We are privileged to read what was only set down for a beloved brother to see, but perhaps we can feel a little more justified if we use her impressions as he did. They inspired and guided Wordsworth as a poet; by returning his poetry back to this source, we perhaps fulfil Dorothy's original purpose, and come a little nearer to the heart of life at Grasmere.

ARRIVAL AT GRASMERE

Extracts from William Wordsworth's letter to Samuel Taylor Coleridge describing the journey to Grasmere.

Christmas Eve, Grasmere, 1799

My dearest Coleridge,

We arrived here last Friday, and have now been four days in our new abode without writing to you, a long time! but we have been in such confusion as not to have had a moment's leisure.

I arrived at Sockburn the day after you quitted it, I scarcely knew whether to be sorry or no that you were no longer there, as it would have been a great pain to me to have parted from you. I was sadly disappointed in not finding Dorothy; Mary was a solitary house-keeper and overjoyed to see me. D is now sitting by me racked with the tooth-ache. This is a grievous misfortune as she has so much work for her needle among the bedcurtains, etc. that she is absolutely buried in it. We have both caught troublesome colds in our new and almost empty house, but we hope to make it a comfortable dwelling. Our first two days were days of fear as one of the rooms upstairs smoked like a furnace, we have since learned that it is uninhabitable as a sitting room on this account; the other room however which is fortunately the one we intended for our *living* room promises uncommonly well; that is, the chimney draws perfectly, and does not even smoke at the first lighting of the fire. In particular winds most likely we shall have *puffs* of *inconvenience*, but this I believe will be found a curable evil, by means of devils as they are called and other beneficent agents which we shall station at the top of the chimney if their services should be required. D is much pleased with the house and *appurtenances*, the orchard especially; in imagination she has already built a seat with a summer shed on the highest platform in this our little domestic slip of mountain. The spot commands a view over the roof of our house, of the lake, the church, helm cragg, and two thirds of the vale. We mean also to enclose the two or three yards of ground between us and the road, this for the sake of a few flowers, and because it will make it more our own. Besides, am I fanciful when I would extend the obligation of gratitude to insensate things? May not a man have a salutary pleasure in doing something gratuitously for the sake of his house, as for an individual to which he owes so much – The manners of the neighbouring cottagers have far exceeded our expectations; they seem little adulterated; indeed as far as we have seen not at all. The people we have uniformly found kindhearted frank and manly, prompt to serve without servility. This is but an experience of four days, but we have had dealings with persons of various occupations, and have had no reason whatever to complain. We do not think it will be necessary for us to keep a servant. We have agreed to give a woman, who lives in one of the adjoining cottages two shillings a week for attending two or three hours a day to light the fires wash dishes, etc., etc. In addition to this she is to have her victuals likewise on other days if we should have visitors and she is wanted more than usual. We could have had this attendance for eighteen pence a week but we added the sixpence for the sake of the poor woman, who is made happy by it. The weather since our arrival has been a keen frost, one morning two thirds of the lake was covered with ice continued all the day but, to our great surprize, the next morning, though there was no intermission of the frost, had entirely disappeared. The ice had been so thin that the wind had broken it up, and most likely driven it to the outlet of the lake. Rydale is covered with ice, clear as polished steel, I have procured a pair of skates and to-morrow mean to give my body to the wind, – not however without reasonable caution. We are looking for John every day; it will be a pity, if he should come, that D is so much engaged, she has scarcely been out since our arrival; one evening I tempted her forth; the planet Jupiter was on the top of the hugest of the Rydale mountains, but I had reason to repent for having seduced her from her work as she returned with a raging tooth-ache. – We were highly pleased with your last short letter, which we had confidently and eagerly expected at Sockburn. Stuart's conduct is liberal and I hope it will answer for him. You make no mention of your health. I was uneasy on that account when you were with us; upon recollection it seemed to me that the fatigues, accidents, and exposures attendant upon our journey, took greater hold of you than they ought to have done had your habit of body been such as not to render caution necessary for it. You do not speak of your travelling conversations, I shall probably be able to send it to you. I am afraid it will have one fault, that of being too long. – As to the Tragedy and Peter Bell, D will do all in her power to put them forward. Composition I find invariably pernicious to me, and even penmanship if continued for any length of time at one sitting. I shall therefore wish you good night, my beloved friend, a wish, with a thousand others, in which D joins me. I am afraid half of what I have written is illegible, farewell.

Friday Evg: We have been overhead in confusion, painting the rooms, mending the doors, and heaven knows what! This however shall not prevent me from attempting to give you some account of our journey hither. We left Sockburne tuesday before last early in the morning, D on a double horse, behind that good creature George, and I upon Lilly, or Violet as Cottle calls her. We cross'd the Tees in the Sockburn fields by moonlight. George accompanied us eight miles beyond Richmond and there we parted with sorrowful hearts. We were now in Wensley dale and D and I set off side by side to foot it as far as Kendal. A little before sunset we reached one of the waterfalls of which I read you a short description in Mr Taylor's tour. I meant to have attempted to give you a picture of it but I feel myself too lazy to execute the task. Tis a singular scene; such a performance as you might have expected from some giant gardiner employed by one of Queen Elizabeth's Courtiers, if this same giant gardiner had consulted with Spenser and they two had finish'd the work together. By this you will understand that with something of vastness or grandeur it is at once formal and wild. We reach'd the town of Askrigg, 12 miles, about six in the evening, having walked the last three miles in the dark and two of them over hardfrozen road to the great annoyance of our feet and ancles. Next morning the earth was thinly covered with snow, enough to make the road soft and prevent its being slippery. On leaving Askrigg we turned aside to see another waterfall – 'twas a beautiful morning with driving snow showers that disappeared by fits, and unveiled the east which was all one delicious pale mill which we passed and in a moment a sweet little valley opened before us, with an area of grassy ground, and a stream dashing over various lamina of black rocks close under a bank covered with firs. The bank and stream on our left, another woody bank on our right, and the flat meadow in front, from which, as at Buttermere, the stream had retired as it were to hide itself under the shade. As we walked up this delightful valley we were tempted to look back perpetually on the brook which reflected the orange light of the morning among the gloomy rocks with a brightness varying according to the agitation of the current. The steeple of Askrigg was between us and the east, at the bottom of the valley; it was not a quarter of a mile distant, but oh! how far we were from it. The two banks seemed to join before us with a facing of rock common to them both, when we reached this point the valley opened out again, two rocky banks on each side, which, hung with ivy and moss and fringed luxuriantly with brushwood, ran directly parallel to each other and then approaching with a gentle curve, at their point of union presented a lofty waterfall, the termination of the valley. Twas a keen frosty morning, showers of snow threatening us but the sun bright and active; we had a task of twenty one miles to perform in a short winter's day, all this put our minds in such a state of excitation that we were no unworthy spectators of this delightful scene. On a nearer approach the water seemed to fall down a tall arch or rather nitch which had shaped itself by insensible moulderings in the wall of an old castle. We left this spot with reluctance but highly exhilarated. When we had walked about a mile and a half we overtook two men with a string of ponies and some empty carts. I recommended to D to avail herself of this opportunity of husbanding her strength, we rode with them more than two miles, twas bitter cold, the wind driving the snow behind us in the best stile of a mountain storm. We soon reached an Inn at a place called Hardaw, and descending from our vehicles, after warming ourselves by the cottage fire we walked up the brook side to take a view of a third waterfall. We had not gone a few hundred yards between two winding rocky banks before we came full upon it. It appeared to throw itself in a narrow line from a lofty wall of rock; the water which shot manifestly to some distance from the rock seeming from the extreme height of the fall to be dispersed before it reached the bason, into a thin shower of snow that was toss'd about like snow blown from the roof of a house. We were disappointed in the cascade though the introductory and accompanying banks were a noble mixture of grandeur and beauty. We walked up to the fall and what would I not give if I could convey to you the images and feelings which were then communicated to me. After cautiously sounding our way over stones of all colours and sizes encased in the clearest ice formed by the spray of the waterfall, we found the rock which before had seemed a perpendicular wall extending itself over us like the ceiling of a huge cave; from the summit of which water shot directly over our heads into a bason and more fragments of rocks wrinkled over with masses of ice, white as snow, or rather as D says like congealed froth. The water fell at least ten yards from us and we stood directly behind it, the excavation not so deep in the rock as to impress any feelings of darkness, but lofty and magnificent and, in connection with the adjoining banks excluding as much of the sky as could well be spared from a scene so exquisitely beautiful. The spot where we stood was as dry as the chamber in which I am now sitting, and the incumbent rock of which the groundwork was limestone veined and dappled with colours which melted into each other in every possible variety. On the summit of the cave were three festoons or rather wrinkles in the rock which ran parallel to each other like the folds of a curtain when it is drawn up; each of them was hung with icicles of various length, and nearly in the middle of the festoons in the deepest valley made by their waiving line the stream shot from between the rows of icicles in irregular fits of strength and with a body of water that momently varied. Sometimes it threw itself into the bason in one continued curve, sometimes it was interrupted almost midway in its fall and, being blown towards us, part of the water fell at no great distance from our feet like the heaviest thunder shower. In such a situation you have at every moment a feeling of the presence of

21

the sky. Above the highest point of the waterfall large fleecy clouds drove over our heads and the sky appeared of a blue more than usually brilliant. The rocks on each side, which, joining with the sides of the cave, formed the vista of the brook were checquered with three diminutive waterfalls or rather veins of water each of which was a miniature of all that summer and winter can produce of a delicate beauty. The rock in the centre of these falls where the water was most abundant, deep black, the adjoining parts yellow white purple violet and dove-coloured; or covered with water-plants of the most vivid green, and hung with streams and fountains of ice and icicles that in some places seemed to conceal the verdure of the plants and the variegated colours of the rocks and in some places to render their hues more splendid. I cannot express to you the enchanted effect produced by this Arabian scene of colour as the wind blew aside the great waterfall behind which we stood and hid and revealed each of these faery cataracts in irregular succession or displayed them with various gradations of distinctness, as the intervening spray was thickened or dispersed. – In the luxury of our imaginations we could not help feeding on the pleasure which in the heat of a July noon this cavern would spread through a frame exquisitely sensible. That huge rock of ivy on the right, the bank winding round on the left with all its living foliage, and the breeze stealing up the valley and bedewing the cavern with the faintest imaginable spray. And then the murmur of the water, the quiet, the seclusions, and a long summer day to dream in! – Have I not tired you? With difficulty we tore ourselves away, and on returning to the cottage we found we had been absent an hour. Twas a short one to us, we were in high spirits, and off we drove, and will you believe me when I tell you that we walked the next ten miles by the watch over a high mountain road thanks to the wind that drove behind us and the good road, in two hours and a quarter, a marvellous feat of which D will long tell. Well! we rested in a tempting inn, close by Garsdale chapel, a lowly house of prayer in a charming little valley, here we stopp'd a quarter of an hour and then off to Sedbergh, 7 miles farther, in an hour and thirty-five minutes, the wind was still at our backs and the road delightful. I must hurry on, next morning we walked to Kendal, 11 miles, a terrible up and down road, in 3 hours, and after buying and ordering furniture, the next day by half past four we reached Grasmere in a post chaise. So ends my long story. God bless you,

W.W.

Write soon I pray you. God bless you. My love to Mrs Coleridge and a kiss for Hartley.

D.W.

Soon after the Wordsworths had settled at Grasmere, William began a long philosophical poem called 'The Recluse'. He never finished it; but the first part, printed below, serves to set the scene before the Journal begins.

THE RECLUSE

PART FIRST

Book First – Home at Grasmere

Once to the verge of yon steep barrier came
A roving school-boy; what the adventurer's age
Hath now escaped his memory – but the hour,
One of a golden summer holiday
He well remembers, though the year be gone –
Alone and devious from afar he came;
And, with a sudden influx overpowered
At sight of this seclusion, he forgot
His haste, for hasty had his footsteps been
As boyish his pursuits; and sighing said,
'What happy fortune were it here to live!
And, if a thought of dying, if a thought
Of mortal separation, could intrude
With paradise before him, here to die!'
No Prophet was he, had not even a hope,
Scarcely a wish, but one bright pleasing thought,
A fancy in the heart of what might be
The lot of others, never could be his.

The station whence he looked was soft and green,
Not giddy yet aerial, with a depth
Of vale below, a height of hills above.
For rest of body perfect was the spot,
All that luxurious nature could desire;

But stirring to the spirit; who could gaze
And not feel motions there? He thought of clouds
That sail on winds: of breezes that delight
To play on water, or in endless chase
Pursue each other through the yielding plain
Of grass or corn, over and through and through,
In billow after billow, evermore
Disporting – nor unmindful was the boy
Of sunbeams, shadows, butterflies and birds;
Of fluttering sylphs and softly-gliding Fays,
Genii, and winged angels that are Lords
Without restraint of all which they behold.
The illusion strengthening as he gazed, he felt
That such unfettered liberty was his,
Such power and joy; but only for this end,
To flit from field to rock, from rock to field,
From shore to island, and from isle to shore,
From open ground to covert, from a bed
Of meadow-flowers into a tuft of wood;
From high to low, from low to high, yet still
Within the bound of this huge concave; here
Must be his home, this valley be his world.

    Since that day forth the Place to him – *to me*
(For I who live to register the truth
Was the same young and happy Being) became
As beautiful to thought, as it had been
When present, to the bodily sense; a haunt
Of pure affections, shedding upon joy
A brighter joy; and through such damp and gloom
Of the gay mind, as oftimes splenetic youth
Makes for sorrow, darting beams of light
That no self-cherished sadness could withstand;
And now 'tis mine, perchance for life, dear Vale
Beloved Grasmere (let the wandering streams
Take up, the cloud-capt hills repeat, the Name)
One of thy lowly Dwellings is my Home.

    And was the cost so great? and could it seem
An act of courage, and the thing itself
A conquest? who must bear the blame? Sage man

Thy prudence, thy experience, thy desires,
Thy apprehensions – blush thou for them all.
  Yes the realities of life so cold,
So cowardly, so ready to betray,
So stinted in the measure of their grace
As we pronounce them, doing them much wrong,
Have been to me more bountiful than hope,
Less timid than desire – but that is past.
        On Nature's invitation do I come,
By Reason sanctioned. Can the choice mislead,
That made the calmest fairest spot of earth
With all its unappropriated good
My own; and not mine only, for with me
Entrenched, say rather peacefully embowered,
Under yon orchard, in yon humble cot,
A younger Orphan of a home extinct,
The only Daughter of my Parents dwells.
  Ay, think on that, my heart, and cease to stir,
Pause upon that and let the breathing frame
No longer breathe, but all be satisfied.
– Oh, if such silence be not thanks to God
For what hath been bestowed, then where, where then
Shall gratitude find rest? Mine eyes did ne'er
Fix on a lovely object, nor my mind
Take pleasure in the midst of happy thoughts,
But either She whom now I have, who now
Divides with me this loved abode, was there,
Or not far off. Where'er my footsteps turned,
Her voice was like a hidden Bird that sang.
The thought of her was like a flash of light,
Or an unseen companionship, a breath
Of fragrance independent of the Wind.
In all my goings, in the new and old
Of all my meditations, and in this
Favourite of all, in this the most of all.
– What being, therefore, since the birth of Man
Had ever more abundant cause to speak
Thanks, and if favours of the Heavenly Muse
Make him more thankful, then to call on Verse

To aid him and in song resound his joy?
The boon is absolute; surpassing grace
To me hath been vouchsafed; among the bowers
Of blissful Eden this was neither given
Nor could be given, possession of the good
Which had been sighed for, ancient thought fulfilled,
And dear Imagination realised,
Up to their highest measure, yea and more.

    Embrace me then, ye Hills, and close me in;
Now in the clear and open day I feel
Your guardianship; I take it to my heart;
'Tis like the solemn shelter of the night.
But I would call thee beautiful, for mild,
And soft, and gay, and beautiful thou art
Dear Valley, having in thy face a smile
Though peaceful, full of gladness. Thou art pleased,
Pleased with thy crags and woody steeps, thy Lake,
Its one green island and its winding shores;
The multitude of little rocky hills,
Thy Church and cottages of mountain stone
Clustered like stars some few, but single most,
And lurking dimly in their shy retreats,
Or glancing at each other cheerful looks
Like separated stars with clouds between.
What want we? have we not perpetual streams,
Warm woods, and sunny hills, and fresh green fields,
And mountains not less green, and flocks and herds,
And thickets full of songsters, and the voice
Of lordly birds, an unexpected sound
Heard now and then from morn to latest eve,
Admonishing the man who walks below
Of solitude and silence in the sky?
These have we, and a thousand nooks of earth
Have also these, but nowhere else is found,
Nowhere (or it is fancy?) can be found
The one sensation that is here; 'tis here,
Here as it found its way into my heart
In childhood, here as it abides by day,
By night, here only; or in chosen minds

That take it with them hence, where'er they go.
– 'Tis, but I cannot name it, 'tis the sense
Of majesty, and beauty, and repose,
A blended holiness of earth and sky,
Something that makes this individual spot,
This small abiding-place of many men,
A termination, and a last retreat,
A centre, come from wheresoe'er you will,
A whole without dependence or defect,
Made for itself, and happy in itself,
Perfect contentment, Unity entire.

Bleak season was it, turbulent and bleak,
When hitherward we journeyed side by side
Through burst of sunshine and through flying showers;
Paced the long vales – how long they were – and yet
How fast that length of way was left behind,
Wensley's rich Vale, and Sedbergh's naked heights.
The frosty wind, as if to make amends
For its keen breath, was aiding to our steps,
And drove us onward like two ships at sea,
Or like two birds, companions in mid-air,
Parted and reunited by the blast.

Stern was the face of nature; we rejoiced
In that stern countenance, for our souls thence drew
A feeling of their strength. The naked trees,
The icy brook, as on we passed, appeared
To question us. 'Whence come ye, to what end?'
They seemed to say, 'What would ye,' said the shower,
'Wild Wanderers, whither through my dark domain?'
The sunbeam said, 'Be happy.' When this vale
We entered, bright and solemn was the sky
That faced us with a passionate welcoming,
And led us to our threshold. Daylight failed
Insensibly, and round us gently fell
Composing darkness, with a quiet load
Of full contentment, in a little shed
Disturbed, uneasy in itself as seemed,
And wondering at its new inhabitants.
It loves us now, this Vale so beautiful

Begins to love us ! by a sullen storm,
Two months unwearied of severest storm,
It put the temper of our minds to proof,
And found us faithful through the gloom, and heard
The poet mutter his prelusive songs
With cheerful heart, an unknown voice of joy
Among the silence of the woods and hills;
Silent to any gladsomeness of sound
With all their shepherds.

THE GRASMERE JOURNAL

I

'God be thanked, I want not
society by a moonlight lake.'

May 14th, 1800 [*Wednesday*]. Wm. and John set off into York-
shire after dinner at ½ past 2 o'clock, cold pork in their pockets.
I left them at the turning of the Lowwood bay under the trees.
My heart was so full that I could hardly speak to W. when I
gave him a farewell kiss. I sate a long time upon a stone at the
margin of the lake, and after a flood of tears my heart was easier.
The lake looked to me, I knew not why, dull and melancholy,
and the weltering on the shores seemed a heavy sound. I walked
as long as I could amongst the stones of the shore. The wood rich
in flowers; a beautiful yellow, palish yellow, flower, that looked
thick, round, and double, and smelt very sweet – I supposed it
was a ranunculus. Crowfoot, the grassy-leaved rabbit-toothed
white flower, strawberries, geranium, scentless violets, anemones
two kinds, orchise, primroses. The heckberry very beautiful,
the crab coming out as a low shrub. Met a blind man, driving a
very large beautiful Bull, and a cow – he walked with two sticks.
Came home by Clappersgate. The valley very green; many sweet
views up to Rydale head, when I could juggle away the fine
houses; but they disturbed me, even more than when I have been
happier; one beautiful view of the Bridge, without Sir Michael's.
Sate down very often, though it was cold. I resolved to write a
journal of the time till W. and J. return, and I set about keeping
my resolve, because I will not quarrel with myself, and because
I shall give Wm. pleasure by it when he comes home again. At
Rydale, a woman of the village, stout and well dressed, begged
a half-penny; she had never she said done it before, but these
hard times! Arrived at home with a bad headach, set some slips
of privett, the evening cold, had a fire, my face now flame-coloured.
It is nine o'clock. I shall soon go to bed. A young woman begged
at the door – she had come from Manchester on Sunday morn.
with two shillings and a slip of paper which she supposed a Bank

note – it was a cheat. She had buried her husband and three children within a year and a half – all in one grave – burying very dear – paupers all put in one place – 20 shillings paid for as much ground as will bury a man – a stone to be put over it or the right will be lost – 11/6 each time the ground is opened ... Oh! that I had a letter from William!

May 15th, Thursday. A coldish dull morning – hoed the first row of peas, weeded etc. etc., sat hard to mending till evening. The rain which had threatened all day came on just when I was going to walk.

[*May 16th,*] *Friday morning.* Warm and mild, after a fine night of rain. Transplanted radishes after breakfast, walked to Mr Gell's with the books, gathered mosses and plants. The woods extremely beautiful with all autumnal variety and softness. I carried a basket for mosses, and gathered some wild plants. Oh! that we had a book of botany. All flowers now are gay and deliciously sweet. The primroses still pre-eminent among the later flowers of the spring. Foxgloves very tall, with their heads budding. I went forward round the lake at the foot of Loughrigg Fell. I was much amused with the business of a pair of stonechats; their restless voices as they skimmed along the water following each other, their shadows under them, and their returning back to the stones on the shore, chirping with the same unwearied voice. Could not cross the water, so I went round by the stepping-stones. The morning clear but cloudy, that is the hills were not overhung by mists. After dinner Aggy weeded onions and carrots. I helped for a little – wrote to Mary Hutchinson – washed my head – worked. After tea went to Ambleside – a pleasant cool but not cold evening. Rydale was very beautiful, with spear-shaped streaks of polished steel. No letters! – only one newspaper. I returned to Clappersgate. Grasmere was very solemn in the last glimpse of twilight; it calls home the heart to quietness. I had been very melancholy in my walk back. I had many of my saddest thoughts, and I could not keep the tears within me. But when I came to Grasmere I felt that it did me good. I finished my letter to M. H. Ate hasty pudding and went to bed. As I was going out in the morning I met a half crazy old man. He shewed me a pincushion and begged a pin, afterwards a half-penny. He began in a kind of indistinct voice in this manner: 'Matthew Jobson's lost a cow. Tom Nichol has two good horses strayed. Jim Jones's cow's brokken her horn, etc. etc.' He went into Aggy's and persuaded her to give him some whey, and let him boil some porridge. She declares he ate two quarts.

[May 17th,] *Saturday*. Incessant rain from morning till night. T. Ashburner brought us coals. Worked hard, and read *Midsummer Night's Dream*, [and] Ballads – sauntered a little in the garden. The Skobby[1] sate quietly in its nest, rocked by the wind, and beaten by the rain.

[May] 18th, *Sunday*. Went to church, slight showers, a cold air. The mountains from this window look much greener, and I think the valley is more green than ever. The corn begins to shew itself. The ashes are still bare, went part of the way home with Miss Simpson. A little girl from Coniston came to beg. She had lain out all night – her step-mother had turned her out of doors. Her father could not stay at home 'she flights so'. Walked to Ambleside in the evening round the lake, the prospect exceedingly beautiful from Loughrigg Fell. It was so green that no eye could be weary of reposing upon it. The most beautiful situation for a house in the field next to Mr Benson's. It threatened rain all the evening but was mild and pleasant. I was overtaken by 2 Cumberland people on the other side of Rydale who complimented me upon my walking. They were going to sell cloth, and odd things which they make themselves, in Hawkshead and the neighbourhood. The post was not arrived, so I walked thro' the town, past Mrs Taylor's, and met him. Letters from Coleridge and Cottle. John Fisher overtook me on the other side of Rydale. He talked much about the alteration

---

1. Chaffinch.

in the times, and observed that in a short time there would be only two ranks of people, the very rich and the very poor, 'for those who have small estates', says he, 'are forced to sell, and all the land goes into one hand'. Did not reach home till 10 o'clock.

[*May 19th,*] *Monday.* Sauntered a good deal in the garden, bound carpets, mended old clothes. Read *Timon of Athens.* Dried linen. Molly weeded the turnips, John stuck the peas. We had not much sunshine or wind, but no rain till about 7 o'clock, when we had a slight shower just after I had set out upon my walk. I did not return but walked up into the Black Quarter. I sauntered a long time among the rocks above the church. The most delightful situation possible for a cottage, commanding two distinct views of the vale and of the lake, is among those rocks. I strolled on, gathered mosses etc. The quietness and still seclusion of the valley affected me even to producing the deepest melancholy. I forced myself from it. The wind rose before I went to bed. No rain – Dodwell and Wilkinson called in my absence.

[*May 20th,*] *Tuesday Morning.* A fine mild rain. After breakfast the sky cleared and before the clouds passed from the hills I went to Ambleside. It was a sweet morning. Everything green and overflowing with life, and the streams making a perpetual song, with the thrushes and all little birds, not forgetting the stone-chats. The post was not come in. I walked as far as Windermere, and met him there. No letters! no papers. Came home by Clappersgate. I was sadly tired, ate a hasty dinner and had a bad headach – went to bed and slept at least 2 hours. Rain came on in the evening – Molly washing.

May 26th, Monday. A very fine morning, worked in the garden till after 10 when old Mr Simpson came and talked to me till after 12. Molly weeding – wrote letters to J.H.,[1] Coleridge,

---

1. Joanna Hutchinson.

C. Ll.,[1] and W. I walked towards Rydale, and turned aside at my favorite field. The air and the lake were still – one cottage light in the vale, and so much of day left that I could distinguish objects, the woods, trees and houses. Two or three different kinds of birds sang at intervals on the opposite shore. I sate till I could hardly drag myself away. I grew so sad. 'When pleasant thoughts', etc . . .

LINES WRITTEN IN EARLY SPRING

Written at Alfoxden in 1798

I heard a thousand blended notes,
While in a grove I sate reclined,
In that sweet mood when pleasant thoughts
Bring sad thoughts to the mind.

To her fair works did Nature link
The human soul that through me ran;
And much it grieved my heart to think
What man has made of man.

Through primrose tufts, in that green bower,
The periwinkle trailed its wreaths;
And 'tis my faith that every flower
Enjoys the air it breathes.

The birds around me hopped and played,
Their thoughts I cannot measure :–
But the least motion which they made
It seemed a thrill of pleasure.

The budding twigs spread out their fan,
To catch the breezy air;
And I must think, do all I can,
That there was pleasure there.

---

1. Charles Lloyd. He lived at Nether Stowey with Coleridge in 1798 and settled near Clappersgate with his family in 1800.

If this belief from heaven be sent,
If such be Nature's holy plan,
Have I not reason to lament
What man has made of man?

[May] 27th, Tuesday. I walked to Ambleside with letters – met the post before I reached Mr Partridge's, one paper, only a letter for Coleridge. I expected a letter from Wm. It was a sweet morning, the ashes in the valley nearly in full leaf, but still to be distinguished, quite bare on the higher ground. I was warm in returning, and becoming cold with sitting in the house I had a bad headach – went to bed after dinner, and lay till after 5. Not well after tea. I worked in the garden, but did not walk further. A delightful evening before the sun set, but afterwards it grew colder – mended stockings etc.

[May 28th,] Wednesday. In the morning walked up to the rocks above Jenny Dockeray's, sate a long time upon the grass, the prospect divinely beautiful. If I had three hundred pounds, and could afford to have a bad interest for my money, I would buy that estate, and we would build a cottage there to end our days in. I went into her garden and got white and yellow lilies, periwinkle, etc., which I planted. Sate under the trees with my work. No fire in the morning. Worked till between 7 and 8, and then watered the garden, and was about to go up to Mr Simpson's, when Miss S. and her visitors passed the door. I went home with them, a beautiful evening, the crescent moon hanging above Helm Crag.

June 1st, Sunday. Rain in the night – a sweet mild morning. Read Ballads; went to church. Singers from Wytheburn, went part of the way home with Miss Simpson. Walked upon the hill above the house till dinner time – went again to church – Christening and singing which kept us very late. The pewside came down with me. Walked with Mr Simpson nearly home. After tea, went to Ambleside, round the lakes – a very fine warm evening. I lay upon the steep of Loughrigg, my heart dissolved in what I saw, when I was not startled but re-called from my reverie by a noise as of a child paddling without shoes. I looked up and saw a lamb close to me. It approached nearer and nearer, as if to examine me, and stood a long time. I did not move. At last it ran past me, and went bleating along the pathway, seeming to be seeking its mother. I saw a hare on the high road. The post was not come in; waited in the road till John's apprentice came with a letter from Coleridge and 3 papers. The moon shone upon the water – reached home at 10 o'clock, went to bed immediately. Molly brought daisies etc. which we planted.

[*June 2nd,*] *Monday.* A cold dry windy morning. I worked in the garden, and planted flowers, etc. Sate under the trees after dinner till tea time. John Fisher stuck the peas, Molly weeded and washed. I went to Ambleside after tea, crossed the stepping-stone at the foot of Grasmere, and pursued my way on the other side of Rydale and by Clappersgate. I sate a long time to watch the hurrying waves, and to hear the regularly irregular sound of the dashing waters. The waves round about the little Island seemed like a dance of spirits that rose out of the water, round its small circumference of shore. Inquired about lodgings for Coleridge, and was accompanied by Mrs Nicholson as far as Rydale. This was very kind, but God be thanked, I want no society by a moonlight lake. It was near 11 when I reached home. I wrote to Coleridge, and went late to bed.

[*June 3rd,*] *Tuesday.* I sent off my letter by the Butcher. A boisterous drying day. I worked in the garden before dinner. Read R[*ichar*]d *Second* – was not well after dinner and lay down. Mrs Simpson's grandson brought me some gooseberries. I got up and walked with him part of the way home, afterwards went down rambling by the lake side – got Lockety Goldings, strawberries etc., and planted. Afted tea the wind fell. I walked towards Mr Simpson's, gave the newspapers to the Girl, reached home at 10. No letter, no William – a letter from R[*ichar*]d to John.

[*June 4th,*] *Wednesday*. A very fine day. I sate out of doors most of the day, wrote to Mr Jackson. Ambleside Fair. I walked to the lake-side in the morning, took up plants, and sate upon a stone reading Ballads. In the evening I was watering plants when Mr and Miss Simpson called. I accompanied them home, and we went to the waterfall at the head of the valley. It was very interesting in the Twilight. I brought home lemon thyme, and several other plants, and planted them by moonlight. I lingered out of doors in the hope of hearing my Brother's tread.

[*June 5th,*] *Tuesday*. I sate out of doors great part of the day and worked in the garden – had a letter from Mr Jackson, and wrote an answer to Coleridge. The little birds busy making love, and pecking the blossoms and bits of moss off the trees; they flutter about and about, and thrid the trees as I lie under them. Molly went out to tea, I would not go far from home, expecting my Brothers. I rambled on the hill above the house, gathered wild thyme, and took up roots of wild columbine. Just as I was returning with my load, Mr and Miss Simpson called. We went again upon the hill, got more plants, set them, and then went to the Blind Man's for London Pride for Miss Simpson. I went up with them as far as the Blacksmith's, a fine lovely moonlight night.

[*June 6th,*] *Friday*. Sate out of doors reading the whole afternoon, but in the morning I wrote to my aunt Cookson. In the evening I went to Ambleside with Coleridge's letter – it was a lovely night as the day had been. I went by Loughrigg and Clappersgate and just met the post at the turnpike; he told me there were two letters but none for me, so I was in no hurry and went round again by Clappersgate, crossed the stepping-stones and entered Ambleside at Matthew Harrison's. A letter from Jack Hutchinson, and one from Montagu, enclosing a 3£ note. No William! I slackened my pace as I came near home, fearing to hear that he was not come. I listened till after one o'clock to every barking dog, cock-fighting, and other sports: it was Mr Borwick's opening. Foxgloves just coming into blossom.

[*June 7th*,] *Saturday*. A very warm cloudy morning, threatening to rain. I walked up to Mr Simpson's to gather gooseberries – it was a very fine afternoon. Little Tommy came down with me, ate gooseberry pudding and drank tea with me. We went up the hill, to gather sods and plants, and went down to the lake side, and took up orchises, etc. I watered the garden and weeded. I did not leave home, in the expectation of Wm. and John, and sitting at work till after 11 o'clock I heard a foot go to the front of the house, turn round, and open the gate. It was William! After our first joy was over, we got some tea. We did not go to bed till 4 o'clock in the morning, so he had an opportunity of seeing our improvements. The birds were singing, and all looked fresh, though not gay. There was a greyness on earth and sky. We did not rise till near 10 in the morning. We were busy all day in writing letters to Coleridge, Montagu, Douglas, Richard. Mr and Miss Simpson called in the evening, the little boy carried our letters to Ambleside. We walked with Mr and Miss S. home, on their return. The evening was cold and I was afraid of the toothach for William. We met John on our return home.

[*June*] *9th, Monday*. In the morning W. cut down the winter cherry tree. I sowed French beans and weeded. A coronetted Landau went by, when we were sitting upon the sodded wall. The ladies (evidently Tourists) turned an eye of interest upon our little garden and cottage. We went to R. Newton's for pike floats and went round to Mr Gell's boat, and on the lake to fish. We caught nothing – it was extremely cold. The reeds and bullrushes or bullpipes of a tender soft green, making a plain whose surface moved with the wind. The reeds not yet tall. The lake clear to the bottom, but saw no fish. In the evening I stuck peas, watered the garden, and planted brocoli. Did not walk, for it was very cold. A poor girl called to beg, who had no work at home, and was going in search of it to Kendal. She slept in Mr Benson's [?], and went off after breakfast in the morning with 7d. and a letter to the Mayor of Kendal.

[*June*] 10th, Tuesday. A cold, yet sunshiny morning. John carried letters to Ambleside. I made tarts, pies, etc. Wm. stuck peas. After dinner he lay down. John not at home. I stuck peas alone. Molly washing. Cold showers with hail and rain, but at half past five, after a heavy rain, the lake became calm and very beautiful. Those parts of the water which were perfectly unruffled lay like green islands of various shapes. W. and I walked to Ambleside to seek lodgings for C. No letters. No papers. It was a very cold chearless evening. John had been fishing in Langdale and was gone to bed.

On Tuesday, May 27th, a very tall woman, tall much beyond the measure of tall women, called at the door. She had on a very long brown cloak, and a very white cap, without bonnet; her face was excessively brown, but it had plainly once been fair. She led a little bare-footed child about 2 years old by the hand, and said her husband, who was a tinker, was gone before with the other children. I gave her a piece of bread. Afterwards on my road to Ambleside, beside the bridge at Rydale, I saw her husband sitting by the roadside, his two asses feeding beside him, and the two young children at play upon the grass. The man did not beg. I passed on and about ¼ mile further I saw two boys before me, one about 10, the other about 8 years old, at play chasing a butterfly. They were wild figures, not very ragged, but without shoes and stockings; the hat of the elder was wreathed round with yellow flowers, the younger whose hat was only a rimless crown, had stuck it round with laurel leaves. They continued at play till I drew very near, and then they addressed me with the begging cant and the whining voice of sorrow. I said 'I served your mother this morning'. (The Boys were so like the woman who had called at the door that I could not be mistaken.) 'O!' says the elder, 'you could not serve my mother for she's dead, and my father's on at the next town – he's a potter.' I persisted in my assertion, and that I would give them nothing. Says the elder, 'Come, let's away', and away they flew like lightning. They had however sauntered so long in their road that they did not reach Ambleside before me, and I saw them go up to Matthew Harrison's house with their wallet upon the elder's shoulder, and creeping with a beggar's complaining foot. On my return through Ambleside I met in the street the mother driving her asses; in the two panniers of one of which were the two little children, whom she was chiding and threatening with a wand which she used to drive her asses, while the little things hung in wantonness over the pannier's edge. The woman had told me in the morning that she was from Scotland, which her accent fully proved, but that she had lived (I think) at Wigton, that they could not keep a house and so they travelled.

This episode was closely followed by William in his poem 'Beggars' written on 13 and 14 March 1802, where it will be found (p. 176).

June 11th, Wednesday. A very cold morning – we went on the lake to set pike floats with John's fish. W. and J. went first alone. Mr Simpson called, and I accompanied him to the lake side. My Brothers and I again went upon the water, and returned to dinner. We landed upon the island where I saw the whitest hawthorn I have seen this year, the generality of hawthorns are bloomless. I saw wild roses in the hedges. Went to bed in the afternoon and slept till after six – a threatening of the toothach. Wm. and John went to the pike floats – they brought in 2 pikes. I sowed kidney-beans and spinnach. A cold evening. Molly stuck the peas. I weeded a little. Did not walk.

[June 16th,] Monday. Wm. and I went to Brathay by Little Langdale and Collath and Skelleth. It was a warm mild morning with threatening of rain. The vale of Little Langdale looked bare and unlovely. Collath was wild and interesting, from the peat carts and peat gatherers – the valley all perfumed with the gale and wild thyme. The woods about the waterfall veined with rich yellow Broom.

This metaphor of the yellow broom like veins of gold in the woods appears three times in the Journal and Wordsworth uses it in the fortieth line of his poem 'To Joanna'. It is hard to say whether it was Dorothy or William who invented the phrase, because much later, on 8 June 1802, Dorothy uses it again, in quotation marks.

This seems to suggest that she at least attributes it to William, but it was certainly one of the many ideas they shared in common.

A succession of delicious views from Skelleth to Brathay. We met near Skelleth a pretty little boy with a wallet over his shoulder. He came from Hawkshead and was going to 'late a lock' of meal. He spoke gently and without complaint. When I asked him if he got enough to eat, he looked surprized, and said 'Nay'. He was 7 years old but seemed not more than 5. We drank tea at Mr Ibbetson's, and returned by Ambleside. Lent 3 : 9 : 0 to the potter at Kendal. Met John on our return home at about 10 o'clock. Saw a primrose in blossom.

[*June 21st,*] *Saturday.* In the morning W. and I went to Ambleside to get his tooth drawn, and put in. A fine clear morning but cold. W.'s tooth drawn with very little pain – he slept till 3 o'clock. Young Mr S. drank tea and supped with us. They fished in Rydale water and they caught 2 small fishes – W. no bite – John 3. Miss Simpson and 3 children called – I walked with them to Rydale. The evening cold and clear and frosty but the wind was falling as I returned – I staid at home about an hour and then walked up the hill to Rydale lake. Grasmere looked so beautiful that my heart was almost melted away. It was quite calm, only spotted with sparkles of light. The church visible. On our return all distant objects had faded away – all but the hills. The reflection of the light bright sky above Black Quarter was very solemn. Mr S. did not go till 12 o'clock.

[*June 22nd,*] *Sunday.* In the morning W. and I walked towards Rydale and up into the wood but finding it not very pleasant we returned – sauntered in the garden – a showery day. In the evening I planted a honeysuckle round the yew tree. In the evening we walked for letters – no letters. No news of Coleridge. Jimmy Benson came home drunk beside us.

[*June 23rd,*] *Monday.* Mr Simpson called in the morning. Tommy's Father dead. W. and I went into Langdale to fish.

44

The morning was very cold. I sate at the foot of the lake, till my head ached with cold The view exquisitely beautiful, through a gate, and under a sycamore tree beside the first house going into Loughrigg. Elterwater looked barren, and the view from the church less beautiful than in winter. When W. went down to the water to fish, I lay under the [? wind], my head pillowed upon a mossy rock, and slept about 10 minutes, which relieved my headach. We ate our dinner together, and parted again. Wm. was afraid he had lost his line and sought me. An old man saw me just after I had crossed the stepping stones and was going through a copse – 'Ho, wherever were you going?' 'To Elterwater Bridge' – 'Why', says he, 'it's well I saw you; ye were gane to Little Langdale by Wrynose', and several other places which he ran over with a mixture of triumph, good-nature and wit – 'It's well I saw you or you'd ha' been lost.' The [? evening] grew very pleasant – We sate on the side of the hill looking to Elterwater. I was much tired and returned home to tea. W. went to fish for pike in Rydale. John came in when I had done tea, and he and I carried a jug of tea to William. We met him in the old road from Rydale. He drank his tea upon the turf. The setting sun threw a red purple light upon the rocks, and stone walls of Rydale, which gave them a most interesting and beautiful appearance.

[*June 24th*,] *Tuesday*. W. went to Ambleside. John walked out. I made tarts, etc. Mrs B. Simpson called and asked us to tea. I went to the view of Rydale, to meet William. John went to him – I returned. W. and I drank tea at Mr Simpson's. Brought down lemon-thyme, greens, etc. The old woman was very happy to see us, and we were so in the pleasure we gave. She was an affecting picture of patient disappointment, suffering under no particular affliction.

[*June 25th*,] *Wednesday*. A very rainy day. I made a shoe. Wm. and John went to fish in Langdale in the evening. I went above the house, and gathered flowers, which I planted, foxgloves, etc. On Sunday Mr and Mrs Coleridge and Hartley came. The day was very warm. We sailed to the foot of Loughrigg. They staid with us three weeks, and till the Thursday following, i.e. till the 23rd of July. On the Friday preceding their departure we drank tea at the island. The weather very delightful, and on the Sunday we made a great fire, and drank tea in Bainriggs with the Simpsons. I accompanied Mrs C. to Wytheburne, and returned with W. to tea at Mr Simpson's. It was excessively hot, but the day after, Friday 24th July, still hotter. All the morning I was engaged in unpacking our Somersetshire goods and in making pies. The house was a hot oven, but yet we could not bake the pies. I was so weary, I could not walk: so I went and sate with Wm. in the orchard. We had a delightful half-hour in the warm still evening.

[July] 26th, *Saturday*. Still hotter. I sate with W. in the orchard all the morning, and made my shoes. In the afternoon from excessive heat I was ill in the headach and toothach and went to bed – I was refreshed with washing myself after I got up, but it was too hot to walk till near dark, and then I sate upon the wall finishing my shoes.

[July] 27th, *Sunday*. Very warm. Molly ill. John bathed in the lake. I wrote out *Ruth* in the afternoon.

RUTH

When Ruth was left half desolate,
Her Father took another Mate;
And Ruth, not seven years old,
A slighted child, at her own will
Went wandering over dale and hill,
In thoughtless freedom, bold.

And she had made a pipe of straw,
And music from that pipe could draw
Like sounds of winds and floods;
Had built a bower upon the green,
As if she from her birth had been
An infant of the woods.

Beneath her father's roof, alone
She seemed to live; her thoughts her own;
Herself her own delight;
Pleased with herself, nor sad, nor gay;
And, passing thus the live-long day,
She grew to woman's height.

There came a Youth from Georgia's shore –
A military casque he wore,
With splendid feathers drest;
He brought them from the Cherokees;
The feathers nodded in the breeze,
And made a gallant crest.

From Indian blood you deem him sprung:
But no! he spake the English tongue,
And bore a soldier's name;
And, when America was free
From battle and from jeopardy,
He 'cross the ocean came.

With hues of genius on his cheek
In finest tones the Youth could speak:
– While he was yet a boy,
The moon, the glory of the sun,
The streams that murmur as they run,
Had been his dearest joy.

He was a lovely Youth ! I guess
The panther in the wilderness
Was not so fair as he;
And, when he chose to sport and play,
No dolphin ever was so gay
Upon the tropic sea.

Among the Indians he had fought,
And with him many tales he brought
Of pleasure and of fear;
Such tales as told to any maid
By such a Youth, in the green shade
Were perilous to hear.

He told of girls – a happy rout !
Who quit their fold with dance and shout,
Their pleasant Indian town,
To gather strawberries all day long ;
Returning with a choral song
When daylight is gone down.

He spake of plants that hourly change
Their blossoms, through a boundless range
Of intermingling hues ;
With budding, fading, faded flowers
They stand the wonder of the bowers
From morn to evening dews.

He told of the magnolia, spread
High as a cloud, high over head !
The cypress and her spire ;
– Of flowers that with one scarlet gleam
Cover a hundred leagues, and seem
To set the hills on fire.

The Youth of green savannahs spake,
And many an endless, endless lake,
With all its fairy crowds
Of islands, that together lie
As quietly as spots of sky
Among the evening clouds.

'How pleasant,' then he said, 'it were
A fisher or a hunter there,
In sunshine or in shade
To wander with an easy mind ;
And build a household fire, and find
A home in every glade !

'What days and what bright years ! Ah me !
Our life were life indeed, with thee
So passed in quiet bliss,
And all the while,' said he, 'to know
That we were in a world of woe,
On such an earth as this !'

And then he sometimes interwove
Fond thoughts about a father's love;
'For there,' said he, 'are spun
Around the heart such tender ties,
That our own children to our eyes
Are dearer than the sun.

'Sweet Ruth ! and could you go with me
My helpmate in the woods to be,
Our shed at night to rear;
Or run, my own adopted bride,
A sylvan huntress at my side !
And drive the flying deer !

'Beloved Ruth !' – No more he said,
The wakeful Ruth at midnight shed
A solitary tear :
She thought again – and did agree
With him to sail across the sea,
And drive the flying deer.

'And now, as fitting is and right,
We in the church our faith will plight,
A husband and a wife.'
Even so they did; and I may say
That to sweet Ruth that happy day
Was more than human life.

Through dream and vision did she sink,
Delighted all the while to think
That on those lonesome floods,
And green savannahs, she would share
His board with lawful joy, and bear
His name in the wild woods.

But, as you have before been told,
This Stripling, sportive, gay and bold,
And, with his dancing crest,
So beautiful, through savage lands
Had roamed about, with vagrant bands
Of Indians in the West.

The wind, the tempest roaring high,
The tumult of a tropic sky,
Might well be dangerous food
For him, a Youth to whom was given
So much of earth – so much of heaven,
And such impetuous blood.

Whatever in those climes he found
Irregular in sight or sound
Did to his mind impart
A kindred impulse, seemed allied
To his own powers, and justified
The workings of his heart.

Nor less, to feed voluptuous thought,
The beauteous forms of nature wrought,
Fair trees and gorgeous flowers;
The breezes their own languor lent;
The stars had feelings, which they sent
Into those favoured bowers.

Yet, in his worst pursuits, I ween
That sometimes there did intervene
Pure hopes of high intent:
For passions linked to forms so fair
And stately, needs must have their share
Of noble sentiment.

But ill he lived, much evil saw,
With men to whom no better law
Nor better life was known;
Deliberately, and undeceived,
Those wild men's vices he received,
And gave them back his own.

His genius and his moral frame
Were thus impaired, and he became
The slave of low desires:
A Man who without self-control
Would seek what the degraded soul
Unworthily admires.

And yet he with no feigned delight
Had wooed the Maiden, day and night
Had loved her, night and morn:
What could he less than love a Maid
Whose heart with so much nature played?
So kind and so forlorn!

Sometimes, most earnestly, he said,
'O Ruth! I have been worse than dead;
False thoughts, thoughts bold and vain,
Encompassed me on every side
When I, in confidence and pride,
Had crossed the Atlantic main.

'Before me shone a glorious world –
Fresh as a banner bright, unfurled
To music suddenly:
I looked upon those hills and plains,
And seemed as if let loose from chains,
To live at liberty.

'No more of this; for now, by thee
Dear Ruth! more happily set free
With nobler zeal I burn;
My soul from darkness is released,
Like the whole sky when to the east
The morning doth return.'

Full soon that better mind was gone;
No hope, no wish remained, not one, –
They stirred him now no more;
New objects did new pleasure give
And once again he wished to live
As lawless as before.

Meanwhile, as thus with him it fared,
They for the voyage were prepared,
And went to the sea-shore,
But, when they thither came the Youth
Deserted his poor Bride, and Ruth
Could never find him more.

God help thee, Ruth ! – Such pains she had,
That she in half a year was mad,
And in a prison housed;
And there, with many a doleful song
Made of wild words, her cup of wrong
She fearfully caroused.

Yet sometimes milder hours she knew,
Nor wanted sun, nor rain, nor dew,
Nor pastimes of the May;
– They all were with her in her cell;
And a clear brook with cheerful knell
Did o'er the pebbles play.

When Ruth three seasons thus had lain,
There came a respite to her pain;
She from her prison fled;
But of the Vagrant none took thought;
And where it liked her best she sought
Her shelter and her bread.

Among the fields she breathed again :
The master-current of her brain
Ran permanent and free;
And, coming to the Banks of Tone,
There did she rest; and dwell alone
Under the greenwood tree.

The engines of her pain, the tools
That shaped her sorrow, rocks and pools,
And airs that gently stir
The vernal leaves – she loved them still;
Nor ever taxed them with the ill
Which had been done to her.

A Barn her winter bed supplies;
But, till the warmth of summer skies
And summer days is gone,
(And all do in this tale agree)
She sleeps beneath the greenwood tree,
And other home hath none.

An innocent life, yet far astray !
And Ruth will, long before her day,
Be broken down and old :
Sore aches she needs must have ! but less
Of mind, than body's wretchedness,
From damp, and rain, and cold.

If she is prest by want of food,
She from her dwelling in the wood
Repairs to a road-side;
And there she begs at one steep place
Where up and down with easy pace
The horsemen-travellers ride.

That oaten pipe of hers is mute,
Or thrown away; but with a flute
Her loneliness she cheers:
This flute, made of a hemlock stalk,
At evening in his homeward walk
The Quantock woodman hears.

I, too, have passed her on the hills
Setting her little water-mills
By spouts and fountains wild –
Such small machinery as she turned
Ere she had wept, ere she had mourned,
A young and happy Child !

Farewell ! and when thy days are told,
Ill-fated Ruth, in hallowed mould
Thy corpse shall buried be,
For thee a funeral bell shall ring,
And all the congregation sing
A Christian psalm for thee.

In the morning, I read Mr Knight's *Landscape*.[1] After tea we
rowed down to Loughrigg Fell, visited the white foxglove, gath-

1. *The Landscape: a Didactic poem in Three Books*, by Richard
Payne Knight, 1794.

ered wild strawberries, and walked up to view Rydale. We lay a long time looking at the lake: the shores all embrowned with the scorching sun. The ferns were turning yellow, that is, here and there one was quite turned. We walked round by Benson's wood home. The lake was now most still, and reflected the beautiful yellow and blue and purple and grey colours of the sky. We heard a strange sound in the Bainriggs wood, as we were floating on the water; it *seemed* in the wood, but it must have been above it, for presently we saw a raven very high above us. It called out, and the dome of the sky seemed to echo the sound. It called again and again as it flew onwards, and the mountains gave back the sound, seeming as if from their center; a musical bell-like answering to the bird's hoarse voice. We heard both the call of the bird, and the echo, after we could see him no longer.

Passage from THE EXCURSION, BOOK IV

... and often, at the hour
When issue forth the first pale stars, is heard
Within the circuit of this fabric huge,
One voice – the solitary raven, flying
Athwart the concave of the dark blue dome,
Unseen, perchance above all power of sight –
An iron knell! with echoes from afar
Faint – and still fainter – as the cry, with which
The wanderer accompanies her flight
Through the calm region, fades upon the ear,
Diminishing by distance till it seemed
To expire; yet from the abyss is caught again,
And yet again recovered!

These twelve lines may have been written at the time and incorporated later or written with Dorothy's Journal as the source.

[July 28th,] *Monday Morning.* Received a letter from Coleridge enclosing one from Mr Davy about the *Lyrical Ballads.* Intensely hot. I made pies in the morning. William went into the wood, and altered his poems. In the evening it was so very warm that I was too much tired to walk.

[*July 29th,*] *Tuesday.* Still very hot. We gathered peas for dinner. We walked up in the evening to find out Hewetson's cottage but it was too dark. I was sick and weary.

[*July 30th,*] *Wednesday.* Gathered peas for Mrs Simpson – John and I walked up with them – very hot – Wm. had intended going to Keswick. I was obliged to lie down after dinner from excessive heat and headach. The evening excessively beautiful – a rich reflection of the moon, the moonlight, clouds and the hills, and from the Rays gap a huge rainbow pillar. We sailed upon the lake till it was 10 o'clock.

[*July 31st,*] *Thursday.* All the morning I was busy copying poems. Gathered peas, and in the afternoon Coleridge came, very hot; he brought the 2nd volume of the Anthology. The men went to bathe, and we afterwards sailed down to Loughrigg. Read poems on the water, and let the boat take its own course. We walked a long time upon Loughrigg. I returned in the grey twilight. The moon just setting as we reached home.

August 1st, Friday. In the morning I copied *The Brothers.* Coleridge and Wm. went down to the lake. They returned, and we all went together to Mary Point,[1] where we sate in the breeze and the shade, and read Wm.'s poems. Altered *The Whirlblast,* etc.

---

1. See 23 May 1802, p. 242.

A whirl-blast from behind the hill
Rushed o'er the wood with startling sound;
Then – all at once the air was still,
And showers of hailstones pattered round.
Where leafless oaks towered high above,
I sat within an undergrove
Of tallest hollies, tall and green;
A fairer bower was never seen.
From year to year the spacious floor
With withered leaves is covered o'er,
And all the year the bower is green.
But see! where'er the hailstones drop
The withered leaves all skip and hop;
There's not a breeze – no breath of air –
Yet here, and there, and everywhere
Along the floor, beneath the shade
By those embowering hollies made,
The leaves in myriads jump and spring,
As if with pipes and music rare
Some Robin Good-fellow were there,
And all those leaves, in festive glee,
Were dancing to the minstrelsy.

See Alfoxden Journal, 18 March 1798.

From 8 August to 17 August, they were staying with Coleridge at Keswick, but Dorothy, mysteriously enough, gives very few details of the visit.

August 17th, Sunday. Came home. Dined in Borrowdale. A rainy morning, but a fine evening – saw the Bristol prison and Bassenthwaite at the same time – Wm. read us *The Seven Sisters* on a stone.

THE SEVEN SISTERS
or, THE SOLITUDE OF BINNORIE

I

Seven Daughters had Lord Archibald,
All children of one mother :
You could not say in one short day
What love they bore each other.
A garland, of seven lilies, wrought !
Seven Sisters that together dwell;
But he, bold Knight as ever fought,
Their Father, took of them no thought,
He loved the wars so well.
Sing, mournfully, oh ! mournfully,
The solitude of Binnorie !

II

Fresh blows the wind, a western wind,
And from the shores of Erin,
Across the wave, a Rover brave
To Binnorie is steering :
Right onward to the Scottish strand
The gallant ship is borne;
The warriors leap upon the land,
And hark ! the Leader of the band
Hath blown his bugle horn.
Sing, mournfully, oh ! mournfully,
The solitude of Binnorie.

III

Beside a grotto of their own,
With boughs above them closing,
The Seven are laid, and in the shade
They lie like dawns reposing.
But now, upstarting with affright
At noise of man and steed,

Away they fly to left, to right –
Of your fair household, Father-Knight,
Methinks you take small heed !
Sing, mournfully, oh ! mournfully,
The solitude of Binnorie.

IV

Away the seven fair Campbells fly,
And, over hill and hollow,
With menace proud, and insult loud,
The youthful Rovers follow.
Cried they, 'Your Father loves to roam :
Enough for him to find
The empty house when he comes home;
For us your yellow ringlets comb,
For us be fair and kind !'
Sing, mournfully, oh ! mournfully,
The solitude of Binnorie.

V

Some close behind, some side to side,
Like clouds in stormy weather;
They run, and cry, 'Nay, let us die,
And let us die together.'
A lake was near; the shore was steep;
There never foot had been;
They ran, and with a desperate leap
Together plunged into the deep,
Nor ever more were seen.
Sing, mournfully, oh ! mournfully,
The solitude of Binnorie.

VI

The stream that flows out of the lake,
As through the glen it rambles,
Repeats a moan o'er moss and stone,
For those seven lovely Campbells.

Seven little Islands, green and bare,
Have risen from out the deep :
The fishers say, those sisters fair,
By faeries all are buried there,
And there together sleep.
Sing, mournfully, oh ! mournfully,
The solitude of Binnorie.

2

'And She who dwells with me, whom I have loved
With such communion, that no place on earth
Can ever be a solitude to me,
Hath to this lonely Summit given my Name.'

From *Poems on the Naming of Places*, III

[*August 21st,*] *Thursday*. Read *Wallenstein*[1] and sent it off –
worked in the morning – walked with John round the two lakes
– gathered white fox-glove seeds and found Wm. in Bainriggs at
our return.

[*August*] *22nd, Friday*. Very cold. Baking in the morning, gath-
ered pea seeds and took up – lighted a fire upstairs. Walked as
far as Rydale with John intending to have gone on to Amble-
side, but we found the papers at Rydale – Wm. walking in the
wood all the time. John and he went out after our return – I
mended stockings. Wind very high shaking the corn.

[*August*] *23rd, Saturday*. A very fine morning. Wm. was com-
posing all the morning. I shelled peas, gathered beans, and
worked in the garden till ½ past 12. Then walked with Wm. in
the wood. The gleams of sunshine, and the stirring trees, and
gleaming boughs, chearful lake, most delightful. After dinner
we walked to Ambleside – showery – went to see Mr Part-
ridge's house. Came home by Clappersgate. We had intended
going by Rydale woods, but it was cold – I was not well, and
tired. Got tea immediately and had a fire. Did not reach home

---

1. That is, Coleridge's translation of *Wallenstein*, a drama by
Schiller, in two acts, which Coleridge translated with much diffi-
culty during the beginning of the year.

till 7 o'clock – mended stockings and Wm. read *Peter Bell*.[1] He read us the poem of *Joanna*, beside the Rothay by the roadside.

'Joanna', the second poem in the group On the Naming of Places, *was written to Joanna Hutchinson. It should not be taken too literally.*

TO JOANNA

Amid the smoke of cities did you pass
The time of early youth; and there you learned,
From years of quiet industry, to love
The living Beings by your own fireside,
With such a strong devotion, that your heart
Is slow to meet the sympathies of them
Who look upon the hills with tenderness,
And make dear friendships with the streams and groves.
Yet we, who are transgressors in this kind,
Dwelling retired in our simplicity
Among the woods and fields, we love you well,
Joanna! and I guess, since you have been
So distant from us now for two long years,
That you will gladly listen to discourse,
However trivial, if you thence be taught
That they, with whom you once were happy, talk
Familiarly of you and of old times.

While I was seated, now some ten days past,
Beneath those lofty firs, that overtop
Their ancient neighbour, the old steeple-tower,
The Vicar from his gloomy house hard by
Came forth to greet me; and when he had asked,
'How fares Joanna, that wild-hearted Maid!
And when will she return to us?' he paused;
And, after short exchange of village news,
He with grave looks demanded, for what cause,
Reviving obsolete idolatry,
I, like a Runic Priest, in characters

---

1. 'Peter Bell' was begun 20 April 1798. See the Alfoxden Journal.

Of formidable size had chiselled out
Some uncouth name upon the native rock,
Above the Rotha, by the forest-side.
– Now, by those dear immunities of heart
Engendered between malice and true love,
I was not loth to be so catechised,
And this was my reply : – 'As it befell,
One summer morning we had walked abroad
At break of day, Joanna and myself.
– 'Twas that delightful season when the broom,
Full-flowered, and visible on every steep,
Along the copses runs in veins of gold.
Our pathway led us on to Rotha's banks;
And when we came in front of that tall rock
That eastward looks, I there stopped short – and stood
Tracing the lofty barrier with my eye
From base to summit; such delight I found
To note in shrub and tree, in stone and flower
That intermixture of delicious hues,
Along so vast a surface, all at once,
In one impression, by connecting force
Of their own beauty, imaged in the heart.
– When I had gazed perhaps two minutes' space,
Joanna, looking in my eyes, beheld
That ravishment of mine, and laughed aloud.
The Rock, like something starting from a sleep
Took up the Lady's voice, and laughed again;
That ancient Woman seated on Helm-crag
Was ready with her cavern; Hammar-scar,
And the tall Steep of Silver-how, sent forth
A noise of laughter; southern Loughrigg heard,
And Fairfield answered with a mountain tone;
Helvellyn far into the clear blue sky
Carried the Lady's voice, – old Skiddaw blew
His speaking-trumpet; – back out of the clouds
Of Glaramara southward came the voice;
And Kirkstone tossed it from his misty head.
– Now whether (said I to our cordial Friend,
Who in the hey-day of astonishment

Smiled in my face) this were in simple truth
A work accomplished by the brotherhood
Of ancient mountains, or my ear was touched
With dreams and visionary impulses
To me alone imparted, sure I am
That there was a loud uproar in the hills.
And, while we both were listening, to my side
The fair Joanna drew, as if she wished
To shelter from some object of her fear.
– And hence, long afterwards, when eighteen moons
Were wasted, as I chanced to walk alone
Beneath this rock, at sunrise, on a calm
And silent morning, I sat down, and there,
In memory of affections old and true,
I chiselled out in those rude characters
Joanna's name deep in the living stone :
And I, and all who dwell by my fireside,
Have called the lovely rock, JOANNA'S ROCK.'

[*August*] 26th, Tuesday. We walked in the evening to Amble-
side – Wm. not quite well. I bought sacking for the mattrass.
A very fine solemn evening. The wind blew very free from the
islands at Rydale. We went on the other side of Rydale, and
sate a long time looking at the mountains, which were all black
at Grasmere, and very bright in Rydale; Grasmere exceedingly
dark, and Rydale of a light yellow green.

[*August*] 27th, Wednesday. In the morning Wm. walked [?]. We
walked along the shore of the lake in the evening, went over
into Langdale and down to Loughrigg Tarn – a very fine even-
ing calm and still.

[*August* 28th,] Thursday. Still very fine weather. I baked bread
and cakes. In the evening we walked round the Lake by Rydale.
Mr Simpson came to fish.

[*August 29th,*] *Friday Evening.* We walked to Rydale to inquire for letters. We walked over the hill by the firgrove. I sate upon a rock, and observed a flight of swallows gathering together high above my head. They flew towards Rydale. We walked through the wood over the stepping-stones. The lake of Rydale very beautiful, partly still. John and I left Wm. to compose an inscription – that about the path. We had a very fine walk by the gloomy lake. There was a curious yellow reflection in the water, as of corn fields. There was no light in the clouds from which it appeared to come.

The inscription referred to above is now thought to be six lines entitled 'The Orchard Pathway' which W. originally intended to be the motto for the whole group On the Naming of Places.

THE ORCHARD PATHWAY

Orchard Pathway, to and fro,
Ever with thee, did I go,
Weaving Verses, a huge store !
These and many hundreds more,
And, in memory of the same,
This little lot shall bear thy name !

August 30th, Saturday Morning. I was baking bread, pies and dinner. It was very warm. William finished his Inscription of the Pathway, then walked in the wood; and when John returned, he sought him, and they bathed together. I read a little of Boswell's *Life of Johnson.* I had a headach and went to lie down in the orchard. I was roused by a shout that Anthony Harrison was come. We sate in the orchard till tea time. Drank tea early, and rowed down the lake which was stirred by breezes. We looked at Rydale, which was soft, chearful and beautiful. We then went to peep into Langdale. The Pikes were very grand. We walked back to the view of Rydale, which was now a dark mirror. We rowed home over a lake still as glass, and then went to George Mackareth's to hire a horse for John. A fine moonlight night. The beauty of the moon was startling, as it rose to us over

Loughrigg Fell. We returned to supper at 10 o'clock. Thomas Ashburner brought us our 8th cart of coals since May 17th.

[*August*] *31st, Sunday*. Anthony Harrison and John left us at ½ past seven – a very fine morning. A great deal of corn is cut in the vale, and the whole prospect, though not tinged with a general autumnal yellow, yet softened down into a mellowness of colouring, which seems to impart softness to the forms of hills and mountains. At 11 o'clock Coleridge came, when I was walking in the still clear moonshine in the garden. He came over Helvellyn. Wm. was gone to bed, and John also, worn out with his ride round Coniston. We sate and chatted till ½ past three, W. in his dressing gown. Coleridge read us a part of *Christabel*. Talked much about the mountains, etc. etc. Miss Thrale's [?] – Losh's opinion of Southey – the first of poets.

September 1st, Monday Morning. We walked in the wood by the lake. W. read *Joanna*, and the *Firgrove*, to Coleridge. They bathed. The morning was delightful, with somewhat of an autumnal freshness. After dinner, Coleridge discovered a rock-seat in the orchard. Cleared away the brambles. Coleridge obliged to go to bed after tea. John and I followed Wm. up the hill, and then returned to go to Mr Simpson's. We borrowed some bottles for bottling rum. The evening somewhat frosty and grey, but very pleasant. I broiled Coleridge a mutton chop, which he ate in bed. Wm. was gone to bed. I chatted with John and Coleridge till near 12.

'The Firgrove' is probably an early draft of lines 1–83 of 'When to the attractions of a busy world'. The greater part was written in 1802 (see 26 March 1802) and altered just before 11 February 1805 when W.'s brother, to whom the poem is addressed, died in a shipwreck.

When, to the attractions of the busy world
Preferring studious leisure, I had chosen
A habitation in this peaceful Vale,

Sharp season followed of continual storm
In deepest winter; and, from week to week,
Pathway, and lane, and public road, were clogged
With frequent showers of snow. Upon a hill
At a short distance from my cottage, stands
A stately Fir-grove, whither I was wont
To hasten, for I found, beneath the roof
Of that perennial shade, a cloistral place
Of refuge, with an unincumbered floor.
Here, in safe covert, on the shallow snow,
And, sometimes, on a speck of visible earth,
The redbreast near me hopped; nor was I loth
To sympathise with vulgar coppice birds
That, for protection from the nipping blast,
Hither repaired. – A single beech-tree grew
Within this grove of firs ! and, on the fork
Of that one beech, appeared a thrush's nest;
A last year's nest, conspicuously built
At such small elevation from the ground
As gave sure sign that they, who in that house
Of nature and of love had made their home
Amid the fir-trees, all the summer long
Dwelt in a tranquil spot. And oftentimes,
A few sheep, stragglers from some mountain-flock,
Would watch my motions with suspicious stare,
From the remotest outskirts of the grove, –
Some nook where they had made their final stand,
Huddling together from two fears – the fear
Of me and of the storm. Full many an hour
Here did I lose. But in this grove the trees
Had been so thickly planted, and had thriven
In such perplexed and intricate array,
That vainly did I seek, beneath their stems
A length of open space, where to and fro
My feet might move without concern or care;
And, baffled thus, though earth from day to day
Was fettered, and the air by storm disturbed,
I ceased the shelter to frequent, – prized,
Less than I wished to prize, that calm recess.

The snows dissolved, and genial Spring returned
To clothe the fields with verdure. Other haunts
Meanwhile were mine; till, one bright April day,
By chance retiring from the glare of noon
To this forsaken covert, there I found
A hoary pathway traced between the trees,
And winding on with such an easy line
Along a natural opening, that I stood
Much wondering how I could have sought in vain
For what was now so obvious. To abide,
For an allotted interval of ease,
Under my cottage-roof, had gladly come
From the wild sea a cherished Visitant;
And with the sight of this same path – begun,
Begun and ended, in the shady grove,
Pleasant conviction flashed upon my mind
That, to this opportune recess allured,
He had surveyed it with a finer eye,
A heart more wakeful; and had worn the track
By pacing here, unwearied and alone,
In that habitual restlessness of foot
That haunts the Sailor measuring o'er and o'er
His short domain upon the vessel's deck,
While she pursues her course through the dreary sea.

When thou hadst quitted Esthwaite's pleasant shore,
And taken thy first leave of those green hills
And rocks that were the play-ground of thy youth,
Year followed year, my Brother ! and we two,
Conversing not, knew little in what mould
Each other's mind was fashioned; and at length,
When once again we met in Grasmere Vale,
Between us there was little other bond
Than common feelings of fraternal love.
But thou, a Schoolboy, to the sea hadst carried
Undying recollections ! Nature there
Was with thee; she, who loved us both, she still
Was with thee; and even so didst thou become
A *silent* Poet; from the solitude

Of the vast sea didst bring a watchful heart
Still couchant, an inevitable ear,
And an eye practised like a blind man's touch.
– Back to the joyless Ocean thou art gone;
Nor from this vestige of thy musing hours
Could I withhold thy honoured name, – and now
I love the fir-grove with a perfect love.
Thither do I withdraw when cloudless suns
Shine hot, or wind blows troublesome and strong;
And there I sit at evening, when the steep
Of Silver-how, and Grasmere's peaceful lake,
And one green island, gleam between the stems
Of the dark firs, a visionary scene !
And, while I gaze upon the spectacle
Of clouded splendour, on this dream-like sight
Of solemn loveliness, I think on thee,
My Brother, and on all which thou hast lost.
Nor seldom, if I rightly guess, while Thou,
Muttering the verses which I muttered first
Among the mountains, through the midnight watch
Art pacing thoughtfully the vessel's deck
In some far region, here, while o'er my head,
At every impulse of the moving breeze,
The fir-grove murmurs with a sea-like sound,
Alone I tread this path; – for aught I know,
Timing my steps to thine; and, with a store
Of undistinguishable sympathies,
Mingling most earnest wishes for the day
When we, and others whom we love, shall meet
A second time, in Grasmere's happy Vale.

NOTE. – This wish was not granted; the lamented Person not long after perished by shipwreck, in discharge of his duty as Commander of the Honourable East India Company's Vessel, the *Earl of Abergavenny.*

[*September*] 2nd, *Tuesday.* In the morning they all went to Stickle Tarn. A very fine, warm, sunny, beautiful morning. I baked a pie etc. for dinner – Little Sally was with me. The fair-day. Miss Simpson and Mr came down to tea – we walked to the fair. There seemed very few people and very few stalls, yet I believe there were many cakes and much beer sold. My brothers came home to dinner at 6 o'clock. We drank tea immediately after by candlelight. It was a lovely moonlight night. We talked much about a house on Helvellyn. The moonlight shone only upon the village. It did not eclipse the village lights, and the sound of dancing and merriment came along the still air. I walked with Coleridge and Wm. up the lane and by the church, and then lingered with Coleridge in the garden. John and Wm. were both gone to bed, and all the lights out.

September 3rd, Wednesday. Coleridge, Wm., and John went from home, to go upon Helvellyn with Mr Simpson. They set out after breakfast. I accompanied them up near the blacksmith's. A fine coolish morning. I ironed till ½ past 3 – now very hot – I then went to a funeral at John Dawson's. About 10 men and 4 women. Bread, cheese, and ale. They talked sensibly and chear-fully about common things. The dead person, 56 years of age, buried by the parish. The coffin was neatly lettered and painted black, and covered with a decent cloth. They set the corpse down at the door; and, while we stood within the threshold, the men with their hats off sang with decent and solemn countenances a verse of a funeral psalm. The corpse was then borne down the hill, and they sang till they had passed the Town-End. I was affected to tears while we stood in the house, the coffin lying before me. There were no near kindred, no children. When we got out of the dark house the sun was shining, and the prospect looked so divinely beautiful as I never saw it. It seemed more sacred than I had ever seen it, and yet more allied to human life. The green fields, neighbours of the churchyard, were as green as possible; and, with the brightness of the sunshine, looked quite gay. I thought she was going to a quiet spot, and I could not help weeping very much. When we came to the bridge, they began to sing again, and stopped during four lines before they entered the churchyard. The priest met us – he did not look as a man ought to do on such an occasion – I had seen him half-drunk the day before in a pot-house. Before we came with the corpse one of the company observed he wondered what sort of cue our Parson would be in ! N.B. It was the day after the Fair. I had not finished ironing till 7 o'clock. The wind was now high and I did not walk – writing my journal now at 8 o'clock. Wm. and John came home at 10 o'clock.

Wordsworth used this description in 'The Excursion', Book II, lines 370–402 and lines 548–66. It did not seem worth printing them here, as Dorothy's prose is far more alive and touching.

[September] 9th, Tuesday Morning. Mr Marshall came – he dined with us. My Brothers walked with him round the lakes after dinner – windy – we went to the island. W. and I after to tea. John and I went to the B. quarter, before supper went to seek a horse at Dawson's, Firgrove. After supper, talked of Wm.'s poems.

Sept[ember] 10th, Wednesday. After breakfast Mr Marshall, Wm. and John went on horseback to Keswick – I wrote to Mrs Marshall – a fine autumn day.[1] I had a fire. Paid Mr Bonsfield 8:2:11. After tea walked with French Beans to Mr Simpson's – went up to the Forest side above a deserted house – sat till twilight came on. Mr and Miss S. came down with me and supped.

[September] 11th, Thursday. All the morning mending white gown – washed my head – Molly washing. Drank tea at Mr Simpson's. Found Wm. at home at my return – he was unable to go on with Mr Marshall and parted from him in Borrowdale. Made tea after my return.

---

1. See Dorothy's letter to Jane Marshall of 10 September in *Early Letters of William and Dorothy Wordsworth*, in which she gives a long and lively account of their life at Grasmere and describes Mr Marshall's visit. It is one of her best letters and is not printed here only because it adds very little to what we know from the Journal.

Sept[ember] 12th, *Friday.* I worked in the morning. Cut my thumb. Walked in the Firgrove before dinner – after dinner sate under the trees in the orchard – a rainy morning, but very fine afternoon. Miss Simpson called for my packing needle. The Fern of the mountains now spreads yellow veins among the trees,[1] the coppice wood turns brown. William observed some affecting little things in Borrowdale. A decayed house with this inscription [*blank space in MS.*] in the Church yard, the tall silent rocks seen thro' the broken windows. A kind of rough column put upon the gravel end of a house, with a ball stone, smooth from the river placed upon it for an ornament. Near it one stone like it upon an old mansion, carefully hewn.

September 13th, *Saturday Morning.* William writing his Preface – did not walk. Jones,[2] and Mr Palmer came to tea. We walked with them to Borricks – a lovely evening, but the air frosty – worked when I returned home. Wm. walked out. John came home from Mr Marshall. Sent back word to Mrs Clarkson.[3]

[*September*] 29th, *on Monday.* John left us. Wm. and I parted with him in sight of Ulswater. It was a fine day, showery, but with sunshine and fine clouds. Poor fellow, my heart was right sad. I could not help thinking we should see him again, because he was only going to Penrith.

It is this parting which is described in the poem Wordsworth wrote after hearing of his brother's death.

1. See p. 43.
2. The Reverend Robert Jones, fellow of St John's, Cambridge, who accompanied Wordsworth on his Continental tour of 1790 and to whom the *Descriptive Sketches* are dedicated.
3. Catherine Clarkson, who later became one of Dorothy's greatest friends, was the wife of Thomas Clarkson, the slave abolitionist, and lived at Eusemere.

ELEGIAC VERSES

In Memory of my Brother
John Wordsworth.

Commander of the E.I. Company's Ship
the *Earl of Abergavenny*, in
which he perished by calamitous
shipwreck, Feb. 6, 1805.

I

The Sheep-boy whistled loud, and lo!
That instant, startled by the shock,
The Buzzard mounted from the rock
Deliberate and slow:
Lord of the air, he took his flight;
Oh! could he on that woeful night
Have lent his wing, my Brother dear,
For one poor moment's space to Thee,
And all who struggled with the Sea,
When safety was so near.

II

Thus in the weakness of my heart
I spoke (but let that pang be still)
When rising from the rock at will,
I saw the Bird depart.
And let me calmly bless the Power
That meets me in this unknown Flower.
Affecting type of him I mourn!
With calmness suffer and believe,
And grieve, and know that I must grieve,
Not cheerless, though forlorn.

III

Here did we stop; and here looked round
While each into himself descends,
For that last thought of parting Friends
That is not to be found.
Hidden was Grasmere Vale from sight,
Our home and his, his heart's delight,
His quiet heart's selected home.
But time before him melts away,
And he hath feeling of a day
Of blessedness to come.

IV

Full soon in sorrow did I weep,
Taught that the mutual hope was dust,
In sorrow, but for higher trust,
How miserably deep!
All vanished in a single word,
A breath, a sound, and scarcely heard:
Sea – Ship – drowned – Shipwreck – so it came,
The meek, the brave, the good, was gone;
He who had been our living John
Was nothing but a name.

V

That was indeed a parting! oh,
Glad am I, glad that it is past;
For there were some on whom it cast
Unutterable woe.
But they as well as I have gains; –
From many a humble source, to pains
Like these, there comes a mild release;
Even here I feel it, even this Plant
Is in its beauty ministrant
To comfort and to peace.

VI

He would have loved thy modest grace,
Meek Flower ! To Him I would have said,
'It grows upon its native bed
Beside our Parting-place;
There, cleaving to the ground, it lies
With multitude of purple eyes,
Spangling a cushion green like moss;
But we will see it, joyful tide !
Some day, to see it in its pride,
The mountain will we cross.'

VII

– Brother and Friend, if verse of mine
Have power to make thy virtues known,
Here let a monumental Stone
Stand – sacred as a Shrine;
And to the few who pass this way,
Traveller or Shepherd, let it say,
Long as these mighty rocks endure, –
Oh do not Thou too fondly brood,
Although deserving of all good,
On any earthly hope however pure !

September 30th, on Tuesday. Charles Lloyd dined with us. We walked homewards with him after dinner. It rained very hard. Rydale was extremely wild, and we had a fine walk. We sate quietly and comfortably by the fire. I wrote the last sheet of Notes and Preface.

The Preface referred to was for the 1802 edition of the Lyrical Ballads. *This is the most brilliant piece of prose Wordsworth wrote. It shows how deeply he was concerned with his calling as a poet and the profound thought which lies behind the simple poetry he was writing in this period.*

74

October 1st, Wednesday. A fine morning, a showery night. The lake still in the morning; in the forenoon flashing light from the beams of the sun, as it was ruffled by the wind. We corrected the last sheet.

October 2nd, Thursday. A very rainy morning. We walked after dinner to observe the torrents. I followed Wm. to Rydale, he afterwards went to Butterlip How. I came home to receive the Lloyds. They walked with us to see Churnmilk force and the Black quarter. The Black Quarter looked marshy, and the general prospect was cold, but the Force was very grand. The Lichens are now coming out a fresh, I carried home a collection in the afternoon. We had a pleasant conversation about the manners of the rich – avarice, inordinate desires, and the effeminacy, unnaturalness, and the unworthy objects of education. After the Lloyds were gone we walked – a showery evening. The moonlight lay upon the hills like snow.

October 3rd, Friday. Very rainy all the morning. Little Sally learning to mark. Wm. walked to Ambleside after dinner, I went with him part of the way. He talked much about the object of his essay for the second volume of 'L.B.' I returned expecting the Simpsons – they did not come. I should have met Wm. but my teeth ached and it was showery and late – he returned after 10. Amos Cottle's death in the *Morning Post*. Wrote to S. Lowthian.

N.B. When Wm. and I returned from accompanying Jones, we met an old man almost double. He had on a coat, thrown over his shoulders, above his waistcoat and coat. Under this he carried a bundle, and had an apron on and a night-cap. His face was interesting. He had dark eyes and a long nose. John, who afterwards met him at Wytheburn, took him for a Jew. He was of Scotch parents, but had been born in the army. He had had a wife, and 'a good woman, and it pleased God to bless us with ten children'. All these were dead but one, of whom he had not heard for many years, a sailor. His trade was to gather leeches, but now leeches are scarce, and he had not strength for it. He lived by begging, and was making his way to Carlisle, where he should buy a few godly books to sell. He said leeches were very scarce, partly owing to this dry season, but many years they had been scarce – he supposed it owing to their being much sought after, that they did not breed fast, and were of slow growth. Leeches were formerly 2s 6d. [per] 100; they are now 30s. He had been hurt in driving a cart, his leg broke, his body driven over, his skull fractured. He felt no pain till he recovered from his first insensibility. It was then late in the evening, when the light was just going away.

The poem 'Resolution and Independence' based on the incident Dorothy records here was written in its original form (and known as 'The Leech-Gatherer') between 4 and 9 May 1802. For a note on this, see also 14 June 1802, and William's letter to Sarah Hutchinson. The poem was completed in its final form on 4 July 1802, and can be found on p. 266 of this book.

October 4th, 1800, *Saturday*. A very rainy, or rather showery and gusty, morning; for often the sun shines. Thomas Ashburner could not go to Keswick. Read a part of Lamb's Play.[1] The language is often very beautiful, but too imitative in particular phrases, words, etc. The characters, except Margaret's, unintelligible, and, except Margaret's, do not show themselves in action. Coleridge came in while we were at dinner, very wet – we talked till 12 o'clock. He had sate up all the night before, writing Essays for the newspaper. His youngest child had been very ill in convulsion fits. Exceedingly delighted with the second part of *Christabel*.

October 5th, Sunday Morning. Coleridge read a 2nd time *Christabel*; we had increasing pleasure. A delicious morning. Wm. and I were employed all the morning in writing an addition to the Preface. Wm. went to bed, very ill after working after dinner. Coleridge and I walked to Ambleside after dark with the letter. Returned to tea at 9 o'clock. Wm. still in bed, and very ill. Silver How in both lakes.

---

1. *Pride's Cure*. The title was afterwards changed to *John Woodvill*.

[*October 6th,*] *Monday.* A rainy day. Coleridge intending to go, but did not get off. We walked after dinner to Rydale. After tea read *The Pedlar.* Determined not to print *Christabel* with the L.B.

Like William and Dorothy I decided finally not to print 'Christabel' in this book, feeling, perhaps as they did, that Coleridge's marvellous poem had little in common with William's Grasmere poetry and owed nothing to the Grasmere scene.

[*October 7th,*] *Tuesday.* Coleridge went off at eleven o'clock. I went as far as Mrs Simpson's. Returned with Mary. She drank tea here. I was very ill in the evening at the Simpsons – went to bed – supped there. Returned with Miss S. and Mrs J. – heavy showers. Found Wm. at home. I was still weak and unwell – went to bed immediately.

[*October 8th,*] *Wednesday.* A threatening bad morning – We dried the linen. Frequent threatening of showers. Received a £5 note from Montagu. Wm. walked to Rydale. I copied a part of *The Beggar*[1] in the morning. I was not quite well in the evening, therefore I did not walk – Wm. walked. A very mild moonlight night. Glow-worms everywhere.

[*October 9th,*] *Thursday.* I was ironing all the day till tea time. Very rainy. Wm. and I walked in the evening, intending to go to Lloyd's, but it came on so very rainy that we were obliged to shelter at Fleming's. A grand Ball at Rydale. After sitting some time we went homewards and were again caught by a shower and sheltered under the sycamores at the boat-house – a very cold snowlike rain. A man called in a soldier's dress – he was thirty years old, of Cockermouth, had lost a leg and thigh in battle, was going to his home. He could earn more money in travelling with his ass than at home.

---

1. This must refer to 'The Old Cumberland Beggar' written at Alfoxden in 1797. It is a long poem and not of sufficient interest to print here.

October 10th, Friday. In the morning when I arose the mists were hanging over the opposite hills, and the tops of the highest hills were covered with snow. There was a most lovely combination at the head of the vale of the yellow autumnal hills wrapped in sunshine, and overhung with partial mists, the green and yellow trees, and the distant snow-topped mountains. It was a most heavenly morning. The Cockermouth traveller came with thread, hardware, mustard, etc. She is very healthy; has travelled over the mountains these thirty years. She does not mind the storms, if she can keep her goods dry. Her husband will not travel with an ass, because it is the tramper's badge; she would have one to relieve her from the weary load. She was going to Ulverston, and was to return to Ambleside Fair. After I had finished baking I went out with Wm., Mrs Jameson and Miss Simpson towards Rydale – the fern among the rocks exquisitely beautiful. We turned home and walked to Mr Gell's. After dinner Wm. went to bed – I read Southey's letter. Miss Simpson and Mrs Jameson came to tea. After tea we went to Lloyd's – a fine evening as we went, but rained in returning – we were wet – found them not at home. I wrote to Mrs Clarkson. Sent off *The Beggar*, etc., by Thomas Ashburner who went to fetch our 9th cart of coals. William sat up after me, writing *Point Rash Judgment*.

> A narrow girdle of rough stones and crags,
> A rude and natural causeway, interposed
> Between the water and a winding slope
> Of copse and thicket, leaves the eastern shore
> Of Grasmere safe in its own privacy :
> And there myself and two beloved Friends,
> One calm September morning, ere the mist
> Had altogether yielded to the sun,
> Sauntered on this retired and difficult way.
> – Ill suits the road with one in haste : but we
> Played with our time; and, as we strolled along,
> It was our occupation to observe
> Such objects as the waves had tossed ashore –
> Feather, or leaf, or weed, or withered bough,
> Each on the other heaped, along the line

Of the dry wreck. And, in our vacant mood,
Not seldom did we stop to watch some tuft
Of dandelion seed or thistle's beard,
That skimmed the surface of the dead calm lake,
Suddenly halting now – a lifeless stand!
And starting off again with freak as sudden;
In all its sportive wanderings, all the while,
Making report of an invisible breeze
That was its wings, its chariot, and its horse,
Its playmate, rather say, its moving soul.
– And often, trifling with a privilege
Alike indulged to all, we paused, one now,
And now the other, to point out, perchance
To pluck, some flower or water-weed, too fair
Either to be divided from the place
On which it grew, or to be left alone
To its own beauty. Many such there are,
Fair ferns and flowers, and chiefly that tall fern,
So stately, of the queen Osmunda named;
Plant lovelier, in its own retired abode
On Grasmere's beach, than Naiad by the side
Of Grecian brook, or Lady of the Mere,
Sole-sitting by the shores of old romance.
– So fared we that bright morning: from the fields
Meanwhile, a noise was heard, the busy mirth
Of reapers, men and women, boys and girls.
Delighted much to listen to those sounds,
And feeding thus our fancies, we advanced
Along the indented shore; when suddenly,
Through a thin veil of glittering haze was seen
Before us, on a point of jutting land,
The tall and upright figure of a Man
Attired in peasant's garb, who stood alone,
Angling beside the margin of the lake.
'Improvident and reckless,' we exclaimed,
'The Man must be, who thus can lose a day
Of the mid harvest, when the labourer's hire
Is ample, and some little might be stored
Wherewith to cheer him in the winter time.'

Thus talking of that Peasant, we approached
Close to the spot where with his rod and line
He stood alone; whereat he turned his head
To greet us – and we saw a Man worn down
By sickness, gaunt and lean, with sunken cheeks
And wasted limbs, his legs so long and lean
That for my single self I looked at them,
Forgetful of the body they sustained. –
Too weak to labour in the harvest field,
The Man was using his best skill to gain
A pittance from the dead unfeeling lake
That knew not of his wants. I will not say
What thoughts immediately were ours, nor how
The happy idleness of that sweet morn,
With all its lovely images, was changed
To serious musing and to self-reproach.
Nor did we fail to see within ourselves
What need there is to be reserved in speech,
And temper all our thoughts with charity.
– Therefore, unwilling to forget that day,
My friend, Myself, and She who then received
The same admonishment, have called the place
By a memorial name, uncouth indeed
As e'er by mariner was given to bay
Or foreland, on a new discovered coast;
And POINT RASH-JUDGMENT is the name it bears.

The friends spoken of were Coleridge and my Sister, and the facts
occurred strictly as recorded.

3

'Among the rocks
He went, and still looked up to sun and cloud,
And listened to the wind;'

[*October*] 11*th, Saturday*. A fine October morning. Sat in the house working all the morning. William composing. Sally Ashburner learning to mark. After dinner we walked up Greenhead Gill in search of a sheepfold.

This was the start of almost two months' work on 'Michael' which Wordsworth finished on 9 December, and which can be found on p. 90 of this book. The poem was based on incidents he had heard of locally but it embodies many of Wordsworth's most deeply held convictions. In a note of 1802–5, he tells us 'a sheepfold in these mountains is an unroofed building of stone walls with different divisions ... generally placed by the side of a brook'.

We went by Mr Olliff's, and through his woods. It was a delightful day, and the views looked excessively chearful and beautiful, chiefly that from Mr Olliff's field, where our house is to be built. The colours of the mountains soft and rich, with orange fern; the cattle pasturing upon the hill-tops; kites sailing in the sky above our heads; sheep bleating and in lines and chains and patterns scattered over the mountains. They come down and feed on the little green islands in the beds of the torrents, and so may be swept away. The sheepfold is falling away. It is built nearly in the form of a heart unequally divided. Look down the brook, and see the drops rise upwards and sparkle in the air at the little falls, the higher sparkles the tallest. We walked along the turf of the mountain till we came to a cattle track, made by the cattle which come upon the hills. We drank tea at Mr Simpson's, returned at about nine – a fine mild night.

October 12th, Sunday. Beautiful day. Sate in the house writing in the morning while Wm. went into the wood to compose. Wrote to John in the morning, copied poems for the L.B.; in the evening wrote to Mrs Rawson. Mary Jameson and Sally Ashburner dined. We pulled apples after dinner, a large basket full. We walked before tea to Bainriggs to observe the many-coloured foliage. The oaks dark green with yellow leaves, the birches generally still green, some near the water yellowish, the sycamore crimson and crimson-tufted, the mountain ash a deep orange, the common ash lemon-colour, but many ashes still fresh in their summer green. Those that were discoloured chiefly near the water. William composing in the evening. Went to bed at 12 o'clock.

October 13th, Monday. A grey day. Mists on the hills. We did not walk in the morning. I copied poems on the Naming of Places. A fair at Ambleside. Walked in the Black Quarter at night.

[*October*] *14th, Tuesday*. Wm. lay down after dinner – I read Southey's Spain. The wind rose very high at evening. Wm. walked out just at bedtime – I went to bed early. We walked before dinner to Rydale.

[*October 15th,*] *Wednesday*. A very fine clear morning. After Wm. had composed a little, I persuaded him to go into the orchard. We walked backwards and forwards. The prospect most divinely beautiful from the seat; all colours, all melting into each other. I went in to put bread in the oven, and we both walked within view of Rydale. Wm. again composed at the sheepfold after dinner. I walked with him to Wytheburn, and he went on to Keswick. I drank tea, and supped at Mr Simpson's. A very cold frosty air and a spangled sky in returning. Mr and Miss S. came with me. Wytheburn looked very wintry, but yet there was a foxglove blossoming by the roadside.

[*October 18th,*] *Saturday.* A very fine October morning. William worked all the morning at the sheepfold, but in vain. He lay down in the afternoon till 7 o'clock, but could not sleep. I slept, my head better – he unable to work. We did not walk all day.

[*October 19th,*] *Sunday morning.* We rose late, and walked directly after breakfast. The top of G[ras]mere mountains cut off. Rydale was very, very beautiful. The surface of the water quite still, like a dim mirror. The colours of the large island exquisitely beautiful, and the trees still fresh and green were magnified by the mists. The prospects on the west side of the Lake were very beautiful. We sate at the 'two points' looking up to Park's. The lowing of the cattle was echoed by a hollow voice in Knab Scar. We went up Loughrigg Fell and were disappointed with G[ras]mere – It did not look near so beautiful as Rydale. We returned home over the stepping-stones. Wm. got to work. We are not to dine till 4 o'clock. – Dined at ½ past 5 – Mr Simpson dined and drank tea with us. We went to bed immediately after he left us.

[*October*] *20th, Monday.* William worked in the morning at the sheepfold. After dinner we walked to Rydale, crossed the stepping-stones, and while we were walking under the tall oak trees the Lloyds called out to us. They went with us on the western side of Rydale. The lights were very grand upon the woody Rydale hills. Those behind dark and topp'd with clouds. The two lakes were divinely beautiful. Grasmere excessively solemn and the whole lake was calm, and dappled with soft grey ripples. The Lloyds staid with us till 8 o'clock. We then walked to the top of the hill at Rydale. Very mild and warm. About 6 glow-worms shining faintly. We went up as far as the grove. When we came home the fire was out. We ate our supper in the dark, and went to bed immediately. William was disturbed in the night by the rain coming into his room, for it was a very rainy night. The ash leaves lay across the road.

[October] 21st, Tuesday. We walked in the morning past Mr Gell's – a very fine clear sharp sunny morning. We drank tea at the Lloyds. It was very cold in the evening, quite frosty and starlight. Wm. had been unsuccessful in the morning at the sheepfold. The reflection of the ash scattered, and the tree stripped.

[October 22nd,] Wednesday Morning. We walked to Mr Gell's – a very fine morning. Wm. composed without much success at the sheepfold. Coleridge came in to dinner. He had done nothing. We were very merry. C. and I went to look at the prospect from his seat. In the evening Stoddart[1] came in when we were at tea, and after tea Mr and Miss Simpson with large potatoes and plumbs. Wm. read after supper, Ruth, etc.; Coleridge Christabel.

[October] 23rd, Thursday. Coleridge and Stoddart went to Keswick. We accompanied them to Wytheburn – a wintry grey morning from the top of the Raise. Grasmere looked like winter, and Wytheburn still more so. We called upon Mrs Simpson and sate 10 minutes in returning. Wm. was not successful in composition in the evening.

[October] 24th, Friday. A very fine morning. We walked before Wm. began to work to the top of the Rydale hills. He was afterwards only partly successful in composition. After dinner we walked round Rydale lake, rich, calm, streaked, very beautiful. We went to the top of Loughrigg. Grasmere sadly inferior. We were much tired – Wm. went to bed till ½ past seven. The ash in the garden green, one close to it bare, the next nearly so.

[October 25th,] Saturday. A very rainy day. Wm. again unsuccessful. We could not walk, it was so very rainy. We read Rogers, Miss Seward, Cowper, etc.

---

1. Sir John Stoddart (1773–1856), a prominent journalist. Hazlitt married his sister.

[*October 26th,*] *Sunday*. Heavy rain all night, a fine morning after 10 o'clock. Wm. composed a good deal in the morning. The Lloyds came to dinner and were caught in a shower. Wm. read some of his poems after dinner. A terrible night. I went with Mrs Lloyd to Newton's to see for lodgings. Mr Simpson in coming from Ambleside called in for a glass of rum just before we went to bed.

October 27th, Monday. Not a rainy morning. The Hill tops covered with snow. Charles Lloyd came for his wife's glass. I walked home with him past Rydale. When he came I met him as I was carrying some cold meat to Wm. in the Fir-grove, I had before walked with him there for some time. It was a fine shelter from the wind. The coppices now nearly of one brown. An oak tree in a sheltered place near John Fisher's, not having lost any of its leaves, was quite brown and dry. We did not walk after dinner. It was a fine wild moonlight night. Wm. could not compose much, fatigued himself with altering.

[*October*] *28th, Tuesday*. A very rainy night. I was baking bread in the morning and made a giblet pie. We walked out before dinner to our favourite field. The mists sailed along the mountains, and rested upon them, enclosing the whole vale. In the evening the Lloyds came. We drank tea with them at Borwick's and played a rubber at whist – stayed supper. Wm. looked very well – A fine moonlight night when we came home.

[*October 31st,*] *Friday*. W. and I did not rise till 1 o'clock. W. very sick and very ill. S. and I drank tea at Lloyds and came home immediately after. A very fine moonlight night – The moon shone like herrings in the water.

[*November 4th,*] *Tuesday*. Stoddart left us – I walked a little way with Wm. and him. W. went to the Tarn, afterwards to the top of Seat Sandal. He was obliged to lie down in the tremendous

wind. The snow blew from Helvellyn horizontally like smoke –
the spray of the unseen waterfall like smoke. Miss Lloyd called
upon me – I walked with her past Rydale. Wm. sadly tired –
threatenings of the piles.

[November 5th,] Wednesday. Wm. not well. A very fine clear
beautiful winter's day. I walked after dinner to Lloyd's – drank
tea and Mrs and Miss Lloyd came to Rydale with me. The moon
was rising but the sky was all over cloud. I made tea for Wil-
liam.

November 6th, Thursday. A very rainy morning and night. I
was baking bread, dinner and parkins. Charles and P. Lloyd
called. Wm. somewhat better. Read *Point Rash Judgment*. The
lake calm and very beautiful – a very rainy afternoon and night.

November 7th, Friday. A cold rainy morning. Wm. still unwell.
I working and reading *Amelia*. The Michaelmas daisy droops, the
pansies are full of flowers, the ashes opposite are green all but
one, but they have lost many of their leaves. The copses are
quite brown. The poor woman and child from Whitehaven drank
tea – nothing warm that day. A very rainy morning. It cleared
up in the afternoon. We expected the Lloyds but they did not
come. Wm. still unwell. A rainy night.

[November 10th,] Monday. I baked bread. A fine clear frosty
morning. We walked after dinner to Rydale village. Jupiter over
the hilltops, the only star, like a sun, flashed out at intervals from
behind a black cloud.

[November 11th,] Tuesday Morning. Walked to Rydale before
dinner for letters. William had been working at the sheepfold.
They were salving sheep. A rainy morning. The Lloyds drank
tea with us. Played at cards – Priscilla not well. We walked

after they left us to the top of the Rydale hill – then towards Mr Olliff's and towards the village. A mild night, partly cloudy, partly starlight. The cottage lights, the mountains not very distinct.

[November 12th,] Wednesday. We sate in the house all the day. Mr Simpson called and found us at dinner – a rainy evening – he staid the evening and supper. I lay down after dinner with a headach.

[November 13th,] Thursday. A stormy night. We sate in the house all the morning. Rainy weather. Old Mr Simpson, Mrs J. and Miss S. drank tea and supped, played at cards, found us at dinner. A poor woman from Hawkshead begged, a widow of Grasmere. A merry African from Longtown.

[November 14th,] Friday. I had a bad headach. Much wind, but a sweet mild morning. I nailed up trees. Sent Molly Ashburner to excuse us to Lloyds. Two letters from Coleridge, very ill. One from Sara H. One from S. Lowthian – I wrote to S. Hutchinson and received £3 from her.

[November 15th,] Saturday Morning. A terrible rain, so William prevented from going to Coleridge's. The afternoon fine and mild – I walked to the top of the hill for a headach. We both set forward at five o'clock after tea. A fine wild but not cold night. I walked with W. over the Raise. It was starlight. I parted with him very sad, unwilling not to go on. The hills, and the stars, and the white waters, with their ever varying yet ceaseless sound, were very impressive. I supped at the Simpsons'. Mr P. walked home with me.

November 16th, Sunday. A very fine warm sunny morning. A letter from Coleridge, and one from Stoddart. Coleridge better.

My head aching very much – I sent to excuse myself to Lloyds – then walked to the Cottage beyond Mr Gell's. One beautiful ash tree sheltered, with yellow leaves, one low one quite green. Some low ashes green. A noise of boys in the rocks hunting some animal. Walked a little in the garden when I came home – very pleasant. Now rain came on. Mr Jackson called in the evening when I was at tea, brought me a letter from C. and W. C. better.

[November 26th,] Wednesday. Well in the morning. Wm. very well. We had a delightful walk up into Easedale. The tops of the mountains covered with snow, frosty and sunny, the roads slippery. A letter from Mary. The Lloyds drank tea. We walked with them near to Ambleside. A beautiful moonlight night. Sara and I walked before [? home]. William very well, and highly poetical.

November 27th, Thursday. Wrote to Tom Hutchinson to desire him to bring Mary with him from Stockton. A thaw, and the ground covered with snow. Sara and I walked before dinner.

[November 28th,] Friday. Coleridge walked over. Miss Simpson drank tea with us. William walked home with her. Coleridge was very unwell. He went to bed before Wm's return. Great boils upon his neck.

[December 4th,] Thursday. Coleridge came in just as we finished dinner. Pork from the Simpsons. Sara and I walked round the 2 lakes – a very fine morning. C. ate nothing, to cure his boils. We walked after tea by moonlight to look at Langdale covered with snow, the Pikes not grand, but the Old Man very impressive. Cold and slippery, but exceedingly pleasant. Sat up till half past one.

[*December 5th,*] *Friday Morning*. Terribly cold and rainy. Coleridge and Wm. set forwards towards Keswick, but the wind in Coleridge's eyes made him turn back. Sara and I had a grand bread and cake baking. We were very merry in the evening, but grew sleepy soon, though we did not go to bed till twelve o'clock.

[*December 6th,*] *Saturday*. Wm. accompanied Coleridge to the foot of the Rays. A very pleasant morning. Sara and I accompanied him half-way to Keswick. Thirlmere was very beautiful even more so than in summer. William was not well, had laboured unsuccessfully. Charles Lloyd had called. Sara and I drank tea with Mrs Simpson. A sharp shower met us – it rained a little when we came home – Mr B.S. accompanied us. Miss S. at Ambleside. Wm. tired and not well. A letter from M.H.

[*December 7th,*] *Sunday*. A fine morning. I read. Sara wrote to Hartley, Wm. to Mary, I to Mrs C. We walked just before dinner to the lakeside, and found out a seat in a tree. Windy, but pleasant. Sara and Wm. walked to the waterfalls at Rydale. I was unwell and went to bed till 8 o'clock – a pleasant mild evening – went to bed at 12. Miss Simpson called.

December 8th, Monday. A sweet mild morning. I wrote to Mrs Cookson, and Miss Griffith.

[*December*] *9th, Tuesday*. I dined at Lloyd's. Wm. drank tea. Walked home. A pleasant starlight frosty evening. Reached home at one o'clock. Wm. finished his poem to-day.

MICHAEL

A *Pastoral Poem*

If from the public way you turn your steps
Up the tumultuous brook of Greenhead Ghyll,
You will suppose that with an upright path
Your feet must struggle; in such bold ascent
The pastoral mountains front you, face to face.
But, courage! for around the boisterous brook
The mountains have all opened out themselves
And made a hidden valley of their own.
No habitation can be seen; but they
Who journey thither find themselves alone
With a few sheep, with rocks and stones, and kites
That overhead are sailing in the sky.
It is in truth an utter solitude;
Nor should I have made mention of this Dell
But for one object which you might pass by,
Might see and notice not. Beside the brook
Appears a straggling heap of unhewn stones!
And to that simple object appertains
A story – unenriched with strange events,
Yet not unfit, I deem, for the fireside,
Or for the summer shade. It was the first
Of those domestic tales that spake to me
Of shepherds, dwellers in the valleys, men
Whom I already loved; not verily
For their own sakes, but for the fields and hills
Where was their occupation and abode.
And hence this Tale, while I was yet a Boy
Careless of books, yet having felt the power
Of Nature, by the gentle agency
Of natural objects, led me on to feel
For passions that were not my own, and think
(At random and imperfectly indeed)
On man, the heart of man, and human life.
Therefore, although it be a history
Homely and rude, I will relate the same
For the delight of a few natural hearts;

And, with yet fonder feeling, for the sake
Of youthful Poets, who among these hills
Will be my second self when I am gone.

Upon the forest-side in Grasmere Vale
There dwelt a Shepherd, Michael was his name;
An old man, stout of heart, and strong of limb.
His bodily frame had been from youth to age
Of an unusual strength : his mind was keen,
Intense, and frugal, apt for all affairs,
And in his shepherd's calling he was prompt
And watchful more than ordinary men.
Hence had he learned the meaning of all winds,
Of blasts of every tone; and, oftentimes,
When others heeded not, He heard the South
Make subterraneous music, like the noise
Of bagpipes on distant Highland hills.
The Shepherd, at such warning, of his flock
Bethought him, and he to himself would say,
'The winds are now devising work for me !'
And truly, at all times, the storm, that drives
The traveller to a shelter, summoned him
Up to the mountains : he had been alone
Amid the hearts of many thousand mists,
That came to him, and left him, on the heights.
So lived he till his eightieth year was past.
And grossly that man errs, who should suppose
That the green valleys, and the streams and rocks,
Were things indifferent to the Shepherd's thoughts.
Fields, where with cheerful spirits he had breathed
The common air; hills, which with vigorous step
He had so often climbed; which had impressed
So many incidents upon his mind
Of hardship, skill or courage, joy or fear;
Which, like a book, preserved the memory
Of the dumb animals, whom he had saved,
Had fed or sheltered, linking to such acts
The certainty of honourable gain;
Those fields, those hills – what could they less? had laid

Strong hold on his affections, were to him
A pleasurable feeling of blind love,
The pleasure which there is in life itself.

His days had not been passed in singleness.
His Helpmate was a comely matron, old –
Though younger than himself full twenty years.
She was a woman of a stirring life,
Whose heart was in her house: two wheels she had
Of antique form; this large, for spinning wool;
That small, for flax; and if one wheel had rest
It was because the other was at work.
The Pair had but one inmate in their house,
An only Child, who had been born to them
When Michael, telling o'er his years, began
To deem that he was old – in shepherd's phrase,
With one foot in the grave. This only Son,
With two brave sheep-dogs tried in many a storm,
The one of an inestimable worth,
Made all their household. I may truly say,
That they were as a proverb in the vale
For endless industry. When day was gone,
And from their occupations out of doors
The Son and Father were come home, even then,
Their labour did not cease; unless when all
Turned to the cleanly supper-board, and there,
Each with a mess of pottage and skimmed milk,
Sat round the basket piled with oaten cakes,
And their plain home-made cheese. Yet when the meal
Was ended, Luke (for so the son was named)
And his old Father both betook themselves
To such convenient work as might employ
Their hands by the fireside; perhaps to card
Wool for the Housewife's spindle, or repair
Some injury done to sickle, flail, or scythe,
Or other implement of house or field.

Down from the ceiling, by the chimney's edge,
That in our ancient uncouth country style

With huge and black projection overbrowed
Large space beneath, as duly as the light
Of day grew dim the Housewife hung a lamp;
An aged utensil, which had performed
Service beyond all others of its kind.
Early at evening did it burn – and late,
Surviving comrade of uncounted hours,
Which, going by from year to year, had found,
And left, the couple neither gay perhaps
Nor cheerful, yet with objects and with hopes,
Living a life of eager industry.
And now, when Luke had reached his eighteenth year,
There by the light of this old lamp they sate,
Father and Son, while far into the night
The Housewife plied her own peculiar work,
Making the cottage through the silent hours
Murmur as with the sound of summer flies.
This light was famous in its neighbourhood,
And was a public symbol of the life
That thrifty Pair had lived. For, as it chanced,
Their cottage on a plot of rising ground
Stood single, with large prospects, north and south,
High into Easedale, up the Dunmail-Raise,
And westward to the village near the lake;
And from this constant light, so regular
And so far seen, the House itself, by all
Who dwelt within the limits of the vale,
Both old and young, was named the EVENING STAR.

    Thus living on through such a length of years,
The Shepherd, if he loved himself, must needs
Have loved his Helpmate; but to Michael's heart
This son of his old age was yet more dear –
Less from instinctive tenderness, the same
Fond spirit that blindly works in the blood of all –
Than that a child, more than all other gifts
That earth can offer to declining man,
Brings hope with it, and forward-looking thoughts,
And stirrings of inquietude, when they

By tendency of nature needs must fail.
Exceeding was the love he bare to him,
His heart and his heart's joy ! For oftentimes
Old Michael, while he was a babe in arms,
Had done him female service, not alone
For pastime and delight, as is the use
Of fathers, but with patient mind enforced
To acts of tenderness; and he had rocked
His cradle, as with a woman's gentle hand.

And, in a later time, ere yet the Boy
Had put on boy's attire, did Michael love,
Albeit of a stern unbending mind,
To have the Young-one in his sight, when he
Wrought in the field, or on his shepherd's stool
Sate with a fettered sheep before him stretched
Under the large old oak, that near his door
Stood single, and, from matchless depth of shade,
Chosen for the Shearer's covert from the sun,
Thence in our rustic dialect was called
The CLIPPING TREE, a name which yet it bears.
There, while they two were sitting in the shade,
With others round them, earnest all and blithe,
Would Michael exercise his heart with looks
Of fond correction and reproof bestowed
Upon the Child, if he disturbed the sheep
By catching at their legs, or with his shouts
Scared them, while they lay still beneath the shears.
And when by Heaven's good grace the boy grew up
A healthy Lad, and carried in his cheek
Two steady roses that were five years old;
Then Michael from a winter coppice cut
With his own hand a sapling, which he hooped
With iron, making it throughout in all
Due requisites a perfect shepherd's staff,
And gave it to the Boy; wherewith equipt
He as a watchman oftentimes was placed
At gate or gap, to stem or turn the flock;
And, to his office prematurely called,

There stood the urchin, as you will divine,
Something between a hindrance and a help;
And for this cause not always, I believe,
Receiving from his Father hire of praise;
Though nought was left undone which staff or voice,
Or looks, or threatening gestures, could perform.

But soon as Luke, full ten years old, could stand
Against the mountain blasts; and to the heights,
Not fearing toil, nor length of weary ways,
He with his Father daily went, and they
Were as companions, why should I relate
That objects which the Shepherd loved before
Were dearer now? that from the Boy there came
Feelings and emanations – things which were
Light to the sun and music to the wind;
And that the old Man's heart seemed born again?
    Thus in his Father's sight the Boy grew up:
And now, when he had reached his eighteenth year,
He was his comfort and his daily hope.

While in this sort the simple household lived
From day to day, to Michael's ear there came
Distressful tidings. Long before the time
Of which I speak, the Shepherd had been bound
In surety for his brother's son, a man
Of an industrious life, and ample means;
But unforeseen misfortunes suddenly
Had prest upon him; and old Michael now
Was summoned to discharge the forfeiture,
A grievous penalty, but little less
Than half his substance. This unlooked for claim,
At the first hearing, for a moment took
More hope out of his life than he supposed
That any old man ever could have lost.
As soon as he had armed himself with strength
To look his trouble in the face, it seemed
The Shepherd's sole resource to sell at once
A portion of his patrimonial fields.

Such was his first resolve: he thought again,
And his heart failed him. 'Isabel,' said he,
Two evenings after he had heard the news,
'I have been toiling more than seventy years,
And in the open sunshine of God's love
Have we all lived; yet if these fields of ours
Should pass into a stranger's hand, I think
That I could not lie quiet in my grave.
Our lot is a hard lot; the sun himself
Has scarcely been more diligent than I;
And I have lived to be a fool at last
To my own family. An evil man
That was, and made an evil choice, if he
Were false to us; and if he were not false,
There are ten thousand to whom loss like this
Had been no sorrow. I forgive him; – but
'Twere better to be dumb than to talk thus.

'When I began, my purpose was to speak
Of remedies and of a cheerful hope.
Our Luke shall leave us, Isabel; the land
Shall not go from us, and it shall be free;
He shall possess it, free as is the wind
That passes over it. We have, thou know'st,
Another kinsman – he will be our friend
In this distress. He is a prosperous man,
Thriving in trade – and Luke to him shall go,
And with his kinsman's help and his own thrift
He quickly will repair this loss, and then
He may return to us. If here he stay,
What can be done? Where every one is poor,
What can be gained?'
                    At this the old Man paused,
And Isabel sat silent, for her mind
Was busy, looking back into past times.
There's Richard Bateman, thought she to herself,
He was a parish-boy – at the church door
They made a gathering for him, shillings, pence
And halfpennies, wherewith the neighbours bought

A basket, which they filled with pedlar's wares;
And, with this basket on his arm, the lad
Went up to London, found a master there,
Who, out of many, chose the trusty boy
To go and overlook his merchandise
Beyond the seas; where he grew wondrous rich,
And left estates and monies to the poor,
And, at his birth-place, built a chapel, floored
With marble which he sent from foreign lands.
These thoughts, and many others of like sort,
Passed quickly through the mind of Isabel,
And her face brightened. The old Man was glad,
And thus resumed : – 'Well, Isabel ! this scheme
These two days, has been meat and drink to me.
Far more than we have lost is left us yet.
– We have enough – I wish indeed that I
Were younger; – but this hope is a good hope.
– Make ready Luke's best garments, of the best
Buy for him more, and let us send him forth
To-morrow, or the next day, or to-night:
– If he *could* go, the Boy should go to-night.'

Here Michael ceased, and to the fields went forth
With a light heart. The Housewife for five days
Was restless morn and night, and all day long
Wrought on with her best fingers to prepare
Things needful for the journey of her son.
But Isabel was glad when Sunday came
To stop her in her work : for, when she lay
By Michael's side, she through the last two nights
Heard him, how he was troubled in his sleep :
And when they rose at morning she could see
That all his hopes were gone. That day at noon
She said to Luke, while they two by themselves
Were sitting at the door, 'Thou must not go:
We have no other Child but thee to lose
None to remember – do not go away,
For if thou leave thy Father he will die.'
The Youth made answer with a jocund voice;

And Isabel, when she had told her fears,
Recovered heart. That evening her best fare
Did she bring forth, and all together sat
Like happy people round a Christmas fire.

With daylight Isabel resumed her work;
And all the ensuing week the house appeared
As cheerful as a grove in Spring : at length
The expected letter from their kinsman came,
With kind assurances that he would do
His utmost for the welfare of the Boy;
To which, requests were added, that forthwith
He might be sent to him. Ten times or more
The letter was read over; Isabel
Went forth to show it to the neighbours round;
Nor was there at that time on English land
A prouder heart than Luke's. When Isabel
Had to her house returned, the old Man said,
'He shall depart tomorrow.' To this word
The Housewife answered, talking much of things
Which, if at such short notice he should go,
Would surely be forgotten. But at length
She gave consent, and Michael was at ease.

Near the tumultuous brook of Greenhead Ghyll,
In that deep valley, Michael had designed
To build a Sheepfold; and, before he heard
The tidings of his melancholy loss,
For this same purpose he had gathered up
A heap of stones, which by the streamlet's edge
Lay thrown together, ready for the work.
With Luke that evening thitherward he walked :
And soon as they had reached the place he stopped,
And thus the old Man spake to him : – 'My Son,
To-morrow thou wilt leave me : with full heart
I look upon thee, for thou art the same
That wert a promise to me ere thy birth,
And all thy life hast been my daily joy.
I will relate to thee some little part

Of our two histories; 'twill do thee good
When thou art from me, even if I should touch
On things thou canst not know of. – After thou
First cam'st into the world – as oft befalls
To new-born infants – thou didst sleep away
Two days, and blessings from thy Father's tongue
Then fell upon thee. Day by day passed on,
And still I loved thee with increasing love.
Never to living ear came sweeter sounds
Than when I heard thee by our own fireside
First uttering, without words, a natural tune;
While thou, a feeding babe, didst in thy joy
Sing at thy Mother's breast. Month followed month,
And in the open fields my life was passed
And on the mountains; else I think that thou
Hadst been brought up upon thy Father's knees.
But we were playmates, Luke: among these hills,
As well thou knowest, in us the old and young
Have played together, nor with me didst thou
Lack any pleasure which a boy can know.'
Luke had a manly heart; but at these words
He sobbed aloud. The old Man grasped his hand,
And said, 'Nay, do not take it so – I see
That these are things of which I need not speak.
– Even to the utmost I have been to thee
A kind and a good Father: and herein
I but repay a gift which I myself
Received at others' hands; for, though now old
Beyond the common life of man, I still
Remember them who loved me in my youth.
Both of them sleep together: here they lived,
As all their Forefathers had done; and when
At length their time was come, they were not loth
To give their bodies to the family mould.
I wished that thou should'st live the life they lived:
But, 'tis a long time to look back, my Son,
And see so little gain for three score years.
These fields were burthened when they came to me;
Till I was forty years of age, not more

Than half of my inheritance was mine.
I toiled and toiled; God blessed me in my work,
And till these three weeks past the land was free.
– It looks as if it never could endure
Another Master. Heaven forgive me, Luke,
If I judge ill for thee, but it seems good
That thou should'st go.'
                    At this the old Man paused;
Then, pointing to the stones near which they stood,
Thus, after a short silence, he resumed:
'This was a work for us; and now, my Son,
It is a work for me. But, lay one stone –
Here, lay it for me, Luke, with thine own hands.
Nay, Boy, be of good hope; – we both may live
To see a better day. At eighty-four
I still am strong and hale; – do thou thy part;
I will do mine. – I will begin again
With many tasks that were resigned to thee:
Up to the heights, and in among the storms,
Will I without thee go again, and do
All works which I was wont to do alone,
Before I knew thy face. – Heaven bless thee, Boy!
Thy heart these two weeks has been beating fast
With many hopes; it should be so – yes – yes –
I knew that thou could'st never have a wish
To leave me, Luke: thou hast been bound to me
Only by links of love: when thou art gone,
What will be left to us! – But, I forget
My purposes. Lay now the corner-stone,
As I requested; and hereafter, Luke,
When thou art gone away, should evil men
Be thy companions, think of me, my Son,
And of this moment; hither turn thy thoughts,
And God will strengthen thee: amid all fear
And all temptation, Luke, I pray that thou
May'st bear in mind the life thy Fathers lived,
Who, being innocent, did for that cause
Bestir them in good deeds. Now, fare thee well –
When thou return'st, thou in this place wilt see

A work which is not here : a covenant
'Twill be between us; but, whatever fate
Befall thee, I shall love thee to the last,
And bear thy memory with me to the grave.'

The Shepherd ended here; and Luke stooped down,
And, as his Father had requested, laid
The first stone of the Sheepfold. At the sight
The old Man's grief broke from him; to his heart
He pressed his Son, he kissed him and wept;
And to the house together they returned.
– Hushed was that House in peace, or seeming peace,
Ere the night fell : – with morrow's dawn the Boy
Began his journey, and when he had reached
The public way, he put on a bold face;
And all the neighbours, as he passed their doors,
Came forth with wishes and with farewell prayers,
That followed him till he was out of sight.

A good report did from their Kinsman come,
Of Luke and his well-doing : and the Boy
Wrote loving letters, full of wondrous news,
Which, as the Housewife phrased it, were throughout
'The prettiest letters that were ever seen.'
Both parents read them with rejoicing hearts.
So, many months passed on : and once again
The Shepherd went about his daily work
With confident and cheerful thoughts; and now
Sometimes when he could find a leisure hour
He to that valley took his way, and there
Wrought at the Sheepfold. Meantime Luke began
To slacken in his duty; and, at length,
He in the dissolute city gave himself
To evil courses : ignominy and shame
Fell on him, so that he was driven at last
To seek a hiding-place beyond the seas.
There is a comfort in the strength of love;
'Twill make a thing endurable, which else
Would overset the brain, or break the heart :

I have conversed with more than one who well
Remember the old Man, and what he was
Years after he had heard this heavy news.
His bodily frame had been from youth to age
Of an unusual strength. Among the rocks
He went, and still looked up to sun and cloud,
And listened to the wind; and, as before,
Performed all kinds of labour for his sheep,
And for the land, his small inheritance.
And to that hollow dell from time to time
Did he repair, to build the Fold of which
His flock had need. 'Tis not forgotten yet
The pity which was then in every heart
For the old Man – and 'tis believed by all
That many and many a day he thither went,
And never lifted up a single stone.

There, by the Sheepfold, sometimes was he seen
Sitting alone, or with his faithful Dog,
Then old, beside him, lying at his feet.
The length of full seven years, from time to time,
He at the building of this Sheepfold wrought,
And left the work unfinished when he died.
Three years, or little more, did Isabel
Survive her Husband: at her death the estate
Was sold, and went into a stranger's hand.
The Cottage which was named the EVENING STAR
Is gone – the ploughshare has been through the ground
On which it stood; great changes have been wrought
In all the neighbourhood: – yet the oak is left
That grew beside their door; and the remains
Of the unfinished Sheepfold may be seen
Beside the boisterous brook of Greenhead Ghyll.

4

'that noble Chaucer ...
... the first of ours that ere brake
Into the Muses' treasure.'

From Drayton's *Elegy to Henry Reynolds*

These lines head Wordsworth's own manuscript of his translations of Chaucer.

There is a gap between the last entry of 22 December 1800 (which breaks off in the middle of a sentence) and 10 October 1801, so that it looks as if there was another volume of the Journal for the months in between, which is now lost.

[October] 24th, *Saturday*. Attempted Fairfield, but misty, and we went no further than Green Head Gill to the sheepfold; mild, misty, beautiful, soft. Wm. and Tom put out the boat – brought the coat from Mr Luff's. Mr Simpson came in at dinner-time – drank tea with us and played at cards.

[October] 25th, *Sunday*. Rode to Legberthwaite with Tom, expecting Mary – sweet day. Went upon Helvellyn, glorious glorious sights. The sea at Cartmel. The Scotch mountains beyond the sea to the right: Whiteside large, and round, and very soft, and green, behind us. Mists above and below, and close to us, with the Sun amongst them. They shot down to the coves. Left John Stanley's at 10 minutes past 12. Returned thither ¼ past 4, drank tea, ate heartily. Before we went on Helvellyn we got bread and cheese – Paid 4/- for the whole. Reached home at nine o'clock. A soft grey evening; the light of the moon, but she did not shine on us.

[*November 9th, Monday*] ... The mountains for ever varying, now hid in the clouds, and now with their tops visible while perhaps they were half concealed below – Legberthwaite beautiful. We ate bread and cheese at John Stanley's, and reached Keswick without fatigue just before dark. We enjoyed ourselves in the study and were *at home*. Supped at Mr Jackson's. Mary and I sate in C.'s room a while.

[*November*] 10*th, Tuesday*. Poor C. left us, and we came home together. We left Keswick at 2 o'clock and did not arrive at G. till 9 o'clock. Drank tea at John Stanley's very comfortably. I burnt myself with Coleridge's aquafortis. Mary's feet sore. C. had a sweet day for his ride. Every sight and every sound reminded me of him – dear, dear fellow, of his many walks to us by day and by night, of all dear things. I was melancholy, and could not talk, but at last I eased my heart by weeping – nervous blubbering, says William. It is not so. O! how many, many reasons have I to be anxious for him.

[*November*] 11*th, Wednesday*. Baked bread and giblet pie – put books in order – mended stockings. Put aside dearest C.'s letters, and now at about 7 o'clock we are all sitting by a nice fire. Wm. with his book and a candle, and Mary writing to Sara.

November 12*th, Thursday*. A beautiful still sunshiny morning. We rose very late. I put the rag-boxes into order. We walked out while the goose was roasting – we walked to the top of the hill. M. and I followed Wm. – he was walking upon the turf between John's Grove and the lane. It was a most sweet noon. We did not go into John's Grove, but we walked among the rocks and there we sate. Mr Oliff passed Mary and me upon the road – Wm. still among the rocks. The lake beautiful from the orchard. Wm. and I walked out before tea – The crescent moon – we sate in the slate quarry – I sate there a long time alone. Wm. reached home before me – I found them at tea. There were a thousand stars in the sky.

[*November 13th,*] *Friday Morning.* Dullish, damp and cloudy – a day that promises not to dry our clothes. We spent a happy evening – went to bed late, and had a restless night – Wm. better than I expected.

[*November 14th,*] *Saturday Morning.* Still a cloudy dull day, very dark. I lay in bed all the day very unwell: they made me some broth and I rose better, after it was dark we spent a quiet evening by the fire.

[*November*] *15th, Sunday.* I walked in the morning, to Churnmilk Force nearly, and went upon Heifer Crags. The valley of its winter yellow, but the bed of the brook still in some places almost *shaded* with leaves – the oaks brown in general, but one that might be almost called green – the whole prospect was very soft, and the distant view down the vale very impressive, a long vale down to Ambleside, the hills at Ambleside in mist and sunshine – all else grey. We sate by the fire and read Chaucer (Thomson; Mary read) and Bishop Hall. Letters from Sara and Mrs Clarkson late at night.

November 16th, Monday. A very darkish misty wettish morning. Mary and Molly ironed all day. I made bread and called at Mr Olliff's – Mrs O. at home – the prospect soft from the windows. Mrs O. observed that it was beautiful *even* in winter! The Luffs passed us. We walked backwards and forwards in the Church field. Wm. somewhat weakish, but upon the whole pretty well; he is now, at 7 o'clock, reading Spenser. Mary is writing beside me. The little syke murmurs. We are quiet and happy, but poor Peggy Ashburner is very ill and in pain. She coughs, as if she would cough her life away. I am going to write to Coleridge and Sara. Poor C.! I hope he was in London yesterday. Molly has been very witty with Mary all day. She says: 'ye may say what ye will, but there's naething like a gay auld man for behaving weel to a young wife. Ye may laugh, but this wind blows no [?] and where there's no love there's no favour.' On Sunday

105

I lectured little John Dawson for telling lies – I told him I had heard that he charged Jenny Baty falsely with having beaten him. Says Molly: 'she says it's not so, that she never lifted hand till him, and she *should* speak truth you would think in her condition' – she is with child. Two Beggars to-day.

[November] 17th, Tuesday. A very rainy morning. We walked into Easedale before dinner. Miss S. came in at dinner time – we went to Mr Gell's cottage – then returned. The coppices a beautiful brown. The oaks many, a very fine leafy shade. We stood a long time to look at the corner birch tree. The wind was among the light thin twigs, and they yielded to it, this way and that. Drank tea and supper at the Simpsons – a moonlight wettish night. Dirty roads.

[November] 18th, Wednesday. We sate in the house in the morning reading Spenser. I was unwell and lay in bed all the afternoon. Wm. and Mary walked to Rydale. Very pleasant moonlight. The Lakes beautiful. The church an image of peace. Wm. wrote some lines upon it in bed when they came home. Mary and I walked as far as Sara's Gate before supper. We stood there a long time, the whole scene impressive, the mountains indistinct, the Lake calm and partly ruffled. Large Island, a sweet sound of water falling into the quiet Lake. A storm was gathering in Easedale, so we returned; but the moon came out and opened to us the church and village. Helm Crag in shade, the larger mountains dappled like a sky. We stood long upon the bridge. Wished for Wm., he had stayed at home being sickish – found him better; we went to bed.

Nov[embe]r 19th, Thursday. A beautiful sunny, frosty morning. We did not walk all day. Wm. said he would put it off till the fine moonlight night, and then it came on a heavy rain and wind. Charles and Olivia Lloyd called in the morning.

[*November*] 20*th, Friday*. We walked in the morning to Easedale. In the evening we had chearful letters from Coleridge and Sara.

[*November*] 21*st, Saturday*. We walked in the morning, and paid one pound and 4d. for letters. William out of spirits. We had a pleasant walk and spent a pleasant evening. There was a furious wind and cold at night. Mr Simpson drank tea with us, and helped William out with the boat. Wm. and Mary walked to the Swan, homewards, with him. A keen clear frosty night. I went into the orchard while they were out.

[*November*] 22*nd, Sunday*. We wrote to Coleridge and sent our letter by the boy. Mr and Miss Simpson came in at tea time. We went with them to the Blacksmith's and returned by Butterlip How – a frost and wind with bright moonshine. The vale looked spacious and very beautiful – the level meadows seemed very large and some nearer us, unequal ground, heaving like sand, the Cottages beautiful and quiet, we passed one near which stood a cropped ash with upright forked branches like the Devil's horns frightening a guilty conscience. We were happy and chearful when we came home – we went early to bed.

Nov[*ember*] 23*rd, Monday*. A beautiful frosty morning. Mary was making William's woollen waistcoat. Wm. unwell, and did not walk. Mary and I sate in our cloaks upon the bench in the orchard. After dinner I went to bed unwell. Mary had a headach at night. We all went to bed soon.

[*November*] 24*th, Tuesday*. A rainy morning. We all were well except that my head ached a little, and I took my breakfast in bed. I read a little of Chaucer, prepared the goose for dinner, and then we all walked out. I was obliged to return for my fur tippet and spencer, it was so cold. We had intended going to Easedale, but we shaped our course to Mr Gell's cottage. It was very windy, and we heard the wind everywhere about us as we went along the lane, but the walls sheltered us. John Green's house looked pretty under Silver How. As we were going along we were stopped at once, at the distance perhaps of 50 yards from our favourite birch tree. It was yielding to the gusty wind with all its tender twigs, the sun shone upon it, and it glanced in the wind like a flying sunshiny shower. It was a tree in shape, with stem and branches, but it was like a Spirit of water. The sun went in, and it resumed its purplish appearance, the twigs still yielding to the wind, but not so visibly to us. The other birch trees that were near it looked bright and chearful, but it was a creature by its own self among them. We could not get into Mr Gell's grounds – the old tree fallen from its undue exaltation above the gate. A shower came on when we were at Benson's. We went through the wood – it became fair. There was a rainbow which spanned the lake from the island-house to the foots of Bainriggs. The village looked populous and beautiful. Catkins are coming out; palm trees budding; the alder, with its plumb-coloured buds. We came home over the stepping-stones. The lake was foamy with white waves. I saw a solitary butterflower in the wood. I found it not easy to get over the stepping stones. Reached home at dinner time. Sent Peggy Ashburner some goose. She sent me some honey, with a thousand thanks. 'Alas ! the gratitude of men has', etc.[1] I went in to set her right about this, and sate a while with her. She talked about Thomas's having sold his land. 'Ay,' says she, 'I said many a time he's not come fra London to buy our land, however.' Then she told me with what pains and industry they had made up their taxes, interest, etc. etc., how they all got up at 5 o'clock in the morning to spin and Thomas carded, and that they had paid off a hundred pounds of interest. She said she used to take such pleasure in the cattle and sheep. 'O how pleased I used to be when they fetched them down, and when I had been a bit poorly I would gang out upon a hill and look ower 't fields and see them, and it used to do me so much good you cannot think.' Molly said to me when I came in, 'Poor body ! she's very ill, but one does not know how long she may last. Many a fair face may gang before her'.

---

1. 'Simon Lee', lines 95–6.

Wordsworth remembered this conversation with Peggy Ash-
burner in 1804 and wrote the poem 'Repentance'. It was a theme
which deeply affected him and he had already used it in 'Michael'
and 'The Last of the Flock'.

REPENTANCE

A Pastoral Ballad

The fields which with covetous spirit we sold,
Those beautiful fields, the delight of the day,
Would have brought us more good than a burthen of gold,
Could we but have been as contented as they.

When the troublesome Tempter beset us, said I,
'Let him come, with his purse proudly grasped in his hand;
But, Allan, be true to me, Allan, – we'll die
Before he shall go with an inch of the land!'

There dwelt we, as happy as birds in their bowers;
Unfettered as bees that in gardens abide;
We could do what we liked with the land, it was ours;
And for us the brook murmured that ran by its side.

But now we are strangers, go early or late;
And often, like one overburthened with sin
With my hand on the latch of the half opened gate,
I look at the fields, but I cannot go in!

When I walk by the hedge on a bright summer's day,
Or sit in the shade of my grandfather's tree,
A stern face it puts on, as if ready to say,
'What ails you, that you must come creeping to me!'

With our pastures about us, we could not be sad;
Our comfort was near if we ever were crost;
But the comfort, the blessings, and wealth that we had,
We slighted them all, – and our birth-right was lost.

Oh, ill-judging sire of an innocent son
Who must now be a wanderer ! but peace to that strain !
Think of evening's repose when our labour was done,
The sabbath's return; and its leisure's soft chain !

And in sickness, if night had been sparing of sleep,
How cheerful, at sunrise, the hill where I stood,
Looking down on the kine, and our treasure of sheep
That besprinkled the field; 'twas like youth in my blood !

Now I cleave to the house, and am dull as a snail;
And, oftentimes, hear the church-bell with a sigh,
That follows the thought – We've no land in the vale,
Save six feet of earth where our forefathers lie !

We sate by the fire without working for some time, then Mary
read a poem of Daniel upon Learning. After tea Wm. read
Spenser, now and then a little aloud to us. We were making his
waistcoat. We had a note from Mrs C., with bad news from poor
C. – very ill. William went to John's Grove. I went to meet him.
Moonlight, but it rained. I met him before I had got as far as
John Baty's – he had been surprized and terrified by a sudden
rushing of winds, which seemed to bring earth sky and lake to-
gether, as if the whole were going to enclose him in; he was
glad he was in a high road.
  In speaking of our walk on Sunday evening, the 22nd Novem-
ber, I forgot to notice one most impressive sight. It was the moon
and the moonlight seen through hurrying driving clouds immedi-
ately behind the Stone-Man upon the top of the hill on the
Forest Side. Every tooth and every edge of rock was visible, and
the Man stood like a Giant watching from the roof of a lofty
castle. The hill seemed perpendicular from the darkness below
it. It was a sight that I could call to mind at any time, it was so
distinct.

November 25th, Wednesday. It was a showery morning and
threatened to be a wettish day, but the sun shone once or twice.

We were engaged to the Lloyds and Wm. and Mary were deter-
mined to go that it might be over. I accompanied them to the
thorn beside Rydale water. I parted from them first at the top
of the hill, and they called me back. It rained a little, and rained
afterwards all the afternoon. I baked pies and bread, and wrote to
Sara Hutchinson and Coleridge. I passed a pleasant evening, but
the wind roared so, and it was such a storm that I was afraid for
them. They came in at nine o'clock, no worse for their walk, and
chearful, blooming and happy.

[November] 26th, Thursday. Mr Olliff called before Wm. was
up to say that they would drink tea with us this afternoon. We
walked into Easedale, to gather mosses, and to fetch cream. I
went for the cream, and they sate under a wall. It was piercing
cold and a hailstorm came on in the afternoon. The Olliffs ar-
rived at 5 o'clock. We played at cards and passed a decent even-
ing. It was a very still night but piercing cold when they went
away at 11 o'clock – a shower came on.

November 27th, Friday. Snow upon the ground thinly scattered.
It snowed after we got up, and then the sun shone, and it was
very warm though frosty – now the sun shines sweetly. A
woman came who was travelling with her husband; he had been
wounded and was going with her to live at Whitehaven. She
had been at Ambleside the night before, offered 4d at the Cock
for a bed – they sent her to one Harrison's where she and her
husband had slept upon the hearth and bought a pennyworth of
chips for a fire. Her husband was gone before, very lame –
'Aye' says she, 'I was once an officer's wife, I, as you see me
now. My first husband married me at Appleby; I had 18£ a year
for teaching a school, and because I had no fortune his father
turned him out of doors. I have been in the West Indies. I lost
the use of this finger just before he died; he came to me and said
he must bid farewell to his dear children and me. I had a muslin
gown on like yours – I seized hold of his coat as he went from
me, and slipped the joint of my finger. He was shot directly. I
came to London and married this man. He was clerk to Judge

111

Chambray, *that man,* that man that's going on the road now. If he, Judge Chambray, had been at Kendal he would [have] given us a guinea or two, and made nought of it, for he is very generous.' Before dinner we set forward to walk intending to return to dinner, but as we had got as far as Rydale Wm. thought he would go on to Mr Luff's. We accompanied him under Loughrigg, and parted near the stepping stones. It was very cold. Mary and I walked quick home. There was a fine gleam of sunshine upon the eastern side of Ambleside Vale. We came up the old road and turning round we were struck with the appearance. Mary wrote to her aunt. We expected the Simpsons. I was sleepy and weary and went to bed before tea. It came on wet in the evening and was very cold. We expected letters from C. and Sara – Sara's came by the boy, but none from C. – a sad disappointment. We did not go to meet Wm. as we had intended – Mary was at work at Wm.'s warm waistcoat.

December 1st, 1801, Tuesday. A fine sunny and frosty morning. Mary and I walked to Rydale for letters. William was not well and staid at home reading after having lain long in bed. We found a letter from Coleridge, a short one – he was pretty well. We were overtaken by two soldiers on our return – one of them being very drunk we wished them to pass us, but they had too much liquor in them to go very fast so we contrived to pass them – they were very merry and very civil. They fought with the mountains with their sticks. 'Aye' says one, 'that will [?fall] upon us. One might stride over that etc.' They never saw such a wild country, though one of them was a Scotchman. They were honest looking fellows. The Corporal said he was frightened to see the road before them. We met Wm. at Sara's gate – he went back intending to go round the lake, but having attempted to cross the water and not succeeding he came back. The Simpsons, Mr and Miss, drank tea with us – Wm. was very poorly and out of spirits. They stayed supper.

[December] 2nd, Wednesday. A fine grey frosty morning. Wm. rose late. I read the Tale of Phoebus and the Crow, which he

112

afterwards attempted to translate, and did translate a large part of it to-day. Mrs Olliff brought us some yeast and made us promise to go there the next day to meet the Luffs. We were sitting by the fire in the evening when Charles and Olivia Lloyd came in. I had not been very well so I did not venture out with them when they went away – Mary and William went as far as Rydale village. It snowed after it was dark and there was a thin covering over the ground which made it light and soft. They looked fresh and well when they came in. I wrote part of a letter to Coleridge. After his return William went on a little with Chaucer.

Of the three translations Wordsworth did from Chaucer at this time I am only printing 'Phoebus and the Crow' to show how closely he follows the original and how little of his own style he imposes on it. Of the others, 'The Prioress's Tale' has no Wordsworthian character, and 'The Cuckoo and the Nightingale', though a charming poem, is now not thought to be by Chaucer but attributed to Sir Thomas Clanvowe. Wordsworth never printed 'The Manciple's Tale' after his friends objected to its moral tone.

THE MANCIPLE'S TALE

When Phoebus took delight on earth to dwell
Among mankind, as ancient stories tell,
He was the blithest bachelor, I trow,
Of all this world, and the best archer too.
He slew the serpent Python as he lay
Sleeping against the sun upon a day,
And many another noble worthy deed
Wrought with his bow as men the same may read.
He played, all music played on earthly ground,
And 'twas a melody to hear the sound
Of his clear voice, so sweetly would he sing.
Certes Amphion, that old Theban king
Who wall'd a city with his minstrelsy,
Was never heard to sing so sweet as he.
Therewith this Phoebus was the seemliest man
That is or hath been since the world began.

His features to describe I need not strive;
For in this world is none so fair alive.
He was moreover, full of gentleness,
Of honour and of perfect worthiness.

This Phoebus flower in forest and in court,
This comely Bachelor for his disport
And eke in token of his victory earned
Of Python, as is from the story learned,
Was wont to carry in his hand a bow.
Now had this Phoebus in his house a Crow
Which in a cage he fostered many a day
And taught to speak as men will teach a jay.
White was this Crow as is a snow-white Swan,
And counterfeit the speech of every man
He could, when he had mind to tell a tale;
Besides, in all the world no Nightingale
Could ring out of his heart so blithe a peal;
No, not a hundred thousandth part as well.

Now had this Phoebus in his house a Wife
Whom he loved better than he loved his life;
And, night and day, he strove with diligence
To please her, and to do her reverence,
Save only, for 'tis truth, the noble Elf
Was jealous, and would keep her to himself.
For he was loth a laughing stock to be,
And so is every wight in like degree;
But all for nought, for it availeth nought,
A good Wife that is pure in deed and thought
Should not be kept in watch and ward, – and, do
The best you may, you cannot keep a Shrew.
It will not be – vain labour is it wholly;
Lordings, this hold I for an arrant folly
Labour to waste in custody of wives;
And so old Clerks have written in their lives.

But to my purpose as I first began.
This worthy Phoebus doeth all he can

To please her, weening that through such delight
And of his government and manhood's right
No man should ever put him from her grace.
But Man's best plans, God knoweth, in no case
Shall compass to constrain a thing which nature
Hath naturally implanted in a creature.

Take any bird and put it in a cage
And wait upon this bird as nurse or page
To feed it tenderly with meat and drink
And every dainty whereof thou canst think,
And also keep it cleanly as thou may;
Altho' the cage of gold be never so gay
Yet hath the Bird by twenty thousand fold
Rather in forest that is wild and cold
Go feed on worms and such like wretchedness,
For ever will this Bird do more or less
To escape out of his cage whene'er he may;
His liberty the Bird desireth aye.

Go take a Cat and nourish her with milk
And tender fish, and make her couch of silk,
And let her see a mouse go by the wall,
Anon she waiveth milk and flesh and all
And every dainty which is in the house,
Such appetite hath she to eat the mouse.
Behold the domination here of kind,
Appetite drives discretion from her mind.

A she-wolf also in her kind is base;
Meets she the sorriest wolf in field or chase
Him will she take – what matters his estate
In time when she hath liking to a mate?

Examples all for men that are untrue.
With women I have nothing now to do:
For men have still a wayward appetite
With lower things to seek for their delight
Than with their wives, albeit women fair
Never so true, never so debonair.

All flesh is so newfangled, plague upon't
That are we pleased with aught on whose clear front
Virtue is stampt, 'tis but for a brief while.

This Phoebus, he that thought upon no guile,
Deceived was for all his jollity;
For under him another one had she,
One of small note and little thought upon,
Nought worth to Phoebus in comparison.
The more harm is, it happeneth often so
Of which there cometh mickle harm and woe.

And so befel as soon as Phoebus went
From home, his wife hath for her lemman sent,
Her Lemman, certes that's a knavish speech;
Forgive it me and that I you beseech.

Plato the wise hath said, as ye may read,
The word must needs be suited to the deed;
No doubtful meanings in a tale should lurk,
The word must aye be cousin to the work;
I am a bold blunt man, I speak out plain
There is no difference truly, not a grain,
Between a wife that is of high degree
(If of her body she dishonest be)
And every low-born wench no more than this
(If it so be that both have done amiss)
That, as the gentle is in state above,
She shall be called his Lady and his Love
And that the other a poor woman is
She shall be called his harlot and his miss.
And yet, in very truth, mine own dear brother,
Men lay as low that one as lieth that other.
Right so betwixt a haughty tyrant chief
And a rough outlaw or an errant thief,
The same I say, no differences I hold,
(To Alexander was this sentence told)
But, for the Tyrant is of greater might
By force of multitudes to slay downright

And burn both house and home, and make all plain,
Lo ! therefore Captain is he called; again
Since the other heads a scanty company
And may not do so great a harm as he,
Or lay upon the land such heavy grief
Men christen him an Outlaw or a Thief.

But I'm no man of texts and instances,
Therefore I will not give you much of these
But with my tale go on as I was bent.

When Phoebus' wife had for her lemman sent
In their loose dalliance they anon engage;
This white Crow, that hung alway in the cage,
Beheld the shame, and did not say one word;
But soon as home was come Phoebus, the Lord,
The Crow sang Cuckow, Cuckow, Cuckow. 'How
What ! Bird,' quoth Phoebus, 'what song singst thou now,
Wert thou not wont to sing as did rejoice
My inmost heart, so merrily thy voice
Greeted my ear, alas, what song is this?'
'So help me Gods, I do not sing amiss,
Phoebus,' quoth he, 'for all thy worthiness,
For all thy beauty and all thy gentleness,
For all thy song and all thy minstrelsy,
For all thy waiting, hoodwinked is thine eye
By one we know not whom, we know not what,
A man to thee no better than a gnat,
For I full plainly as I hope for life
Saw him in guilty converse with thy wife.'

What would you more, the Crow when he him told
By serious tokens and words stout and bold
How that his wife had played a wanton game
To his abasement, and exceeding shame,
And told him oft he saw it with his eyes,
Then Phoebus turned away in woeful guise
Him thought his heart would burst in two with sorrow,
His bow he bent, and set therein an arrow,

And in his anger he his wife did slay;
This is the effect, there is no more to say.
For grief of which he brake his minstrelsy
Both lute and harp, guitar and psaltery,
And also brake his arrows and his bow
And after that thus spake he to the Crow.

'Thou Traitor! with thy scorpion tongue,' quoth he,
'To my confusion am I brought by thee.
Why was I born, why have I yet a life?
O wife, O gem of pleasure, O dear wife,
That wert to me so stedfast and so true,
Now dead thou liest with face pale of hue
Full innocent, that durst I swear, I wis.
O thou rash hand that wrought so far amiss,
O reckless outrage, O disordered wit
That unadvised didst the guiltless smite,
What in my false suspicion have I done,
Why thro' mistrust was I thus wrought upon?

'Let every Man beware and keep aloof
From rashness, and trust only to strong proof;
Smite not too soon before ye have learnt why,
And be advised well and stedfastly,
Ere ye to any execution bring
Yourselves from wrath or surmise of a thing.
Alas! A thousand folk hath ire laid low
Fully undone and brought to utter woe,
Alas for sorrow I myself will slay.'

And to Crow, 'O vile wretch,' did he say,
'Now will I thee requite for thy false tale.
Whilom thou sang like any Nightingale,
Henceforth, false thief, thy song from thee is gone
And vanished thy white feathers, every one.
In all thy life thou nevermore shalt speak.
Thus on a traitor I men's wrongs do wreak.
Thou and thy offspring ever shall be black,
Never again sweet noises shall ye make,

But ever cry against the storm and rain
In token that through thee my Wife is slain.'

And to the Crow he sprang and that anon
And plucking his white feathers left not one
And made him black, and took from him his song,
And eke his speech, and out of doors him flung
Unto perdition, whither let him go
And for this very reason, you must know,
Black is the colour now of every Crow.

December 3rd, 1801, Thursday. I was not well in the morning –
we baked bread – after dinner I went to bed – Wm. walked
into Easedale. Rain, hail and snow. I rose at ½ past 7, got tea,
then went to sup at Mr Olliff's – I had a glorious sleep and was
quite well. A light night, roads very slippery. We spent a
pleasant evening – Mr and Mrs Luff there – Mrs L. poorly. I
wrote a little bit of my letter to Coleridge before I went to Mr
O.'s. We went to bed immediately after our return – Molly gone.

[December] 4th, Friday. My head bad and I lay long. Mrs Luff
called – Mary went with her to the slate quarry. Mr Simpson
and Charles Lloyd called for the yeast receipt. William trans-
lating *The Prioress's Tale.* William and Mary walked after tea to
Rydale. It snowed and rained and they came in wet. I finished
the letter to Coleridge, and we received a letter from him and
Sara. S.'s letter written in good spirits – C.'s also. A letter of
Lamb's about George Dyer with it.

[December] 5th, Saturday. My head bad and I lay long. Mr
Luff called before I rose. We put off walking in the morning,
dull and misty and grey – very rainy in the afternoon and we
could not go out. Wm. finished *The Prioress's Tale,* and after tea
Mary and he wrote it out. Wm. not well. No parcel from Mrs
Coleridge.

[*December*] *6th, Sunday.* A very fine beautiful sunshiny morning. Wm. worked a while at Chaucer, then we set forward to walk into Easedale. We met Mr and Mrs Olliff who were going to call upon us; they turned back with us and we parted at the White Bridge. We went up into Easedale and walked backwards and forwards in that flat field, which makes the second circle of Easedale, with that beautiful rock in the field beside us, and all the rocks and the woods and the mountains enclosing us round. The sun was shining among them, the snow thinly scattered upon the tops of the mountains. In the afternoon we sate by the fire: I read Chaucer aloud, and Mary read the first canto of *The Fairy Queen.* After tea Mary and I walked to Ambleside for letters – reached home by 11 o'clock – we had a sweet walk. It was a sober starlight evening, the stars not shining as it were with all their brightness when they were visible, and sometimes hiding themselves behind small greyish clouds, that passed soberly along. We opened C.'s letter at Wilcock's door. We thought we saw that he wrote in good spirits, so we came happily homewards where we arrived 2 hours after we left home. It was a sad melancholy letter, and prevented us all from sleeping.

December 7th, Monday Morning. We rose by candlelight. A showery unpleasant morning, after a downright rainy night. We determined, however, to go to Keswick if possible, and we set off at a little after 9 o'clock. When we were upon the Rays, it snowed very much; and the whole prospect closed in upon us like a moorland valley, upon a moor very wild. But when we were at the top of the Rays, we saw the mountains before us. The sun shone upon them, here and there; and Wytheburn vale, though wild, looked soft .The [? day] went on chearfully and pleasantly. Now and then a hail shower attacked us; but we kept up a good heart, for Mary is a famous jockey. We met Miss Barcroft – she had been unwell in the '*Liverpool* complaint', and was riding out for the benefit of her health. She had not seen Mrs C. 'The weather had been such as to preclude all intercourse between neighbours!' We reached Greta Hall at about one o'clock, met Mrs C. in the field, Derwent in the cradle asleep – Hartley at his dinner – Derwent pale, the image of his Father.

Hartley well. We wrote to C. Mrs C. left us at ½ past 2. We drank tea by ourselves, the children playing about us. Mary said to Hartley, 'Shall I take Derwent with me?' 'No,' says H., 'I cannot spare my little Brother,' in the sweetest tone possible, 'and he can't do without his mamma.' 'Well,' says Mary, 'why can't I be his mamma? Can't he have more mammas than one?' 'No,' says H. 'What for?' 'Because they do not love, and mothers do.' 'What is the difference between mothers and mammas?' Looking at his sleeves, 'Mothers wear sleeves like this,' (pulling his own tight down), 'and mammas' (pulling them up, and making a bustle about his shoulders) 'so'. We parted from them at 4 o'clock. It was a little of the dusk when we set off. Cotton mills lighted up. The first star at Nadel Fell, but it was never dark. We rode very briskly. Snow upon the Rays. Reached home far sooner than we expected – at seven o'clock. William at work with Chaucer, *The God of Love*. Sate latish. I wrote a letter to C.

December 8th, 1801, Tuesday. A dullish, rainyish morning. Wm. at work with Chaucer. I read Bruce's *Lochleven* and *Life*. Going to bake bread and pies. After dinner I felt myself unwell having not slept well in the night, so, after we had put up the Bookcases which Charles Lloyd sent us, I lay down – I did not sleep much but I rose refreshed. Mary and William walked to the boat house at Rydale while I was in bed. It rained very hard all night. No company. Wm. worked at *The Cuckow and the Nightingale* till he was tired. Mary very sleepy and not quite well. We both slept sound. Letter from Richard with news of John, dated 7th August.

December 9th, Wednesday Morning. William slept well, but his tongue [? furred]. I read *Palamon and Arcite*. Mary read Bruce. William writing out his alteration of Chaucer's *Cuckow and Nightingale*. After dinner it was agreed that we should walk – when I had finished a letter to C. part of which I had written in the morning by the kitchen fire while the mutton was roasting. Wm. did not go with us but Mary and I walked into Easedale, and backwards and forwards in that large field under George

Rawnson's white cottage. We had intended gathering mosses, and for that purpose we turned into the green lane, behind the tailor's, but it was too dark to see the mosses. The river came galloping past the Church, as fast as it could come; and when we got into Easedale we saw Churn Milk Force, like a broad stream of snow. At the little footbridge we stopped to look at the company of rivers, which came hurrying down the vale this way and that; it was a valley of streams and islands, with that great waterfall at the head, and lesser falls in different parts of the mountains, coming down to these rivers. We could hear the sound of those lesser falls, but we could not *see* them. We walked backwards and forwards till all distant objects, except the white shape of the waterfall and the lines of the mountains, were gone. We had the crescent moon when we went out, and at our return there were a few stars that shone dimly, but it was a grey cloudy night.

December 10th, Thursday. A very fine sunny morning – not frosty. We walked into Easedale to gather mosses, and then we went past to Aggy Fleming's and up the Gill, beyond the little waterfall. It was a wild scene of crag and mountain. One craggy point rose above the rest irregular and rugged, and very impressive it was. We called at Aggy Fleming's – she told us about her miserable house – she looked shockingly with her head tied up. Her mother was there – the children looked healthy. We were very unsuccessful in our search after mosses. Just when the evening was closing in, Mr Clarkson came to the door. It was a fine frosty evening. We played at cards.

[*December*] 11th, *Friday.* Baked pies and cakes. It was a stormy morning with hail showers. The Luffs dined with us – Mrs L. came with Mrs Olliff in the gig. We sate lazily round the fire after dinner. Mr and Mrs Olliff drank tea and supped with us – a hard frost when they came.

[*December*] 12th, *Saturday.* A fine frosty morning – Snow upon the ground. I made bread and pies. We walked with Mrs Luff to Rydale and came home the other side of the Lake, met Townley with his dogs. All looked chearful and bright. Helm Crag rose very bold and craggy, a Being by itself, and behind it was the large ridge of mountains, smooth as marble and snow white. All the mountains looked like solid stone, on our left, going from Grasmere, i.e. White Moss and Nab Scar. The snow hid all the grass, and all signs of vegetation, and the rocks showed themselves boldly everywhere, and seemed more stony than rock or stone. The birches on the crags beautiful, red brown and glittering. The ashes glittering spears with their upright stems. The hips very beautiful, and so good ! ! and, dear Coleridge ! I ate twenty for thee, when I was by myself. I came home first – they walked too slow for me. Wm. went to look at Langdale Pikes. We had a sweet invigorating walk. Mr Clarkson came in before tea. We played at cards – sate up late. The moon shone upon the water below Silver-How, and above it hung, combining with Silver-How on one side, a bowl-shaped moon, the curve downwards; the white fields, glittering roof of Thomas Ashburner's house, the dark yew tree, the white fields gay and beautiful. Wm. lay with his curtains open that he might see it.

[*December*] 17th, *Thursday*. Snow in the night and still snowing. We went to Mr Luff's to dine – met Mrs King. Hard frost and as light as day – we had a delightful walk and reached home a little after twelve. Mrs Luff ill. Ambleside looked excessively beautiful as we came out – like a village in another country; and the light chearful mountains were seen in the long, long distance as bright and as clear as at midday with the blue sky above them. We heard waterfowl calling out by the lake side. Jupiter was very glorious above the Ambleside hills, and one large star hung over the coombe of the hills on the opposite side of Rydale water.

December 20th, *Sunday*. It snowed all day. In the evening we went to tea at Thomas Ashburner's. It was a very deep snow. The brooms were very beautiful, arched feathers with wiry stalks pointed to the end, smaller and smaller. They waved gently with the weight of the snow. We stayed at Thomas A.'s till after 9 o'clock – Peggy better. The lasses neat and clean and rosy.

5

'On Man, on Nature and on Human Life
Thinking in solitude, from time to time
I feel sweet passions traversing my soul
Like Music, unto these, where'er I may
I would give utterance in numerous verse.'

From the first version of the 'Prospectus' for *The
Excursion*

Monday 21st, being the shortest day. Mary walked to Ambleside
for letters. It was a wearisome walk, for the snow lay deep upon
the roads and it was beginning to thaw. I stayed at home and
clapped the small linen. Wm. sate beside me, and read *The Pedlar*.
He was in good spirits, and full of hope of what he should do
with it. He went to meet Mary, and they brought 4 letters – 2
from Coleridge, one from Sara, and one from France. Coleridge's
were melancholy letters, he had been very ill in his bowels. We
were made very unhappy. Wm. wrote to him, and directed the
letter into Somersetshire. I finished it after tea. In the afternoon
Mary and I ironed, afterwards she packed her clothes up, and I
mended Wm.'s stockings while he was reading *The Pedlar*.

*From now until 9 March, Wordsworth is at work on 'The Pedlar'.
This is a version of a long poem entitled 'The Ruined Cottage',
begun at Racedown in 1795, which William worked on until
1804 and which ended up as the first book of* The Excursion. *Be-
cause the first version is less well known, I am printing it in its
original form given in Manuscript B, dated 1787–8. To see what
alterations W. was making to it during these months, the reader
can turn to* The Excursion, Book I, *and decide for himself which of
the two versions he prefers. 'The Ruined Cottage' will be found
on p. 153.*

[December] 22nd, Tuesday. Still thaw. I washed my head. Wm.
and I went to Rydale for letters, the road was covered with dirty

snow, rough and rather slippery. We had a melancholy letter from C., for he had been very ill, though he was better when he wrote. We walked home almost without speaking. Wm. composed a few lines of *The Pedlar*. We talked about Lamb's tragedy[1] as we went down the White Moss. We stopped a long time in going to watch a little bird with a salmon-coloured breast, a white cross or T upon its wings, and a brownish back with faint stripes. It was pecking the scattered dung upon the road. It began to peck at the distance of four yards from us, and advanced nearer and nearer till it came within the length of W.'s stick, without any apparent fear of us. As we came up the White Moss, we met an old man, who I saw was a beggar by his two bags hanging over his shoulder; but, from a half laziness, half indifference, and a wanting to *try* him, if he would speak, I let him pass. He said nothing, and my heart smote me. I turned back, and said, 'You are begging?' 'Ay,' says he. I gave him a halfpenny. William, judging from his appearance, joined in. 'I suppose you were a sailor?' 'Ay', he replied, 'I have been 57 years at sea, 12 of them on board a man of war under Sir Hugh Palmer.' 'Why have you not a pension?' 'I have no pension, but I could have got into Greenwich hospital, but all my officers are dead.' He was 75 years of age, had a freshish colour in his cheeks, grey hair, a decent hat with a binding round the edge, the hat worn brown and glossy, his shoes were small thin shoes low in the quarters, pretty good. They had belonged to a gentleman. His coat was blue, frock shaped, coming over his thighs, it had been joined up at the seams behind with paler blue, to let it out, and there were three bell-shaped patches of darker blue behind, where the buttons had been. His breeches were either of fustian, or grey cloth, with strings hanging down, whole and tight; he had a checked shirt on, and a small coloured handkerchief tied round his neck. His bags were hung over each shoulder, and lay on each side of him, below his breast. One was brownish, and of coarse stuff, the other was white with meal on the outside, and his blue waistcoat was whitened with meal. In the coarse bag I guess he put his scraps

---

1. This must refer to Charles Lamb's great personal tragedy, his sister's periodical insanity which led her in September 1786 to attack her family and kill her mother.

of meat etc. He walked with a slender stick – decently stout, but his legs bowed outwards.

We overtook old Fleming at Rydale, leading his little Dutchman-like grandchild along the slippery road. The same pace seemed to be natural to them both, the old man and the little child, and they went hand in hand, the grandfather cautious, yet looking proud of his charge. He had two patches of new cloth at the shoulder-blades of his faded claret-coloured coat, like eyes at each shoulder not worn elsewhere. I found Mary at home in her riding-habit, all her clothes being put up. We were very sad about Coleridge. Wm. walked further. When he came home he cleared a path to the necessary, called me out to see it, but before we got there a whole housetopfull of snow had fallen from the roof upon the path and it echoed in the ground beneath like a dull beating upon it. We talked of going to Ambleside after dinner to borrow money of Luff, but we thought we would defer our visit to Eusemere a day. Half the seaman's nose was reddish as if he had been in his youth somewhat used to drinking, though he was not injured by it. We stopped to look at the stone seat at the top of the hill. There was a white cushion upon it, round at the edge like a cushion, and the rock behind looked soft as velvet, of a vivid green, and so tempting! The snow too looked as soft as a down cushion. A young foxglove, like a star, in the centre. There were a few green lichens about it, and a few withered brackens of fern here and there upon the ground near, all else was a thick snow; no footmark to it, not the foot of a sheep. When we were at Thomas Ashburner's on Sunday Peggy talked about the Queen of Patterdale. She had been brought to drinking by her husband's unkindness and avarice. She was formerly a very nice tidy woman. She had taken to drinking but that was better than if she had taken to something worse (by this I suppose she meant killing herself). She said that her husband used to be out all night with other women and she used to *hear* him come in in the morning, for they never slept together – 'Many a poor body, a wife like me, has had a working heart for her, as much stuff as she had.' We sate snugly round the fire. I read to them the Tale of Custance and the Syrian monarch, also some of the *Prologues*. It is the Man of Lawe's Tale. We went to bed early. It snowed and thawed.

[*December*] 23rd, *Wednesday*. A downright thaw, but the snow not gone off the ground except on the steep hillsides – it was a thick black heavy air. I baked pies and bread. Mary wrote out the Tales from Chaucer for Coleridge. William worked at *The Ruined Cottage* and made himself very ill. I went to bed without dinner – he went to the other bed – we both slept and Mary lay on the rug before the fire. A broken soldier came to beg in the morning. Afterwards a tall woman, dressed somewhat in a tawdry style, with a long checked muslin apron, a beaver hat, and throughout what are called good clothes. Her daughter had gone before, with a soldier and his wife. She had buried her husband at Whitehaven, and was going back into Cheshire.

[*December*] 24th, *Thursday*. Still a thaw. We walked to Rydale, Wm., Mary and I – left the patterns at Thomas Fleming's for Mrs King. The roads uncomfortable and slippery. We sate comfortably round the fire in the evening, and read Chaucer. Thoughts of last year. I took out my old Journal.[1]

[*December*] 25th, *Friday*. Christmas Day. A very bad day – we drank tea at John Fisher's – we were unable to walk. I went to bed after dinner. The roads very slippery. We received a letter from Coleridge while we were at John Fisher's – a terrible night – little John brought the letter. Coleridge poorly but better – his letter made us uneasy about him. I was glad I was not by myself when I received it.

[*December*] 26th, *Saturday*. My head ached and I lay long in bed and took my breakfast there – soon after I had breakfasted we went to call at Mr Olliff's. They were not at home. It came on very wet. Mary went into the house, and Wm. and I went up to Tom Dawson's to speak about his Grandchild, the rain went off and we walked to Rydale. It was very pleasant – Grasmere

---

1. Perhaps the Alfoxden Journal of 1798, or the first part of this Journal which ended on 22 December 1800.

Lake a beautiful image of stillness, clear as glass, reflecting all things, the wind was up, and the waters sounding. The lake of a rich purple, the fields a soft yellow, the island yellowish-green, the copses red-brown, the mountains purple. The Church and buildings, how quiet they were! Poor Coleridge, Sara, and dear little Derwent here last year at this time. After tea we sate by the fire comfortably. I read aloud *The Miller's Tale*. Wrote to Coleridge. The Olliffs passed in chaise and gig. Wm. wrote part of the poem to Coleridge.

This of course refers to 'The Prelude', written for Coleridge. We only know of certain passages written between 1800 and 1803; Book VII, lines 699–712; Book VIII, lines 221–310; and Book XII, lines 185–204. The story of Shepherd and his son in Book VIII appears in the manuscript of 1802 and was originally used as an incident in the life of Michael and Luke. It was almost certainly composed between October and December 1800. See p. 81.

[December] 27th, Sunday. A fine soft beautiful, mild day, with gleams of sunshine. I lay in bed till 12 o'clock, Mr Clarkson's man came – we wrote to him. We walked up within view of Rydale. William went to take in his Boat. I sate in John's Grove a little while. Mary came home. Mary wrote some lines of the third part of Wm.'s poem, which he brought to read to us, when we came home. Mr Simpson came in at dinner time and stayed tea. They fetched in the boat. I lay down upon the bed in the meantime. A sweet evening.

December 28th, Monday. William, Mary, and I set off on foot to Keswick. We carried some cold mutton in our pockets, and dined at John Stanley's, where they were making Christmas pies. The sun shone, but it was coldish. We parted from Wm. upon the Rays. He joined us opposite Sara's rock. He was busy in composition, and sate down upon the wall. We did not see him again till we arrived at John Stanley's. There we roasted apples in the oven. After we had left John Stanley's, Wm. discovered that he had lost his gloves. He turned back, but they were gone. We were tired and had bad headaches. We rested often. Once he left his Spenser, and Mary turned back for it, and found it upon the bank, where we had last rested. We reached Greta Hall at about ½ past 5 o'clock. The children and Mrs C. well. After tea, message came from Wilkinson, who had passed us on the road, inviting Wm. to sup at the Oak. He went. Met a young man (a predestined Marquis) called Johnston. He spoke to him familiarly of the L.B. He had seen a copy presented by the Queen to Mrs Harcourt. Said he saw them everywhere, and wondered they did not sell. We all went weary to bed – my bowels very bad.

December 29th, Tuesday. A fine morning. A thin fog upon the hills which soon disappeared. The sun shone. Wilkinson went with us to the top of the hill. We turned out of the road at the second mile stone, and passed a pretty cluster of houses at the foot of St John's Vale. The houses were among tall trees, partly of Scotch fir, and some naked forest trees. We crossed a bridge just below these houses, and the river winded sweetly along the meadows. Our road soon led us along the sides of dreary bare hills, but we had a glorious prospect to the left of Saddleback, half-way covered with snow, and underneath the comfortable white houses and the village of Threlkeld. These houses and the village want trees about them. Skiddaw was behind us, and dear Coleridge's desert home. As we ascended the hills it grew very cold and slippery. Luckily, the wind was at our backs, and helped us on. A sharp hail-shower gathered at the head of Martindale, and the view upwards was very grand – the wild cottages, seen through the hurrying hail-shower. The wind drove and eddied about and about, and the hills looked large and swelling through the storm. We thought of Coleridge. O! the bonny nooks and windings and curlings of the beck, down at the bottom of the steep green mossy banks. We dined at the public-house on porridge, with a second course of Christmas pies. We were well received by the Landlady, and her little Jewish daughters were glad to see us again. The husband a very handsome man. While we were eating our dinners a traveller came in. He had walked over

Kirkstone that morning. We were much amused by the curiosity of the landlord and landlady to learn who he was, and by his mysterious manner of letting out a little bit of his errand, and yet telling nothing. He had business further up in the vale. He left them with this piece of information to work upon, and I doubt not they discovered who he was and all his business before the next day at that hour. The woman told us of the riches of a Mr Walker, formerly of Grasmere. We said, 'What, does he do nothing for his relations? He has a sickly sister at Grasmere.' 'Why,' said the man, 'I daresay if they had any sons to put forward he would do it for them, but he has children of his own.' N.B. – His fortune is above £60,000, and he has two children ! ! The landlord went about 1 mile and a ½ with us to put us in the right way. The road was often very slippery, the wind high, and it was nearly dark before we got into the right road. I was often obliged to crawl upon all fours, and Mary fell many a time. A stout young man whom we met on the hills, and who knew Mr Clarkson, very kindly set us into the right road, and we inquired again near some houses, and were directed by a miserable, poverty-struck looking woman, who had been fetching water, to go down a nasty miry lane. We soon got into the main road and reached Mr Clarkson's at tea time. Mary H. spent the next day with us, and we walked on Dunmallet before dinner, but it snowed a little. The day following, being New Year's Eve, we accompanied Mary to Stainton Bridge – met Mr Clarkson with a calf's head in a basket – we turned with him and parted from Mary.

On Sunday the 17th we went to meet Mary. It was a mild gentle thaw. She stayed with us till Friday, 22nd January; she was to have left on Thursday 21st but it was too stormy. On Thursday we dined at Mr Myers's, and on Friday, 22nd, we parted from Mary. Before our parting we sate under a wall in the sun near a cottage above Stainton Bridge. The field in which we sate sloped downwards to a nearly level meadow, round which the Emont flowed in a small half-circle as at Sockburn. The opposite bank is woody, steep as a wall, but not high, and above that bank the fields slope gently and irregularly down to it. These fields are surrounded by tall hedges, with trees among them, and there are clumps or grovelets of tall trees here and there. Sheep and cattle were in the fields. Dear Mary! there we parted from her. I daresay, as often as she passes that road she will turn in at the gate to look at this sweet prospect. There was a barn and I think two or three cottages to be seen among the trees, and slips of lawn and irregular fields. During our stay at Mr Clarkson's we walked every day, except that stormy Thursday, and then we dined at Mr Myers's and I went after dinner on a double horse – Mrs Clarkson was poorly all the time we were there. We dined at Thomas Wilkinson's on Friday the 15th, and walked to Penrith for Mary. The trees were covered with hoar-frost – grasses and trees and hedges beautiful; a glorious sunset; frost keener than ever. Next day thaw. Mrs Clarkson amused us with many stories of her family and of persons whom she had known. I wish I had set them down as I heard them, when they were fresh in my memory. She had two old Aunts who lived at Norwich. The son of one of them (Mrs Barnard) had had a large fortune left him. The other sister, rather piqued that her child had not got it, says to her: 'Well, we have one Squire in the family however'. Mrs Barnard replied with tears rushing out 'Sister Harmer, Sister Harmer, there you sit. My son's no more a Squire than yours. I take it very unkindly of you, Sister Harmer.' She used to say 'Well, I wish it may do him any good'. When her son wished to send his carriage for her she said: 'Nay I can walk to the Tabernacle and surely I may walk to see him'! She kept two maids yet she white-washed her kitchen herself – the two sisters lived together. She had a grand cleaning day twice a week and the sister had a fire made upstairs that all below might be thoroughly cleaned. She gave a great deal away in charity, visited the sick and was very pious. Mrs Clarkson knew a clergyman and his wife who brought up ten children upon a curacy, sent two sons to college, and he left £1000 when he died. The wife was very generous, gave to all poor people victuals and drink. She had a passion for feeding animals. She killed a pig with feeding it over much. When it was dead she said, 'To be sure it's a great loss, but I thank God it did not die *clemmed*' (the Cheshire word for starved). Her husband was very fond of playing Back-gammon, and used to play whenever he could get anybody to play with him. She had played much in her youth, and was an excellent player; but her husband knew nothing of this, till one day she said to him, 'You're fond of Back-gammon, come play with me'. He was surprised. She told him that she had kept it to herself while she had a young family to attend to, but that now she would play with him! So they began to play, and played afterwards every night. Mr C. told us many pleasant stories. His journey from London to Wisbech on foot when a school boy, Irish murderer's knife and stick, postboy, etc., the white horse sleeping at the turnpike gate, snoring of the turnpike man, clock ticking, the burring story, the story of the mastiff, bull-baitings by men at Wisbech.

On Saturday, January 23rd, we left Eusemere at 10 o'clock in the morning, I behind Wm., Mr Clarkson on his Galloway. The morning not very promising, the wind cold. The mountains large and dark, but only thinly streaked with snow; a strong wind. We dined in Grisdale on ham, bread, and milk. We parted from Mr C. at one o'clock – it rained all the way home. We struggled with the wind, and often rested as we went along. A hail shower met us before we reached the Tarn, and the way often was difficult over the snow; but at the Tarn the view closed in. We saw nothing but mists and snow: and at first the ice on the Tarn below us cracked and split, yet without water, a dull grey white. We lost our path, and could see the Tarn no longer. We made our way out with difficulty, guided by a heap of stones which we well remembered. We were afraid of being bewildered in the mists, till the darkness should overtake us. We were long before we knew that we were in the right track, but thanks to William's skill we knew it long before we could see our way before us. There was no footmark upon the snow either of man or beast. We saw 4 sheep before we had left the snow region. The Vale of Grasmere, when the mists broke away, looked soft and grave, of a yellow hue. It was dark before we reached home. We were not very much tired. My inside was sore with the cold – we had both of us been much heated upon the mountains but we caught no cold. O how comfortable and happy we felt ourselves, sitting by our own fire, when we had got off our wet clothes and had dressed ourselves fresh and clean. We found 5£ from Montagu and 20£ from Christopher. We talked about the Lake of Como, read in the *Descriptive Sketches*,[1] looked about us, and

---

1. Begun 1791. See also p. 71, n. 2.

felt that we were happy. We indulged dear thoughts about home – poor Mary! we were sad to think of the contrast for her.

[January] 27th, Wednesday. A beautiful mild morning – the sun shone, the lake was still, and all the shores reflected in it. I finished my letter to Mary, Wm. wrote to Stuart. I copied out sonnets for him. Mr Olliff called and asked us to tea tomorrow. We stayed in the house till the sun shone more dimly and we thought the afternoon was closing in, but though the calmness of the Lake was gone with the bright sunshine, yet it was delightfully pleasant. We found no letter from Coleridge. One from Sara which we sate upon the wall to read – a sweet long letter, with a most interesting account of Mr Patrick.[1] We had ate up the cold turkey before we walked so we cooked no dinner. Sate a while by the fire, and then drank tea at Frank Baty's. As we went past the Nab I was surprised to see the youngest child amongst the rest of them running about by itself, with a canny round fat face, and rosy cheeks. I called in. They gave me some nuts. Everybody surprised that we should come over Grisdale. Paid £1:3:3: for letters come since December 1st. Paid also about 8 shillings at Penrith. The bees were humming about the hive. William raked a few stones off the garden, his first garden labour this year; I cut the shrubs. When we returned from Frank's, Wm. wasted his mind in the Magazines. I wrote to Coleridge, and Mrs C., closed the letters up to [? Samson]. Then we sate by the fire, and were happy, only our tender thoughts became painful. Went to bed at ½ past 11.

January 28th, Thursday. A downright rain. A wet night. Wm. slept better – better this morning – he had [written an] epitaph, and altered one that he wrote when he was a boy.[2] It cleared up

1. David Patrick, with whom Sara Hutchinson stayed as a child and on whose character W. drew for his portrait of the Wanderer in *The Excursion*.
2. It is not known which Epitaph this is. His 'Poet's Epitaph' was written in Germany in 1799.

after dinner. We were both in miserable spirits, and very doubtful about keeping our engagement to the Olliffs. We walked first within view of Rydale, then to Lewthwaite's, then we went to Mr Olliff's. We talked a while. Wm. was tired. We then played at cards. Came home in the rain. Very dark. Came with a lantern. Wm. out of spirits and tired. After we went to bed I heard him continually, he called at ¼ past 3 to know the hour.

January 29th, Friday. Wm. was very unwell. Worn out with his bad night's rest. He went to bed – I read to him, to endeavour to make him sleep. Then I came into the other room, and read the first book of *Paradise Lost.* After dinner we walked to Ambleside – found Lloyd's at Luffs – we stayed and drank tea by ourselves. A heart-rending letter from Coleridge – we were sad as we could be. Wm. wrote to him.

During the past month Dorothy has frequently expressed her concern over Coleridge – see above 21 and 25 December. He was beginning to suffer from those bouts of melancholy and despair which later overshadowed his life and which find their fullest expression in 'Dejection: an Ode', written in the spring of this year – see below, p. 201.

We talked about Wm.'s going to London. It was a mild afternoon – there was an unusual softness in the prospects as we went, a rich yellow upon the fields, and a soft grave purple on the waters. When we returned many stars were out, the clouds were moveless, in the sky soft purple, the Lake of Rydale calm, Jupiter behind, Jupiter at least *we* call him, but William says we always call the largest star Jupiter. When he came home we both wrote to C. I was stupefied.

January 30th, Saturday. A cold dark morning. William chopped wood – I brought it in a basket. A cold wind. Wm. slept better, but he thinks he looks ill – he is shaving now. He asks me to set down the story of Barbara Wilkinson's turtle dove. Barbara is an old maid. She had two turtle doves. One of them died, the first year I think. The other bird continued to live alone in its cage for

9 years, but for one whole year it had a companion and daily visitor – a little mouse, that used to come and feed with it; and the dove would caress it, and cower over it with its wings, and make a loving noise to it. The mouse, though it did not testify equal delight in the dove's company, yet it was at perfect ease. The poor mouse disappeared, and the dove was left solitary till its death. It died of a short sickness, and was buried under a tree with funeral ceremony by Barbara and her maidens, and one or two others.

On *Saturday, 30th,* Wm. worked at *The Pedlar* all the morning. He kept the dinner waiting till four o'clock. He was much tired. We were preparing to walk when a heavy rain came on.

[*January*] *31st, Sunday.* Wm. had slept very ill – he was tired and had a bad headache. We walked round the two lakes. Grasmere was very soft, and Rydale was extremely beautiful from the western side. Nab Scar was just topped by a cloud which, cutting it off as high as it could be cut off, made the mountain look uncommonly lofty. We sate down a long time in different places. I always love to walk that way, because it is the way I first came to Rydale and Grasmere, and because our dear Coleridge did also. When I came with Wm., 6½ years ago, it was just at sunset. There was a rich yellow light on the waters, and the Islands were reflected there. To-day it was grave and soft, but not perfectly calm. William says it was much such a day as when Coleridge came with him. The sun shone out before we reached Grasmere. We sate by the roadside at the foot of the Lake, close to Mary's dear name, which she had cut herself upon the stone. Wm. cut at it with his knife to make it plainer.[1] We amused ourselves for a long time in watching the breezes, some as if they came from the bottom of the lake, spread in a circle, brushing along the surface of the water, and growing more delicate, as it were thinner, and of a *paler* colour till they died away. Others spread out like a peacock's tail, and some went right forward

---

1. See below, p. 232, for note on the Rock of Names.

this way and that in all directions. The lake was still where these breezes were not, but they made it all alive. I found a strawberry blossom in a rock. The little slender flower had more courage than the green leaves, for *they* were but half expanded and half grown, but the blossom was spread full out. I uprooted it rashly, and I felt as if I had been committing an outrage, so I planted it again. It will have but a stormy life of it, but let it live if it can. We found Calvert here. I brought a handkerchief full of mosses, which I planted on the chimneypiece when C. was gone. He dined with us, and carried away the encyclopaedias. After they were gone, I spent some time in trying to reconcile myself to the change, and in rummaging out and arranging some other books in their places. One good thing is this – there is a nice elbow place for William, and he may sit for the picture of John Bunyan any day. Mr Simpson drank tea with us. We paid our rent to Benson. William's head was bad after Mr S. was gone. I petted him on the carpet and began a letter to Sara.

February 1st, Monday. Wm. slept badly. I baked pies and bread. William worked hard at *The Pedlar*, and tired himself. He walked up with me towards Mr Simpson's. There was a purplish light upon Mr Olliff's house, which made me look to the other side of the vale, when I saw a strange stormy mist coming down the side of Silver How of a reddish purple colour. It soon came on a heavy rain. We parted presently – Wm. went to Rydale – I drank tea with Mrs S., the two Mr Simpsons both tipsy. I came home with Jenny as far as the Swan. A cold night, dry and windy – Jupiter above the Forest Side. Wm. pretty well but he worked a little. In the morning a box of clothes with books came from London. I sate by his bedside and read in *The Pleasure of Hope*[1] to him, which came in the box. He could not fall asleep, but I found in the morning that he had slept better than he expected. No letters.

February 2nd, Tuesday. A fine clear morning, but sharp and cold. Wm. went into the orchard after breakfast to chop wood. I

---

1. By the Scottish poet Thomas Campbell, published 1799.

walked backwards and forwards on the platform. Molly called me down to Charles Lloyd – he brought me flower seeds from his Brother. William not quite well. We walked into Easedale – were turned back in the open field by the sight of a cow – every horned cow puts me in terror. We walked as far as we could, having crossed the footbridge, but it was dirty, and we turned back – walked backwards and forwards between Goody Bridge and Butterlip How. William wished to break off composition, and was unable, and so did himself harm. The sun shone, but it was cold. After dinner William worked at *The Pedlar*. After tea I read aloud the eleventh book of *Paradise Lost*. We were much impressed, and also melted into tears. The papers came in soon after I had laid aside the book – a good thing for my Wm. I worked a little to-day at putting the linen into repair that came in the box. Molly washing.

February 6th, Saturday. William had slept badly. It snowed in the night, and was on Saturday, as Molly expressed it, a cauld clash. William went to Rydale for letters – he came home with two very affecting letters from Coleridge – resolved to try another climate. I was stopped in my writing, and made ill by the letters. William had a bad headach; he made up a bed on the floor, but could not sleep – I went to his bed and slept not – better when I rose – wrote again after tea, and translated two or three of Lessing's *Fables*.[1]

[*February*] 7th, Sunday. A fine clear frosty morning. The eaves drop with the heat of the sun all day long. The ground thinly covered with snow. The road black, rocks bluish. Before night the Island was quite green; the sun had melted all the snow upon it. Mr Simpson called before Wm. had done shaving – William had had a bad night and was working at his poem. We sate by the fire, and did not walk, but read *The Pedlar*, thinking it done; but lo! though Wm. could find fault with no one part of it, it was uninteresting, and must be altered. Poor Wm.!

---

1. Gotthold Lessing, German critic and dramatist, 1729–81.

February 8th, 1802, Monday Morning. It was very windy and rained very hard all the morning. William worked at his poem and I read a little in Lessing and the grammar. A chaise came to fetch Ellis the Carrier who had hurt his head.

After dinner (i.e. we set off at about ½ past 4) we went towards Rydale for letters. It was a cold '*cauld clash*'. The rain had been so cold that it hardly melted the snow. We stopped at Park's to get some straw in Wm.'s shoes. The young mother was sitting by a bright wood fire with her youngest child upon her lap, and the other two sate on each side of the chimney. The light of the fire made them a beautiful sight, with their innocent countenances, their rosy cheeks, and glossy curling hair. We sate and talked about poor Ellis, and our journey over the Hawes. It had been reported that we came over in the night. Willy told us of 3 men who were once lost in crossing that way in the night; they had carried a lantern with them; the lantern went out at the Tarn, and they all perished. Willy had seen their cloaks drying at the public-house in Patterdale the day before their funeral. We walked on very wet through the clashy cold roads in bad spirits at the idea of having to go as far as Rydale, but before we had come again to the shore of the Lake, we met our patient bow-bent Friend, with his little wooden box at his back. 'Where are you going?' said he. 'To Rydale for letters.' 'I have two for you in my box.' We lifted up the lid, and there they lay. Poor fellow, he straddled and pushed on with all his might; but we soon outstripped him far away when we had turned back with our letters. We were very thankful that we had not to go on, for we should have been sadly tried. In thinking of this I could not help comparing lots with him ! He goes at that slow pace every morning, and after having wrought a hard day's work returns at night, however weary he may be, takes it all quietly, and, though perhaps he neither feels thankfulness nor pleasure, when he eats his supper, and has no luxury to look forward to but falling asleep in bed, yet I daresay he neither murmurs nor thinks it hard. He seems mechanized to labour. We broke the seal of Coleridge's letter, and I had light enough just to see that he was not ill. I put it in my pocket, but at the top of the White Moss I took it to my bosom, a safer place for it. The night was wild. There was a strange mountain lightness, when we were at the top of the White Moss. I have often observed it there in the evenings, being between the two valleys. There is more of the sky there than any other place. It has a strange effect sometimes along with the obscurity of evening or night. It seems almost like a peculiar *sort* of light. There was not much wind till we came to John's Grove, then it roared right out of the grove; all the trees were tossing about. C.'s letter somewhat damped us, it spoke with less confidence about France. Wm. wrote to him. The other letter was from Montagu, with £8. Wm. was very unwell, tired when he had written. He went to bed, and left me to write to M. H., Montagu, and Calvert, and Mrs Coleridge. I had written in his letter to Coleridge. We wrote to Calvert to beg him not to fetch us on Sunday. Wm. left me with a *little* peat fire – it grew less. I wrote on, and was starved. At 2 o'clock I went to put my letters under Fletcher's door. I never felt such a cold night. There was a strong wind and it froze very hard. I collected together all the clothes I could find (for I durst not go into the pantry for fear of waking William). At first when I went to bed I seemed to be warm. I suppose because the cold air, which I had just left, no longer touched my body; but I soon found that I was mistaken. I could not sleep from sheer cold. I had baked pies and bread in the morning. Coleridge's letter contained prescriptions.

N.B. The moon came out suddenly when we were at John's Grove, and a star or two besides.

[*February* 9th,] *Tuesday.* Wm. had slept better. He fell to work, and made himself unwell. We did not walk. A funeral came by of a poor woman who had drowned herself, some say because she was hardly treated by her husband; others that he was a very decent respectable man, and *she* but an indifferent wife. However this was, she had only been married to him last Whitsuntide and had had very indifferent health ever since. She had got up in the night, and drowned herself in the pond. She had requested to be buried beside her mother, and so she was brought in a hearse. She was followed by several decent-looking men on horseback, her sister, Thomas Fleming's wife, in a chaise, and some others with her, and a cart full of women. Molly says folks thinks o' their mothers. Poor body, *she* has been little thought of by any body else. We did a little of Lessing. I attempted a fable, but my head ached; my bones were sore with the cold of the day before, and I was downright stupid. We went to bed, but not till Wm. had tired himself.

[*February*] 10th, *Wednesday*. A very snowy morning. It cleared up a little however for a while but we did not walk. We sent for our letters by Fletcher and for some writing paper etc. He brought us word there were none. This was strange for I depended on Mary. While I was writing out the poem, as we hope for a final writing, a letter was brought me by John Dawson's daughter, the letter written at Eusemere. I paid Wm. Jackson's bill by John Fisher, sent off a letter to Montagu by Fletcher. After Molly went we read the first part of the poem and were delighted with it, but Wm. afterwards got to some ugly places, and went to bed tired out. A wild, moonlight night.

[*February*] 11th, *Thursday*. A very fine clear sunny frost, the ground white with snow – William rose before Molly was ready for him, I rose at a little after nine. William sadly tired and working still at *The Pedlar*. Miss Simpson called when he was worn out – he escaped and sate in his own room till she went. She was very faint and ill, had had a tooth drawn and had suffered greatly. I walked up with her past Gawain's. The sun was very warm till we got past Lewthwaite's – then it had little power, and had not melted the roads. As I came back again I felt the vale like a different climate. The vale was bright and beautiful. Molly had linen hung out. We had pork to dinner sent us by Mrs Simpson. William still poorly. We made up a good fire after dinner, and Wm. brought his mattress out, and lay down on the floor. I read to him the life of Ben Jonson, and some short poems of his, which were too *interesting* for him, and would not let him go to sleep. I had begun with Fletcher, but he was too *dull* for me. Fuller says, in his *Life of Jonson* (speaking of his plays), 'If his latter be not so spriteful and vigorous as his first pieces, all that are old, and all who desire to be old, should excuse him therein'. He says he 'beheld' wit-combats between Shakespeare and Jonson, and compares Shakespeare to an English man-of-war, Jonson to a Spanish great galleon. There is one affecting line in Jonson's epitaph on his first daughter –

> Here lies to each her parents ruth,
> Mary the daughter of their youth.
> At six months' end she parted hence,
> In safety of her innocence.

I have been writing this journal while Wm. has had a nice little sleep. Once he was waked by Charles Lloyd who had come to see about lodging for his children in the hooping cough. It is now 7 o'clock – I have a nice coal fire – Wm. is still on his bed. Two beggars to-day. I continued to read to him. We were much delighted with the poem of *Penshurst*.[1] Wm. rose better. I was cheerful and happy. But he got to work again, and went to bed unwell.

[February] 12th, Friday. A very fine, bright, clear, hard frost. Wm. working again. I recopied *The Pedlar*, but poor Wm. all the time at work. Molly tells me 'What! little Sally's gone to visit at Mr Simpson's. They say she's very smart, she's got on a new bed-gown that her Cousin gave her, it's a very bonny one, they tell me, but I've not seen it. Sally and me's in luck.' In the afternoon a poor woman came, *she said*, to beg some rags for her husband's leg, which had been wounded by a slate from the roof in the great wind – but she had been used to go a-begging, for she has often come here. Her father lived to the age of 105. She is a woman of strong bones, with a complexion that has been beautiful, and remained very fresh last year, but now she looks broken, and her little boy – a pretty little fellow, and whom I have loved for the sake of Basil[2] – looks thin and pale. I observed

---

1. An enchanting poem by Ben Jonson to the country seat where Sir Philip Sidney was born.

2. Basil Montagu, the small son of a friend of William's who was cared for by Dorothy during their years at Racedown and Alfoxden, 1795–8.

this to her. 'Aye,' says she, 'we have all been ill. Our house was unroofed in the storm nearly, and so we lived in it so for more than a week.' The child wears a ragged drab coat and a fur cap, poor little fellow, I think he seems scarcely at all grown since the first time I saw him. William was with me; we met him in a lane going to Skelwith Bridge. He looked very pretty. He was walking lazily, in the deep narrow lane, overshadowed with the hedgerows, his meal poke hung over his shoulder. He said he 'was going a laiting'. Poor creatures! He now wears the same coat he had on at that time. When the woman was gone, I could not help thinking that we are not half thankful enough that we are placed in that condition of life in which we are. We do not so often bless God for this, as we wish for this £50, that £100, etc. etc. We have not, however, to reproach ourselves with ever breathing a murmur. This woman's was but a *common* case. The snow still lies upon the ground. Just at the closing in of the day, I heard a cart pass the door, and at the same time the dismal sound of a crying infant. I went to the window, and had light enough to see that a man was driving a cart, which seemed not to be very full, and that a woman with an infant in her arms was following close behind and a dog close to her. It was a wild and melancholy sight. Wm. rubbed his table after candles were lighted, and we sate a long time with the windows unclosed; I almost finished writing The Pedlar; but poor Wm. wore himself and me out with labour. We had an affecting conversation. Went to bed at 12 o'clock.

February 13th, Saturday. It snowed a little this morning. Still at work at The Pedlar, altering and refitting. We did not walk, though it was a very fine day. We received a present of eggs and milk from Janet Dockeray, and just before she went, the little boy from the Hill brought us a letter from Sara H., and one from the Frenchman in London. I wrote to Sara after tea, and Wm. took out his old newspapers, and the new ones came in soon after. We sate, after I had finished the letter, talking; and Wm. read parts of his Recluse aloud to me. We did not drink tea till ½ past 7.

Dorothy is still referring to 'The Pedlar' and The Recluse *as two separate poems.* The Recluse *was the title of a long philosophical poem Wordsworth always intended to write, of which* The Excursion *was to be only one part. Only one book of* The Recluse *and the Prospectus to it were ever completed. The first part was written soon after the Wordsworths arrived at Grasmere and I have used it to set the scene before the journal begins.*

February 14th, Sunday. A fine morning. The sun shines but it has been a hard frost in the night. There are some little snowdrops that are afraid to pop their white heads quite out, and a few blossoms of hepatica that are half-starved. Wm. left me at work altering some passages of *The Pedlar*, and went into the orchard. The fine day pushed him on to resolve; and as soon as I had read a letter to him, which I had just received from Mrs Clarkson, he said he would go to Penrith, so Molly was despatched for the horse. I worked hard, got the backs pasted, the writing finished, and all quite trim. I wrote to Mrs Clarkson, and put up some letters for Mary H., and off he went in his blue spencer, and a pair of *new* pantaloons fresh from London. He turned back when he had got as far as Frank's to ask if he had his letters safe, then for some apples, then fairly off. We had money to borrow for him. It was a pleasant afternoon. I ate a little bit of cold mutton without laying cloth and then sate over the fire, reading Ben Jonson's *Penshurst*,[1] and other things. Before sunset I put on my shawl and walked out. The snow-covered mountains were spotted with rich sunlight, a palish buffish colour. The roads were very dirty for, though it was a keen frost, the sun had melted the snow and water upon them. I stood at Sara's gate, and when I came in view of Rydale, I cast a long look upon the mountains beyond. They were very white, but I concluded that Wm. would have a very safe passage over Kirkstone, and I was quite easy about him. After dinner, a little before sunset, I walked out about 20 yards above Glowworm Rock. I met a carman, a Highlander I suppose, with 4 carts, the first 3 belonging to himself, the last evidently to a

1 See p. 141

man and his family who had joined company with him, and who I guessed to be potters. The carman was cheering his horses, and talking to a little lass about 10 years of age who seemed to make him her companion. She ran to the wall, and took up a large stone to support the wheel of one of his carts, and ran on before with it in her arms to be ready for him. She was a beautiful creature, and there was something uncommonly impressive in the lightness and joyousness of her manner. Her business seemed to be all pleasure – pleasure in her own motions, and the man looked at her as if he too was pleased, and spoke to her in the same tone in which he spoke to his horses. There was a wildness in her whole figure, not the wildness of a Mountain lass, but a *Road* lass, a traveller from her birth, who had wanted neither food nor clothes. Her Mother followed the last cart with a lovely child, perhaps about a year old, at her back, and a good-looking girl, about 15 years old, walked beside her. All the children were like the mother. She had a very fresh complexion, but she was blown with fagging up the hill, with the steepness of the hill and the bairn that she carried. Her husband was helping the horse to drag the cart up by pushing it with his shoulder. I got tea when I reached home, and read German till about 9 o'clock. Then Molly went away and I wrote to Coleridge. Went to bed at about 12 o'clock. Slept in Wm.'s bed and I slept badly, for my thoughts were full of William.

February 15th, Monday. I was starching small linen all the morning. It snowed a great deal, and was terribly cold. After dinner it was fair, but I was obliged to run all the way to the foot of the White Moss, to get the least bit of warmth into me. I found a letter from C. – he was much better – this was very satisfactory, but his letter was not an answer to Wm.'s which I expected. A letter from Annette. I got tea when I reached home and then set on to reading German. I wrote part of a letter to Coleridge, went late to bed and slept badly.

[*February*] 16th, Tuesday. A fine morning, but I had persuaded myself not to expect Wm.; I believe because I was afraid of being disappointed. I ironed all day. He came in just at tea time, had only seen Mary H. for a couple of hours between Eamont Bridge and Hartshorn Tree. Mrs C. better. He had had a difficult journey over Kirkstone, and came home by Threlkeld – his mouth and breath were very cold when he kissed me. We spent a sweet evening. He was better, had altered *The Pedlar*. We went to bed pretty soon. Mr Graham said he wished Wm. had been with him the other day – he was riding in a post-chaise and he heard a strange cry that he could not understand, the sound continued, and he called to the chaise driver to stop. It was a little girl crying as if her heart would burst. She had got up behind the chaise, and her cloak had been caught by the wheel, and was jammed in, and it hung there. She was crying after it. Poor thing. Mr Graham took her into the chaise, and the cloak was released from the wheel, but the child's misery did not cease, for her cloak was torn to rags; it had been a miserable cloak before, but she had no other, and it was the greatest sorrow that could befal her. Her name was Alice Fell. She had no parents, and belonged to the next town. At the next town, Mr G. left money with some respectable people in the town, to buy her a new cloak.

ALICE FELL: or POVERTY

'Written to gratify Mr Graham of Glasgow, brother of the Author of "The Sabbath". He was a zealous coadjutor of Mr Clarkson, and a man of ardent humanity. The incident had happened to himself, and he urged me to put it into verse, for humanity's sake.'

> The post-boy drove with fierce career,
> For threatening clouds the moon had drowned;
> When, as we hurried on, my ear
> Was smitten with a startling sound.
>
> As if the wind blew many ways,
> I heard the sound, – and more and more,
> It seemed to follow with the chaise,
> And still I heard it as before.

At length I to the boy called out;
He stopped his horses at the word,
But neither cry, nor voice, nor shout,
Nor aught else like it, could be heard.

The boy then smacked his whip, and fast
The horses scampered through the rain;
But, hearing soon upon the blast
The cry, I bade him halt again.

Forthwith alighting on the ground,
'Whence comes,' said I, 'this piteous moan?'
And there a little Girl I found,
Sitting behind the chaise, alone.

'My cloak!' no other word she spake,
But loud and bitterly she wept,
As if her innocent heart would break;
And down from off her seat she leapt.

'What ails you, child?' – she sobbed 'Look here!'
I saw it in the wheel entangled,
A weather-beaten rag as e'er
From any garden scare-crow dangled.

There, twisted between nave and spoke,
It hung, nor could at once be freed;
But our joint pains unloosed the cloak,
A miserable rag indeed!

'And whither are you going, child,
To-night along these lonesome ways?'
'To Durham,' answered she, half wild –
'Then come with me into the chaise.'

Insensible to all relief
Sat the poor girl, and forth did send
Sob after sob, as if her grief
Could never, never have an end.

'My child, in Durham do you dwell?'
She checked herself in her distress,
And said, 'My name is Alice Fell;
I'm fatherless and motherless.

'And I to Durham, Sir, belong.'
Again, as if the thought would choke
Her very heart, her grief grew strong;
And all was for her tattered cloak!

The chaise drove on; our journey's end
Was nigh; and sitting by my side,
As if she had lost her only friend
She wept, nor would be pacified.

Up to the tavern-door we post;
Of Alice and her grief I told;
And I gave money to the host
To buy a new cloak for the old.

'And let it be of duffil grey,
As warm a cloak as man can sell!'
Proud creature was she the next day,
The little orphan, Alice Fell!

[*February*] 22nd, *Monday*. A wet morning. I lay down, as soon
as breakfast was over, very unwell. I slept. Wm. brought me
4 letters to bed – from Annette and Caroline, Mary and Sara,
and Coleridge. C. had had another attack in his bowels; other-
wise mending – M. and S. both well. M. reached Middleham the
Monday night before at 12 o'clock – Tom there. In the evening
we walked to the top of the hill, then to the bridge, we hung
over the wall, and looked at the deep stream below; it came with
a full, steady, yet very rapid flow down to the lake. The sykes
made a sweet sound everywhere, and looked very interesting in
the twilight. That little one above Mr Olliff's house was very
impressive. A ghostly white serpent line, it made a sound most

distinctly heard of itself. The mountains were black and steep – the tops of some of them having yet snow visible, but it rained so hard last night much of it has been washed away. After tea I was just going to write to Coleridge when Mr Simpson came in. Wm. began to read *Peter Bell*[1] to him, so I carried my writing to the kitchen fire. Wm. called me upstairs to read the 3rd part. Mr S. had brought his first engraving to let us see – he supped with us. Wm. was tired with reading and talking and went to bed in bad spirits.

[*February*] 23rd, *Tuesday*. A misty rainy morning – the lake calm. I baked bread and pies. Before dinner worked a little at Wm.'s waistcoat – after dinner read German Grammar. Before tea we walked into Easedale. We turned aside in the Parson's field, a pretty field with 3 pretty prospects. Then we went to the first large field, but such a cold wind met us that we turn'd again. The wind seemed warm when we came out of our own door. That dear thrush was singing upon the topmost of the smooth branches of the ash tree at the top of the orchard. How long it had been perched on that same tree I cannot tell, but we had heard its dear voice in the orchard the day through, along with a chearful undersong made by our winter friends, the robins. We came home by Goan's. I picked up a few mosses by the roadside, which I left at home. We then went to John's Grove, there we sate a little while looking at the fading landscape. The lake, though the objects on the shore were fading, seemed brighter than when it is perfect day, and the Island pushed itself upwards, distinct and large. All the shores marked. There was a sweet, sea-like sound in the trees above our heads. We walked backwards and forwards some time for dear John's sake, then walked to look at Rydale. Darkish when we reached home, and we got tea immediately with candles. William now reading in Bishop Hall[2] – I going to read German. We have a nice singing fire, with one piece of wood. Fletcher's carts are arrived but no papers from Mrs Coleridge.

---

1. See above, page 61 n. 1.
2. Bishop Joseph Hall, 1574–1656, satirist and poet.

[*February*] 24th, *Wednesday*. A rainy day – we were busy all day unripping William's coats for the tailor. William wrote to Annette, to Coleridge and the Frenchman – I received a letter from Mrs Clarkson, a very kind affecting letter, which I answered telling her I would go to Eusemere when William went to Keswick – I wrote a little bit to Coleridge. We sent off these letters by Fletcher. It was a tremendous night of wind and rain. Poor Coleridge! a sad night for a traveller such as he. God be praised he was in safe quarters. Wm. went out, and put the letters under the door – he never felt a colder night.

[*March* 1st,] *Monday*. A fine pleasant day, we walked to Rydale. I went on before for the letters, brought 2 from M. and S.H. We climbed over the wall and read them under the shelter of a mossy rock. We met Mrs Lloyd in going – Mrs Olliff's child ill. The catkins are beautiful in the hedges, the ivy is very green. Robert Newton's paddock is greenish – that is all we see of Spring; finished and sent off the letter to Sara, and wrote to Mary. Wrote again to Sara, and Wm. wrote to Coleridge. Mrs Lloyd called when I was in bed.

[*March* 2nd,] *Tuesday*. A fine grey morning. I was baking bread and pies. After dinner I read German, and a little before dinner Wm. also read. We walked on Butterlip How under the wind. It rained all the while, but we had a pleasant walk. The mountains of Easedale, black or covered with snow at the tops, gave a peculiar softness to the valley, the clouds hid the tops of some of them. The valley was populous and enlivened with the streams. Mrs Lloyd drove past without calling.

[*March* 3rd,] *Wednesday*. I was so unlucky as to propose to re-write *The Pedlar*. Wm. got to work, and was worn to death. We did not walk. I wrote in the afternoon.

[*March* 4th,] *Thursday*. Before we had quite finished breakfast Calvert's man brought the horses for Wm. We had a deal to do, to shave, pens to make, poems to put in order for writing, to settle the dress, pack up etc., and the man came before the pens were made, and he was obliged to leave me with only two. Since he has left me at half past 11 (it is now 2) I have been putting the drawers into order, laid by his clothes which we had thrown here and there and everywhere, filed two months' newspapers and got my dinner, 2 boiled eggs and 2 apple tarts. I have set Molly on to clear the garden a little, and I myself have helped. I transplanted some snowdrops – the Bees are busy. Wm. has a nice bright day. It was hard frost in the night. The Robins are singing sweetly. Now for my walk. I will be busy. I will look well, and be well when he comes back to me. O the Darling ! Here is one of his bitten apples. I can hardly find in my heart to throw it into the fire. I must wash myself, then off. I walked round the two Lakes, crossed the stepping-stones at Rydale foot. Sate down where we always sit. I was full of thoughts about my darling. Blessings on him. I came home at the foot of our own hill under Loughrigg. They are making sad ravages in the woods. Benson's wood is going, and the wood above the River. The wind has blown down a small fir tree on the Rock that terminates John's path – I suppose the wind of Wednesday night. I read German after my return till tea time. I worked and read the L.B., enchanted with the *Idiot Boy*. Wrote to Wm., then went to bed. It snowed when I went to bed.

'The Idiot Boy', written at Alfoxden in 1798, is one of the finest examples of Wordsworth's early style and he and Dorothy attached great importance to it. But it is written in the spirit of the first edition of the Lyrical Ballads of 1798 and would in any case be too long to print here.

[March 5th,] Friday. First walked in the garden and orchard, a frosty sunny morning. After dinner I gathered mosses in Easedale. I saw before me sitting in the open field upon his sacks of rags the old Ragman that I know. His coat is of scarlet in a thousand patches. His breeches' knees were untied. The breeches have been given him by some one – he has a round hat, pretty good, small crowned but large rimmed. When I came to him, he said 'Is there a brigg yonder that'll carry me ow'r t' watter?' He seemed half stupid. When I came home Molly had shook the carpet and cleaned everything upstairs. When I see her so happy in her work, and exulting in her own importance, I often think of that affecting expression which she made use of to me one evening lately. Talking of her good luck in being in this house, 'Aye, Mistress, them 'at's low laid would have been a proud creature could they but have [seen] where I is now, fra what they thought mud be my doom'. I was tired when I reached home. I sent Molly Ashburner to Rydale. No letters! I was sadly mortified. I expected one fully from Coleridge. Wrote to William, read the L.B., got into sad thoughts, tried at German, but could not go on. Read L.B. Blessings on that Brother of mine! Beautiful new moon over Silver How.

[*March 6th,*] *Saturday Morning.* I awoke with a bad headache and partly on that account, partly for ease I lay in bed till one o'clock. At one I pulled off my nightcap – ½ past one sate down to breakfast. A very cold sunshiny frost. I wrote *The Pedlar*, and finished it before I went to Mr Simpson's to drink tea. Miss S. at Keswick, but she came home. Mrs Jameson came in – I stayed supper. Fletcher's carts went past and I let them go with William's letter. Mr B.S. came nearly home with me. I found letters from Wm., Mary, and Coleridge. I wrote to C. Sate up late, and could not fall asleep when I went to bed.

[*March 7th,*] *Sunday Morning.* A very fine, clear frost. I stitched up *The Pedlar*; wrote out *Ruth*; read it with the alterations; then wrote Mary H. Read a little German, got my dinner. Mrs Lloyd called at the door, and in came William. I did not expect him till tomorrow. How glad I was. After we had talked about an hour, I gave him his dinner, a beef steak. We sate talking and happy. Mr and Miss Simpson came in at tea time. William came home very well – he had been a little fatigued with reading his poems. He brought two new stanzas of *Ruth*. We went to bed pretty soon and slept well. A mild grey evening.

These are the two new verses of 'Ruth' which William brought home and which are to be found in one of the notebooks Dorothy used for her Journal. They were not included in the final form of the poem which is printed on p. 46. The first of these two was to be placed between verses 10 and 11, and the second between verses 31 and 32.

I. Of march and ambush, siege and fight,
   Then did he tell; and with delight
   The heart of Ruth would ache;
   Wild histories they were, and dear:
   But 'twas a thing of heaven to hear
   When of himself he spake.

II. It was a purer, better mind:
   O Maiden innocent and kind
   What sights I might have seen!
   Even now upon my eyes they break!
   And he again began to speak
   Of lands where he had been.

[*March 8th*,] *Monday Morning*. A soft rain and mist. We walked to Rydale for letters. The Vale looked very beautiful in excessive simplicity, yet, at the same time, in uncommon obscurity. The Church stood alone, no mountains behind. The meadows looked calm and rich, bordering on the still lake. Nothing else to be seen but lake and island. Found a very affecting letter from Montagu, also one from Mary. We read Montagu's in walking on – sate down to read Mary's. I came home with a bad headach and lay down – I slept, but rose little better. I have got tea and am now much relieved. On Friday evening the moon hung over the northern side of the highest point of Silver How, like a gold ring snapped in two, and shaven off at the ends, it was so narrow. Within this ring lay the circle of the round moon, as *distinctly* to be seen as ever the enlightened moon is. William had observed the same appearance at Keswick, perhaps at the very same moment, hanging over the Newland Fells. Sent off a letter to Mary H., also Coleridge and Sara, and rewrote in the evening the alterations of *Ruth*, which we sent off at the same time.

[*March 9th,*] *Tuesday Morning.* William was reading in Ben Jonson – he read me a beautiful poem on Love. We then walked. The first part of our walk was melancholy – we went within view of Rydale – then we sate on Sara's seat – we walked afterwards into Easedale. It was cold when we returned. We met Sally Newton and her water dog. We sate by the fire in the evening, and read *The Pedlar* over. William worked a little, and altered it in a few places.

For the reasons given at the beginning of this section, the original version of 'The Pedlar' follows. But the poem they read over was probably closer to the first book of The Excursion *on 9 March as we have it now.*

THE RUINED COTTAGE

Part 1st

'Twas Summer, and the sun was mounted high,
Along the south the uplands feebly glared
Through a pale steam, and all the northern downs
In clearer air ascending shewed far off
Their surfaces on which the shadows lay
Of many clouds far as the sight could reach
Along the horizon's edge, that lay in spots
Determined and unmoved; with steady beams
Of clear and pleasant sunshine interposed;
Pleasant to him who on the soft cool grass
Extends his careless limbs beside the root
Of some huge oak whose aged branches make
A twilight of their own, a dewy shade
Where the wren warbles, while the dreaming man,
Half conscious of that soothing melody,
With sidelong eye looks out upon the scene
By those impending branches made [more soft]
More soft and distant. Other lot was mine;
Across a bare wide Common I had toiled
With languid feet which by the slippery ground
Were baffled still; and when I stretched myself
On the brown earth, my limbs from very heat

153

Could find no rest, nor my weak arm disperse
The insect host which gathered round my face
And joined their murmurs to the tedious noise
Of seeds of bursting gorse which crackled round.
I rose and turned towards a group of trees
Which midway in that level stood alone,
And thither come at length beneath a shade
Of clustering elms that sprang from the same root
I found a ruined Cottage – four clay walls
That stared upon each other. 'Twas a spot
The wandering gypsey in a stormy night
Would pass it with his moveables to house
On the open plain beneath the imperfect arch
Of a cold lime-kiln. As I looked around
Beside the door I saw an aged Man
Stretched on a bench whose edge with short bright moss
Was green, and studded o'er with fungus flowers.
An iron-pointed staff lay at his side.
Him had I seen the day before, alone
And in the middle of the public way
Standing to rest himself. His eyes were turned
Towards the setting sun, while, with that staff
Behind him fixed, he propped a long white pack
Which crossed his shoulders; wares for maids who live
In lonely villages or straggling huts.
I knew him – he was born of lowly race
On Cumbrian hills, and I have seen the tear
Stand in his luminous eye when he described
The house in which his early youth was passed
And found I was no stranger to the spot.
I loved to hear him talk of former days
And tell how when a child, ere yet of age
To be a shepherd, he had learned to read
His bible in a school that stood alone,
Sole building on a mountain's dreary edge,
Far from the sight of city spire, or sound
Of Minster clock. From that bleak tenement
He many an evening to his distant home
In solitude returning saw the hills

Grow larger in the darkness, all alone
Beheld the stars come out above his head,
And travelled through the wood, no comrade near,
To whom he might confess the things he saw.
So the foundations of his mind were laid
In such communion, not from terror free.
While yet a child, and long before his time
He had perceived the presence and the power
Of greatness, and deep feelings had impressed
Great objects on his mind, with portraiture
And colour so distinct [that on his mind]
They lay like substances, and almost seemed
To haunt the bodily sense. He had received
A precious gift, for as he grew in years
With these impressions would he still compare
All his ideal stores, his shapes and forms,
And being still unsatisfied with aught
Of dimmer character, he thence attained
An active power to fasten images
Upon his brain, and on their pictured lines
Intensely brooded, even till they acquired
The liveliness of dreams. Nor did he fail,
While yet a child, with a child's eagerness,
Incessantly to turn his ear and eye
On all things which the rolling seasons brought
To feed such appetite. Nor this alone
Appeased his yearning; in the after day
 Of boyhood, many an hour in caves forlorn
And in the hollow depth of naked crags
He sate, and even in their fixed lineaments,
Or from the power of a peculiar eye,
Or by creative feeling overborne,
Or by predominance of thought oppressed,
Even in their fixed and steady lineaments
He traced an ebbing and a flowing mind,
Expression ever varying. In his heart
 Love was not yet, nor the pure joy of love,
By sound diffused, or by the breathing air,
Or by the silent looks of happy things,

Or flowing from the universal face
Of earth and sky. But he had felt the power
Of nature, and already was prepared
By his intense conceptions to receive
Deeply the lesson deep of love, which he
Whom Nature, by whatever means, has taught
To feel intensely, cannot but receive.
Ere his ninth summer he was sent abroad
To tend his father's sheep, such was his task
Henceforward till the later day of youth.
Oh! then what soul was his when on the tops
Of the high mountains he beheld the sun
Rise up and bathe the world in light. He looked,
The ocean and the earth beneath him lay
In gladness and deep joy. The clouds were touched
And in their silent faces did he read
Unutterable love. Sound needed none
Nor any voice of joy; his spirit drank
The spectacle. Sensation, soul and form
All melted into him. They swallowed up
His animal being; in them did he live
And by them did he live. They were his life.
In such access of mind, in such high hour
Of visitation from the living God,
He did not feel the God; he felt his works;
Thought was not. In enjoyment it expired.
Such hour by prayer or praise was unprofaned,
He neither prayed, nor offered thanks or praise,
His mind was a thanksgiving to the power
That made him. It was blessedness and love.
A shepherd on the lonely mountain tops,
Such intercourse was his, and in this sort
Was his existence oftentimes possessed.
Ah! *then* how beautiful, how bright appeared
The written promise; he had early learned
To reverence the volume which displays
The mystery, the life which cannot die;
But in the mountains did he *feel* his faith
There did he see the writing – All things there

Looked immortality, revolving life,
And greatness still, revolving, infinite;
There littleness was not, the least of things
Seemed infinite, and there his spirit shaped
Her prospects, nor did he *believe* – he saw.
What wonder if his being thus became
Sublime and comprehensive. Low desires
Low thoughts had there no place, yet was his heart
Lowly; for he was meek in gratitude
Oft as he called to mind those ecstasies,
And whence they flowed, and from them he acquired
Wisdom which works through patience; thence he learned
In many a calmer hour of sober thought
To look on nature with an humble heart
Self-questioned where it did not understand,
And with a superstitious eye of love.
Small need had he of books; for many a tale
Traditionary round the mountains hung,
And many a legend peopling the dark woods
Nourished Imagination in her growth,
And gave the mind that apprehensive power
By which she is made quick to recognize
The moral properties and scope of things.
Yet greedily he read and read again
What'er the rustic Vicar's shelf supplied,
The life and death of Martyrs who sustained
Intolerable pangs, and here and there
A straggling volume torn and incomplete
Which left half-told the preternatural tale,
Romance of giants, chronicle of fiends
Profuse in garniture of wooden cuts
Strange and uncouth, dire faces, figures dire
Sharp-kneed, sharp-elbowed, and lean-ankled too
With long and ghostly shanks, forms which once seen
Could never be forgotten. Things though low
Though low and humble, not to be despised
By such as have observed the curious links
With which the perishable hours of life
Are bound together, and the world of thought

Exists and is sustained. A different store,
The annual savings of a toilsome life,
The Schoolmaster supplied; books that explain
The purer elements of truth involv'd
In lines and numbers, and by charm severe,
Especially perceived where Nature droops
And feeling is suppress'd, preserve the mind
Busy, in solitude and poverty.
And thus employed he many a time forgot
The listless [creeping] hours when in the hollow vale,
Hollow and green, he lay on the green turf
In lonesome idleness. What could he do?
Nature was at his heart, and he perceived
Though yet he knew not how, a wasting power
In all things which from her sweet influence
Might tend to wean him, therefore with her hues
Her forms and with the spirit of her forms
He cloathed the nakedness of austere truth.
While yet he linger'd in the elements
Of science, and among her simplest laws,
His triangles, they were the stars of heaven,
The *silent* stars; his altitudes the crag
Which is the eagle's birthplace; or some peak
Familiar with forgotten years, which shews,
Inscribed, as with the silence of the thought,
Upon its bleak and visionary side,
The history of many a winter storm,
Of obscure records of the path of fire.
Yet with these linesome sciences he still
Continued to amuse the heavier hours
Of solitude, and solitary thought.
But now, before his twentieth year was pass'd
Accumulated feelings press'd his heart
With an encreasing weight; he was o'erpower'd
By Nature, and his mind became disturbed,
And many a time he wished the winds might rage
When they were silent: from his intellect,
And from the stillness of abstracted thought,
In vain he sought repose, in vain he turned

To science for a cure. I have heard him say
That at this time he scann'd the laws of light
With a strange pleasure of disquietude
Amid the din of torrents, when they send
From hollow clefts, up to the clearer air
A cloud of mist which in the shining sun
Varies its rainbow hues. But vainly thus
And vainly by all other means he strove
To mitigate the fever of his heart.
From Nature and her overflowing soul
He had received so much, that all his thoughts
Were steeped in feeling. He was only then
Contented, when, with bliss ineffable
He felt the sentiment of being, spread
O'er all that moves, and all that seemeth still,
O'er all which, lost beyond the reach of thought,
And human knowledge, to the human eye
Invisible, yet liveth to the heart,
O'er all that leaps, and runs, and shouts, and sings,
Or beats the gladsome air, o'er all that glides
Beneath the wave, yea in the wave itself
And mighty depth of waters. Wonder not
If such his transports were; for in all things
He saw one life, and felt that it was joy.
One song they sang, and it was audible,
Most audible then, when the fleshly ear
O'ercome by grosser prelude of that strain,
Forgot its functions, and slept undisturbed.
These things he had sustained in solitude
Even till his bodily strength began to yield
Beneath their weight. The mind within him burnt
And he resolved to quit his native hills.
He asked his father's blessing, and assumed
This lowly occupation. The old man
Bless'd him and prayed for him, yet with a heart
Foreboding evil. He from his native hills
Had wandered far, much had he seen of men
Their manners, their enjoyments and pursuits
Their passions and their feelings, chiefly those

Essential and eternal in the heart
Which mid the simpler forms of rural life
Exist more simple in their elements
And speak a plainer language. He possessed
No vulgar mind though he had passed his life
In this poor occupation, first assumed
From impulses of curious thought, from such
Continued many a year and now pursued
From habit and necessity. His eye
Flashing poetic fire he would repeat
The songs of Burns and as we trudged along
Together did we make the hollow grove
Ring with our transports: though he was untaught,
In the dead lore of schools undisciplined,
Why should he grieve? he was a chosen son
To him was given an ear which deeply felt
The voice of Nature in the obscure wind
The sounding mountain and the running stream.
To every natural form, rock, fruit and flower
Even the loose stones that cover the highway
He gave a moral life, he saw them feel
Or linked them to some feeling. In all shapes
He found a secret and mysterious soul,
A fragrance and a spirit of strange meaning.
Though poor in outward shew he was most rich,
He had a world about him, 'twas his own
He made it, for it only lived to him
And to the God who looked into his mind.
Such sympathies would often bear him far
In outward gesture, and in invisible look,
Beyond the common seeming of mankind.
Some called it madness – such it might have been
But that he had an eye that evermore
Looked deep into the shades of difference
As they lie hid in all exterior forms
Near or remote, minute or vast, an eye
Which from a stone, a tree, a withered leaf,
To the broad ocean and the azure heavens
Spangled with kindred multitudes of stars

Could find no surface where its power might sleep,
Which spake perpetual logic to his soul,
And by an unrelenting agency
Did bind his feelings even as in a chain.
    So was he framed. Now on the Bench he lay
Stretched at his ease [length], and with that weary load
Pillowed his head. I guess he had no thought
Of his way-wandering life. His eyes were shut,
The shadows of the breezy elms above
Dappled his face. With thirsty heat oppressed
At length I hailed him, glad to see his hat
Bedewed with water-drops, as if the brim
Had newly scooped a running stream. He rose
And, pointing to a sun-flower, bade me climb
The [   ] wall where the same gaudy flower
Looked out upon the road. It was a plot
Of garden ground now wild, its matted weeds
Marked with the steps of those whom as they pass'd
The gooseberry trees that shot in long [lank slips]
Of currants hanging from their leafless stems
In scanty strings had tempted to o'erleap
The broken wall. Within that chearless spot
Where two tall hedgrows of thick willow boughs
Joined in a damp cold nook I found a well
Half choaked
I slaked my thirst and to the shady bench
Returned, and while I stood unbonneted
To catch the current of the breezy air
The old man said 'I see around me [here]
Things which you cannot see. We die, my Friend,
Nor we alone, but that which each man loved
And prized in his peculiar nook of earth
Dies with him or is changed, and very soon
Even of the good is no memorial left.
The Waters of that spring if they could feel
Might mourn. They are not as they were, the bond
Of brotherhood is broken; time has been
When every day the touch of human hand
Disturbed their stillness, and they ministered

161

To human comfort. As I stopped to drink
Few minutes gone at that deserted well
What feelings came to me ! A spider's web
Across its mouth hung to the water's edge
And on the wet and slimy foot-stone lay
The useless fragment of a wooden bowl.
It moved my very heart. The day has been
When I would never pass this road but she
Who lived within these walls, when I appeared,
A daughter's welcome gave me, and I loved her
As my own child. Oh Sir ! The good die first
And they whose hearts are dry as summer dust
Burn to the socket. Many a passenger
Has blessed poor Margaret for her gentle looks
When she upheld the cool refreshment drawn
From that forsaken well, and no one came
But he was welcome – no one went away
But that it seemed she loved him. She is dead,
The worm is on her cheek, and this poor hut
Stripped of its outward garb of household flowers
Of rose and sweetbriar [jasmine] offers to the wind
A cold bare wall whose earthy top is tricked
With weeds and the rank spear-grass; she is dead
And nettles rot and adders sun themselves
Where we have sate together while she nursed
Her infant at her bosom. The wild colt
The unstalled heifer and the Potter's ass
Find shelter now within the chimney wall
Where I have seen her evening hearth-stone blaze
And through the window spread upon the road
Its chearful light. You will forgive me, Sir,
I feel I play the truant with my tale.
She had a husband, an industrious man
Sober and steady. I have heard her say
That he was up and busy at his loom
In summer ere the mower's scythe had swept
The dewy grass, and in the early spring
Ere the last star had vanished. They who passed
At evening from behind the garden fence

Might hear his busy spade which he would ply
After his daily work till the day-light
Was gone, and every leaf and flower were lost
In the dark hedges. So they passed their days
In peace and comfort, and two pretty babes
Were their best hope next to the God in Heaven.
– You may remember, now some ten years gone,
Two blighting seasons, when the fields were left
With half a harvest [tillage]; it pleased heaven to add
A worse affliction in the plague of war.
A happy land was stricken to the heart.
'Twas a sad time of sorrow and distress.
A wanderer among the cottages
I with my pack of winter raiment saw
The hardship of that season; many rich
Sank down as in a dream among the poor,
And of the poor did many cease to be,
And their place knew them not. Meanwhile abridged
Of daily comforts, gladly reconciled
To numerous self-denials, Margaret
Went struggling on through those calamitous years
With cheerful hope, but ere the second spring
A fever seized her husband. In disease
He lingered long, and when his strength returned
He found the little he had stored to meet
The hour of accident or crippling age
Was all consumed. As I have said, 'twas now
A time of trouble – shoals of artizans
Were from their daily labour turned away
To hang for bread on parish charity
They and their wives and children, happier far
Could they have lived as do the little birds
That peck along the hedges, or the kite
That makes his dwelling in the mountain rocks.
Ill fared it now with Robert, he who dwelt
In this poor cottage; at his door he stood
And whistled many a snatch of merry tunes
That had no mirth in them, or with his knife
Carved uncouth figures on the heads of sticks,

Then idly sought about through every nook
Of house or garden any casual task
Of use or ornament, and with a strange
Amusing but uneasy novelty
He blended where he might the various tasks
Of summer, autumn, winter, and of spring.
The passenger might see him at the door
With his small hammer on the threshold stone
Pointing lame buckle-tongues and rusty nails,
The treasured store of an old household box,
Or braiding cords or weaving bells and caps
Of rushes, playthings for his babes.
But this endured not, his good-humour soon
Became a weight in which no pleasure was
And poverty brought on a petted mood
And a sore temper, day by day he drooped,
And he would leave his home, and to the town
Without an errand would he turn his steps,
Or wander here and there among the fields.
One while he would speak lightly of his babes
And with a cruel tongue, at other times
He played with them wild freaks of merriment;
And 'twas a piteous thing to see the looks
Of the poor innocent children. "Every smile",
said Margaret to me, here beneath these trees,
"Made my heart bleed." ' At this the old man paused
And looking up to those enormous elms
He said, ''tis now the hour of deepest noon,
At this still season of repose and peace,
This hour when all things which are not at rest
Are chearful, while this multitude of flies
Fills all the air with happy melody,
Why should a tear be in an old Man's eye?
Why should we thus with an untoward mind,
And in the weakness of humanity,
From natural wisdom turn our hearts away,
To natural comfort shut our eyes and ears,
And, feeding on disquiet, thus disturb
[This calm] of Nature with our restless thoughts?'

He spake with somewhat of a solemn tone
But when he ended there was in his face
Such easy chearfulness, a look so mild
That for a little time it stole away
All recollection and that simple tale
Passed from my mind like a forgotten sound.
A while on trivial things we held discourse
To me soon tasteless. In my own despite
I thought of that poor woman as of one
Whom I had known and loved. He had rehearsed
Her homely tale with such familiar power
With such a tender countenance, an eye
So busy, that the things of which he spake
Seemed present, and attention now relaxed
There was a heartfelt chillness in my veins.
I rose and turning from that breezy shade
Went out into the open air, and stood
To drink the comfort of the warmer sun.
Long time I had not stayed ere looking round
Upon that tranquil ruin, and impelled
By a mild form of curious pensiveness
I begg'd of the old man that for my sake
He would resume his story. He replied
'It were a wantonness, and would demand
Severe reproof, if we were men whose hearts
Could hold vain dalliance with the misery
Even of the dead, contented thence to draw
A momentary pleasure, never marked
By reason, barren of all future good.
But we have known that there is often found
In mournful thoughts, and always might be found,
A power to virtue friendly; were't not so
I am a dreamer among men – indeed
An idle dreamer. 'Tis a common tale
By moving accidents uncharactered
A tale of silent suffering, hardly clothed
In bodily form, and to the grosser sense

But ill adapted, scarcely palpable
To him who does not think. But at your bidding
I will proceed.

      While thus it fared with them
To whom this Cottage till that hapless year
Had been a blessed home, it was my chance
To travel in a country far remote,
And glad I was when, halting by yon gate
Which leads from the green lane, again I saw
These lofty elm-trees. Long I did not rest,
With many pleasant thoughts I cheared my way
O'er the flat common. At the door arrived
I knocked, and when I entered with the hope
Of usual greeting Margaret looked at me
A little while, then turned her head away
Speechless, and sitting down upon a chair
Wept bitterly. I wist not what to do
Or how to speak to her. Poor wretch ! at last
She rose from off her seat, and then, Oh Sir !
I cannot *tell* how she pronounced my name,
With fervent love and with a face of grief
Unutterably helpless, and a look
That seemed to cling upon me, she inquired
If I had seen her husband. As she spake
A strange surprize and fear came to my heart,
And I could make no answer. Then she told
That he had disappeared; just two months gone
He left his house; two wretched days had passed,
And on the third by the first break of light
Within her casement full in view she saw
A purse of gold. "I trembled at the sight",
Said Margaret, "for I knew it was his hand
That placed it there, and on that very day
By one a stranger, from my husband sent,
The tidings came that he had joined a troop
Of soldiers going to a distant land.
He left me thus. Poor Man ! he had not heart
To take a farewell of me, and he feared
That I should follow with my babes and sink

Beneath the misery of a soldier's life."
This tale did Margaret tell with many tears;
And when she ended I had little power
To give her comfort, and was glad to take
Such words of hope from her own mouth as served
To chear us both; but long we had not talked
Ere we built up a pile of better thoughts
And with a brighter eye she looked around
As if she had been shedding tears of joy.
We parted. It was then the early spring;
I left her busy with her garden tools;
And well remember, o'er that fence she looked,
And while I paced along the foot-way path,
Called out, and sent a blessing after me,
With tender chearfulness, and with a voice
That seemed the very sound of happy thoughts.
I roved o'er many a hill and many a dale
With this my weary load, in heat and cold,
Through many a wood, and many an open ground
In sunshine or in shade, in wet or fair,
Now blithe, now drooping, as it might befal,
My best companions now the driving winds
And now the "trotting" brooks and whispering trees,
And now the music of my own sad steps
With many a short-lived thought that passed between
And disappeared. I measured back this road
Towards the wane of summer, when the wheat
Was yellow, and the soft and bladed grass
Sprung up afresh and o'er the hay-field spread
Its tender green. When I had reached the door
I found that she was absent. In the shade
Where now we sit I waited her return.
Her cottage in its outward look appeared
As chearful as before; in any shew
Of neatness little changed, but that I thought
The honeysuckle crowded round the door
And from the wall hung down in heavier loads
And knots of worthless stone-crop started out
Along the window's edge, and grew like weeds

Against the lower panes. I turned aside
And strolled into her garden. It was changed,
The unprofitable bindweed spread his bells
From side to side, and with unwieldy wreaths
Had dragged the rose from its sustaining wall
And bent it down to earth; the border tufts,
Daisy, and thrift, and lowly camomile
And thyme had straggled out into the paths
Which they were used to deck. Ere this an hour
Was wasted, back I turned my restless steps
And as I walked before the door it chanced
A stranger passed, and guessing whom I sought
He said that she was used to ramble far.
The sun was sinking in the west, and now
I sate with sad impatience. From within
Her solitary infant cried aloud;
The spot though fair seemed very desolate
The longer I remained more desolate. .
And looking round I saw the corner stones
Till then unmarked, on either side the door
With dull red stains discoloured and stuck o'er
With tufts and hairs of wool as if the sheep
That feed upon the commons thither came
As to a couching-place and rubbed their sides
Even at her threshold. The church-clock struck eight,
I turned and saw her distant a few steps.
Her face was pale and thin, her figure too
Was changed. As she unlocked the door she said
"It grieves me you have waited here so long
But in good truth I've wandered much of late;
And sometimes, to my shame I speak, have need
Of my best prayers to bring me back again."
While on the board she spread our evening meal
She told me she had lost her elder child,
That he for months had been a serving boy
Apprenticed by the parish. "I am changed,
And to myself," said she, "have done much wrong,
And to this helpless infant. I have slept
Weeping, and weeping have I waked; my tears

168

Have flowed as if my body were not such
As others are, and I could never die.
But I am now in mind and in my heart
More easy, and I hope," said she, "that heaven
Will give me patience to endure the things
Which I behold at home." It would have grieved
Your very soul to see her. Sir, I feel
The story linger in my heart. I fear
'Tis long and tedious, but my spirit clings
To that poor woman, so familiarly
Do I perceive her manner and her look
And presence, and so deeply do I feel
Her goodness that a vision of the mind,
A momentary trance comes over me
And to myself I seem to muse on one
By sorrow laid asleep, or borne away,
A human being destined to awake
A human life or something very near
To human life, when he shall come again
For whom she suffered. Sir, it would have grieved
Your very heart to see her, evermore
Her eyelids drooped, her eyes were downward cast,
And when she at her table gave me food
She did not look at me, her voice was low,
Her body was subdued. In every act
Pertaining to her house-affairs appeared
The careless stillness which a thinking soul
Gives to an idle matter. Still she sighed,
But yet no motion of the breast was seen,
No heaving of the heart. While by the fire
We sate together, sighs came on my ear
I knew not how, and scarcely whence they came.
I took my staff, and when I kissed her babe
The tears were in her eyes. I left her then
With the best hope and comfort I could give.
She thanked me for my will, for my hope
It seemed she did not thank me. I returned,
And took my rounds along this road again,
Ere on its sunny bank the primrose flower

Had chronicled the earliest day of spring.
I found her sad and drooping; she had learned
No tidings of her husband, if he lived
She knew not that he lived; if he were dead
She knew not he was dead. She seemed not changed
In person or appearance. but her house
Bespoke a sleepy hand of negligence,
The floor was neither dry nor neat, the hearth
Was comfortless
The windows they were dim, and her few books
Which one upon the other heretofore
Had been piled up against the corner panes
In seemly order, now with straggling leaves
Lay scattered here and there, open or shut,
As they had chanced to fall. Her infant babe
Had from its mother caught the trick of grief,
And sighed among its playthings; once again
I turned towards the garden gate, and saw
More plainly still that poverty and grief
Were now come nearer to her; the earth was hard
With weeds defaced and knots of withered grass;
No ridges there appeared of clear black mould,
No winter greenness. Of her herbs and flowers
It seemed the better part were gnawed away
Or trampled on the earth; a chain of straw
Which had been twisted round the tender stem
Of a young apple-tree lay at its root,
The bark was nibbled round by truant sheep.
Margaret stood near, her infant in her arms
And seeing that my eye was on the tree
She said, "I fear it will be dead and gone
Ere Robert come again." Towards the house
Together we returned and she enquired
If I had any hope. But for her babe
And for her little friendless Boy, she said,
She had no wish to live, that she must die
Of sorrow. Yet I saw the idle loom
Still in its place. His Sunday garments hung
Upon the self-same nail – his very staff

Stood undisturbed behind the door, and when
I passed this way, beaten by autumn winds,
She told me that her little babe was dead
And she was left alone. That very time,
I yet remember, through the miry lane
She walked with me a mile when the bare trees
Trickled with foggy damps, and in such sort
That any heart had ached to hear her, begged
That wheresoe'er I went I still would ask
For him whom she had lost. We parted then,
Our final parting, for from that time forth
Did many seasons pass ere I return'd
Into this tract again. Five tedious years
She lingered in unquiet widowhood
A wife and widow. Needs must it have been
A sore heart-wasting. I have heard, my Friend,
That in that broken arbour she would sit
The idle length of half a sabbath day
There – where you see the toadstool's lazy head,
And when a dog passed by she still would quit
The shade and look abroad. On this old Bench
For hours she sate, and evermore, her eye
Was busy in the distance, shaping things
Which made her heart beat quick. Seest thou that path?
The greensward now has broken its grey line;
There to and fro she paced through many a day
Of the warm summer, from a belt of flax
That girt her waist spinning the long-drawn thread
With backward steps – yet ever as there passed
A Man whose garments shewed the Soldier's red
Or crippled Mendicant in Sailor's garb
The little child who sate to turn the wheel
Ceased from his toil, and she with faltering voice
Expecting still to learn her husband's fate,
Made many a fond enquiry, and when they,
Whose presence gave no comfort, were gone by
Her heart was still more sad. And by yon gate
Which bars the traveller's road she often stood
And when a stranger horseman came, the latch

Would lift, and in his face look wistfully
Most happy if from aught discovered there
Of tender feeling she might dare repeat
The same sad question. Meanwhile her poor hut
Sank to decay, for he was gone, whose hand
At the first nippings of October frost
Closed up each chink, and with fresh bands of straw
Chequered the green-grown thatch. And so she lived
Through the long winter, reckless and alone;
Till this reft house, by frost, and thaw, and rain
Was sapped, and, when she slept, the nightly damps
Did chill her breast, and in the stormy day
Her tattered clothes were ruffled by the wind
Even at the side of her own fire. Yet still
She loved this wretched spot, nor would for worlds
Have parted hence, and still that length of road
And this rude bench one torturing hope endeared,
Fast rooted at her heart; and here, my friend,
In sickness she remained, and here she died,
Last human tenant of these ruined walls.'

6

'Low and rustic life was generally chosen, because, in that situation, the essential passions of the heart find a better soil in which they can attain their maturity . . .'

From the 1800 version of Wordsworth's 'Preface to the Second Edition of the *Lyrical Ballads*'

[*March* 11*th*,] *Thursday*. A fine morning. William worked at the poem of *The Singing Bird*. Just as we were sitting down to dinner we heard Mr Clarkson's voice. I ran down, William followed. He was so finely mounted that William was more intent upon the horse than the rider, an offence easily forgiven, for Mr Clarkson was as proud of it himself as he well could be. We ate our dinner, then Mr Clarkson came. We walked with him round by the White Bridge after dinner. The vale in mist, rather the mountains, big with the rain, soft and beautiful. Mr C. was sleepy and went soon to bed.

[*March* 12*th*,] *Friday*. A very fine morning. We went to see Mr Clarkson off. Then we went up towards Easedale but a shower drove us back. The sun shone while it rained, and the stones of the walls and the pebbles on the road glittered like silver. When William was at Keswick I saw Jane Ashburner driving the cow along the high road from the well where she had been watering it – she had a stick in her hand and came tripping along in the jig-step, as if she were dancing. Her presence was bold and graceful, her cheeks flushed with health, and her countenance was free and gay. William finished his poem of *The Singing Bird*.

THE SAILOR'S MOTHER

(Title given to 'The Singing Bird' in 1807)

One morning (raw it was and wet –
A foggy day in winter time)
A Woman on the road I met,
Not old, though something past her prime:
Majestic in her person, tall and straight;
And like a Roman matron's was her mien and gait.

The ancient spirit is not dead;
Old times, thought I, are breathing there;
Proud was I that my country bred
Such strength, a dignity so fair:
She begged an alms, like one in poor estate;
I looked at her again, nor did my pride abate.

When from these lofty thoughts I woke,
'What is it,' said I, 'that you bear,
Beneath the covert of your Cloak,
Protected from this cold damp air?'
She answered, soon as she the question heard
'A simple burthen, Sir, a little Singing-bird.'

And, thus continuing, she said,
'I had a Son, who many a day
Sailed on the seas, but he is dead;
In Denmark he was cast away:
And I have travelled weary miles to see
If aught which he had owned might still remain for me.

'The bird and cage they both were his:
'Twas my Son's bird; and neat and trim
He kept it: many voyages
The singing-bird had gone with him;
When last he sailed, he left the bird behind;
From bodings, as might be, that hung upon his mind.

'He to a fellow-lodger's care
Had left it, to be watched and fed,
And pipe its song in safety; – there
I found it when my Son was dead;
And now, God help me for my little wit!
I bear it with me, Sir; – he took so much delight in it.'

In the meantime I read the remainder of Lessing. In the evening
after tea William wrote *Alice Fell*[1] – he went to bed tired, with
a wakeful mind and a weary body. A very sharp clear night.

[*March 13th,*] *Saturday Morning.* It was as cold as ever it has
been all winter, very hard frost. I baked pies bread and seed cake
for Mr Simpson. William finished *Alice Fell,* and then he wrote
the poems of *The Beggar Woman,* taken from a woman whom I
had seen in May (now nearly 2 years ago) when John and he
were at Gallow Hill.[2] I sate with him at intervals all the morning,
took down his stanzas, etc. After dinner we walked to Rydale for
letters – it was terribly cold – we had 2 or 3 brisk hail showers –
the hail stones looked clean and pretty upon the dry clean road.
Little Peggy Simpson was standing at the door catching the hail
stones in her hand – she grows very like her mother. When she is
sixteen years old I dare say that to her Grandmother's eye she
will seem as like to what her mother was, as any rose in her gar-
den is like the rose that grew there years before. No letters at
Rydale. We drank tea as soon as we reached home. After tea I
read to William that account of the little boy belonging to the
tall woman, and an unlucky thing it was, for he could not es-
cape from those very words, and so he could not write the poem.
He left it unfinished, and went tired to bed. In our walk from
Rydale he had got warmed with the subject, and had half cast the
poem.

---

1. See above under 16 February, p. 145.
2. See above, p. 42.

She had a tall man's height or more;
Her face from summer's noontide heat
No bonnet shaded, but she wore
A mantle, to her very feet
Descending with a graceful flow,
And on her head a cap as white as newfallen snow.

Her skin was of Egyptian brown:
Haughty, as if her eyes had seen
Its own light to a distance thrown,
She towered, fit person for a Queen
To lead those ancient Amazonian files;
Or ruling Bandit's wife among the Grecian isles.

Advancing, forth she stretched her hand
And begged an alms with doleful plea
That ceased not; on our English land
Such woes, I knew, could never be;
And yet a boon I gave her, for the creature
Was beautiful to see – a weed of glorious feature.

I left her, and pursued my way;
And soon before me did espy
A pair of little Boys at play,
Chasing a crimson butterfly;
The taller followed with his hat in hand,
Wreathed round with yellow flowers the gayest of the land.

The other wore a rimless crown
With leaves of laurel stuck about;
And, while both followed up and down,
Each whooping with a merry shout,
In their fraternal features I could trace
Unquestionable lines of that wild Suppliant's face.

Yet *they*, so blithe of heart, seemed fit
For finest tasks of earth or air :
Wings let them have, and they might flit
Precursors to Aurora's car,
 Scattering fresh flowers; though happier far, I ween,
To hunt their fluttering game o'er rock and level green.

They dart across my path – but lo,
Each ready with a plaintive whine !
Said I, 'not half an hour ago
Your Mother has had alms of mine.'
'That cannot be,' one answered – 'she is dead :'
I looked reproof – they saw – but neither hung his head.

'She has been dead, Sir, many a day.' –
'Hush, boys ! you're telling me a lie;
It was your Mother, as I say !'
And, in the twinkling of an eye,
'Come ! Come !' cried one, and without more ado,
 Off to some other play the joyous Vagrants flew !

[*March* 14th,] *Sunday Morning*. William had slept badly – he got up at nine o'clock, but before he rose he had finished *The Beggar Boys*, and while we were at breakfast that is (for I had breakfasted) he, with his basin of broth before him untouched, and a little plate of bread and butter he wrote the Poem to a Butterfly ! He ate not a morsel, nor put on his stockings, but sate with his shirt neck unbuttoned, and his waist coat open while he did it. The thought first came upon him as we were talking about the pleasure we both always feel at the sight of a butterfly. I told him that I used to chase them a little, but that I was afraid of brushing the dust off their wings, and did not catch them. He told me how they used to kill the white ones when he went to school because they were Frenchmen. Mr Simpson came in just as he was finishing the Poem. After he was gone I wrote it down and the other poems, and I read them over to him. We then called at Mr Olliff's – Mr O. walked with us to within sight of Rydale – the sun shone very pleasantly, yet it was extremely cold. We

dined and then Wm. went to bed. I lay upon the fur gown before
the fire, but I could not sleep – I lay there a long time. It is now
halfpast 5 – I am going to write letters – I began to write to Mrs
Rawson. William rose without having slept – we sate comfort-
ably by the fire till he began to try to alter The Butterfly, and
tired himself – he went to bed tired.

TO A BUTTERFLY

Stay near me – do not take thy flight !
A little longer stay in sight !
Much converse do I find in thee,
Historian of my infancy !
Float near me; do not yet depart !
Dead times revive in thee :
Thou bring'st, gay creature as thou art !
A solemn image to my heart,
My father's family !
Oh ! pleasant, pleasant were the days,
The time, when, in our childish plays,
My sister Emmeline and I
Together chased the butterfly !
A very hunter did I rush
Upon the prey : – with leaps and springs
I followed on from brake to bush ;
But she, God love her, feared to brush
The dust from off its wings.

[March 15th,] Monday Morning. We sate reading the poems, and
I read a little German. Mr Luff came in at one o'clock. He had a
long talk with William – he went to Mr Olliff's after dinner and
returned to us to tea. During his absence a sailor who was travel-
ling from Liverpool to Whitehaven called; he was faint and pale
when he knocked at the door – a young man very well dressed.
We sate by the kitchen fire talking with him for 2 hours. He told
us interesting stories of his life. His name was Isaac Chapel. He
had been at sea since he was 15 years old. He was by trade a sail-

maker. His last voyage was to the coast of Guinea. He had been on board a slave ship, the captain's name Maxwell, where one man had been killed, a boy put to lodge with the pigs and was half eaten, one boy set to watch in the hot sun till he dropped down dead. He had been cast away in North America and had travelled thirty days among the Indians, where he had been well treated. He had twice swum from a King's ship in the night and escaped. He said he would rather be in hell than be pressed. He was now going to wait in England to appear against Captain Maxwell. 'O he's a Rascal, Sir, he ought to be put in the papers!' The poor man had not been in bed since Friday night. He left Liverpool at 2 o'clock on Saturday morning; he had called at a farm house to beg victuals and had been refused. The woman said she would give him nothing. 'Won't you? Then I can't help it.' He was excessively like my brother John. A letter was brought us at tea time by John Dawson from M.H. I wrote to her, to Sara about Mr Olliff's gig, and to Longman and Rees – I wrote to Mrs Clarkson by Mr Luff.

[*March 16th,*] *Tuesday.* A very fine morning. Mrs Luff called – William went up into the orchard while she was here and wrote a part of *The Emigrant Mother.* After dinner I read him to sleep. I read Spenser while he leaned upon my shoulder. We walked to look at Rydale. Then we walked towards Goan's. The moon was a good height above the mountains. She seemed far and distant in the sky; there were two stars beside her, that twinkled in and out, and seemed almost like butterflies in motion and lightness. They looked to be far nearer to us than the moon.

[*March 17th,*] *Wednesday.* William went up into the orchard and finished the Poem. Mrs Luff and Mrs Olliff called. I went with Mrs O. to the top of the White Moss – Mr O. met us and I went to their house – he offered me manure for the garden. I went and sate with W. and walked backwards and forwards in the orchard till dinner time. He read me his poem. I broiled beef-steaks. After dinner we made a pillow of my shoulder – I read to him and my Beloved slept. I afterwards got him the pillows, and he was lying with his head on the table when Miss Simpson came in. She stayed tea. I went with her to Rydale – no letters! A sweet evening as it had been a sweet day, a grey evening, and I walked quietly along the side of Rydale Lake with quiet thoughts – the hills and the lake were still – the Owls had not begun to hoot, and the little birds had given over singing. I looked before me and I saw a red light upon Silver How as if coming out of the vale below,

> There was a light of most strange birth,
> A light that came out of the earth,
> And spread along the dark hill-side.

Thus I was going on when I saw the shape of my Beloved in the road at a little distance. We turned back to see the light but it was fading – almost gone. The owls hooted when we sate on the wall at the foot of White Moss; the sky broke more and more, and we saw the moon now and then. John Green passed us with his cart – we sate on. When we came in sight of our own dear Grasmere, the vale looked fair and quiet in the moonshine; the Church was there and all the cottages. There were huge slow-travelling clouds in the sky, that threw large masses of shade upon some of the mountains. We walked backwards and forwards, between home and Olliff's, till I was tired. William kindled, and began to write the poem. We carried cloaks into the orchard, and sate a while there. I left him, and he nearly finished the poem. I was tired to death, and went to bed before him – he came down to me, and read the poem to me in bed.

THE EMIGRANT MOTHER

Once in a lonely hamlet I sojourned
In which a Lady driven from France did dwell;
The big and lesser griefs with which she mourned,
In friendship she to me would often tell.
This Lady, dwelling upon British ground,
Where she was childless, daily would repair
To a poor neighbouring cottage; as I found,
For sake of a young Child whose home was there.

Once having seen her clasp with fond embrace
This Child, I chanted to myself a lay,
Endeavouring, in our English tongue, to trace
Such things as she unto the Babe might say:
And thus, from what I heard and knew, or guessed,
My song the workings of her heart expressed.

I

'Dear Babe, thou daughter of another,
One moment let me be thy mother!
An infant's face and looks are thine,
And sure a mother's heart is mine:
Thy own dear mother's far away,
At labour in the harvest field:
Thy little sister is at play; –
What warmth, what comfort would it yield
To my poor heart, if thou wouldst be
One little hour a child to me!

II

'Across the waters I am come,
And I have left a babe at home:
A long, long way of land and sea!
Come to me – I'm no enemy:
I am the same who at thy side
Sate yesterday, and made a nest
For thee, sweet Baby! – thou hast tried,
Thou know'st the pillow of my breast;
Good, good art thou: – alas! to me
Far more than I can be to thee.

III

'Here, little Darling, dost thou lie;
An infant thou, a mother I!
Mine wilt thou be, thou hast no fears;
Mine art thou – spite of these my tears.

Alas! before I left the spot,
My baby and its dwelling-place;
The nurse said to me "Tears should not
Be shed upon an infant's face,
It was unlucky" – no, no, no;
No truth is in them who say so!

IV

'My own dear little-one will sigh,
Sweet Babe! and they will let him die.
"He pines," they'll say, "it is his doom,
And you may see his hour is come."
Oh! had he but thy cheerful smiles,
Limbs stout as thine, and lips as gay,
Thy looks, thy cunning, and thy wiles,
And countenance like a summer's day,
They would have hopes of him; – and then
I should behold his face again!

V

''Tis gone – like dreams that we forget;
There was a smile or two – yet – yet
I can remember them, I see
The smiles, worth all the world to me.
Dear Baby! I must lay thee down;
Thou troublest me with strange alarms;
Smiles hast thou, bright ones of thy own;
I cannot keep thee in my arms;
For they confound me; – where – where is
That last, that sweetest smile of his?

VI

'Oh! how I love thee! – we will stay
Together here this one half day.
My sister's child, who bears my name,
From France to sheltering England came;

She with her mother crossed the sea;
The babe and mother near me dwell:
Yet does my yearning heart to thee
Turn rather, though I love her well:
Rest, little Stranger, rest thee here!
Never was any child more dear!

VII

'– I cannot help it; ill intent
I've none, my pretty Innocent!
I weep – I know they do thee wrong,
These tears – and my poor idle tongue.
Oh, what a kiss was that! my cheek
How cold it is! but thou art good;
Thine eyes are on me – they would speak,
I think to help me if they could.
Blessings upon that soft, warm face,
My heart again is in its place!

VIII

'While thou art mine, my little Love,
This cannot be a sorrowful grove;
Contentment, hope, and mother's glee,
I seem to find them all in thee:
Here's grass to play with, here are flowers;
I'll call thee by my darling's name;
Thou hast, I think, a look of ours,
Thy features seem to me the same;
His little sister thou shalt be;
And, when once more my home I see,
I'll tell him many tales of Thee.'

7

'. . . a tale of visionary hours.'

[*March 18th,*] *Thursday.* A very fine morning. The sun shone, but it was far colder than yesterday. I felt myself weak and William charged me not to go to Mrs Lloyd's. I seemed indeed to myself unfit for it, but when he was gone I thought I would get the visit over if I could, so I ate a beefsteak thinking it would strengthen me; so it did, and I went off. I had a very pleasant walk – Rydale was full of life and motion. The wind blew briskly, and the lake was covered all over with bright silver waves, that were there each the twinkling of an eye, then others rose up and took their places as fast as they went away. The rocks glittered in the sunshine, the crows and the ravens were busy, and the thrushes and little birds sang. I went through the fields, and sate ½ an hour afraid to pass a cow. The cow looked at me, and I looked at the cow, and whenever I stirred the cow gave over eating. I was not very much tired when I reached Lloyd's – I walked in the garden – Charles is all for agriculture – Mrs L. in her kindest way. A parcel came in from Birmingham, with Lamb's play for us, and for C. They came with me as far as Rydale. As we came along Ambleside vale in the twilight it was a grave evening. There was something in the air that compelled me to serious thought – the hills were large, closed in by the sky. It was nearly dark when I parted from the Lloyds, that is night was come on, and the moon was overcast. But, as I climbed Moss, the moon came out from behind a mountain mass of black clouds. O, the unutterable darkness of the sky, and the earth below the moon! and the glorious brightness of the moon itself ! There was a vivid sparkling streak of light at this end of Rydale water, but the rest was very dark, and Loughrigg Fell and Silver How were white and bright, as if they were covered with hoar frost. The moon retired again, and appeared and disappeared several times before I reached home. Once there was no moonlight to be seen but upon the island-house and the promontory of the island where it stands. 'That needs must be a holy place', etc. etc. I had many very exquisite feelings, and when I saw this lowly Building in the waters, among the dark and lofty hills, with that bright, soft light upon it, it made me more than half a poet. I was tired when I reached home, and could not sit down to reading, and tried to write verses, but alas! I gave up expecting William, and went soon to bed. Fletcher's carts came home late.

[*March* 19th,] *Friday.* A very rainy morning. I went up into the lane to collect a few green mosses to make the chimney gay against my darling's return. Poor C. I did not wish for, or expect him, it rained so. Mr Luff came in before my dinner. We had a long talk. He left me before 4 o'clock, and about half an hour after Coleridge came in – his eyes were a little swollen with the wind. I was much affected with the sight of him, he seemed half stupefied. William came in soon after. Coleridge went to bed late, and William and I sate up till four o'clock. A letter from Sara sent by Mary. They disputed about Ben Jonson. My spirits were agitated very much.

[*March* 20th,] *Saturday.* A tolerably fine morning after 11 o'clock but when I awoke the whole vale was covered with snow. William and Coleridge walked to Borwick's. I followed but did not find them – came home and they were here. We had a little talk about going abroad. We sate pleasantly enough. After tea William read *The Pedlar.* After supper we talked about various things – christening the children, etc. etc. Went to bed at 12 o'clock.

[*March* 21st,] *Sunday.* A showery day. Coleridge and William lay long in bed. We sent up to Mackareth's for the horse to go to Keswick, but we could not have it. Went with C. to Borwick's where he left us. William was very unwell this evening. We had a sweet and tender conversation. I wrote to Mary and Sara.

[*March 22nd,*] Monday. A rainy day. William very poorly. Mr Luff came in after dinner and brought us 2 letters from Sara H. and one from poor Annette. I read Sara's letters while he was here, I finished my letters to M. and S. and wrote to my brother Richard. We talked a good deal about C. and other interesting things. We resolved to see Annette, and that Wm. should go to Mary. Wm. wrote to Coleridge not to expect us till Thursday or Friday.

[*March 23rd,*] Tuesday. A mild morning. William worked at *The Cuckow* poem. I sewed beside him. After dinner he slept, I read German, and, at the closing-in of day, went to sit in the orchard – he came to me, and walked backwards and forwards. We talked about C. Wm. repeated the poem to me. I left him there, and in 20 minutes he came in, rather tired with attempting to write. He is now reading Ben Jonson. I am going to read German. It is about 10 o'clock, a quiet night. The fire flutters, and the watch ticks. I hear nothing else save the breathing of my Beloved, and he now and then pushes his book forward, and turns over a leaf. Fletcher is not come home. No letter from C.

[*March 24th,*] Wednesday. We walked to Rydale for letters. It was a beautiful spring morning – warm, and quiet with mists. We found a letter from M. H. I made a vow that we would not leave this country for G. Hill – Sara and Tom not being going to the Wolds. I wrote to Mary in the evening. I went to bed after dinner. William walked out and wrote [to] Peggy Ashburner – I rose better. Wm. altered *The Butterfly*[1] as we came from Rydale.

[*March 26th,*] Friday. A beautiful morning. William wrote to Annette, then worked at *The Cuckow*.

---

1. See under 14 March, p. 178.

TO THE CUCKOO

O blithe New-comer ! I have heard,
I hear thee and rejoice.
O Cuckoo ! shall I call thee Bird,
Or but a wandering Voice?

While I am lying on the grass
Thy twofold shout I hear,
From hill to hill it seems to pass,
At once far off, and near.

Though babbling only to the Vale,
Of sunshine and of flowers,
Thou bringest unto me a tale
Of visionary hours.

Thrice welcome, darling of the Spring !
Even yet thou art to me
No bird, but an invisible thing,
A voice, a mystery.

The same whom in my school-boy days
I listened to; that Cry
Which made me look a thousand ways
In bush, and tree, and sky.

To seek thee did I often rove
Through woods and on the green;
And thou wert still a hope, a love;
Still longed for, never seen.

And I can listen to thee yet;
Can lie upon the plain
And listen, till I do beget
That golden time again.

O blessed Bird ! the earth we pace
Again appears to be
An unsubstantial, faery place;
That is fit home for Thee !

I was ill and in bad spirits – After dinner I sate 2 hours in the orchard. William and I walked together after tea, first to the top of White Moss, then to Mr Olliff's. I left Wm. and while he was absent wrote out poems. I grew alarmed, and went to seek him – I met him at Mr Olliff's. He has been trying, without success, to alter a passage – in *Silver How* poem.[1] He had written a conclusion just before he went out. While I was getting into bed, he wrote *The Rainbow*.

My heart leaps up when I behold
   A rainbow in the sky:
So was it when my life began;
So it is now I am a man;
So be it when I shall grow old,
   Or let me die!
The Child is father of the Man;
   And I could wish my days to be
Bound each to each by natural piety.

[*March 27th,*] *Saturday*. A divine morning. At breakfast William wrote part of an ode.

ODE

Intimations of Immortality from Recollections of Early Childhood

I

There was a time when meadow, grove and stream,
The earth, and every common sight,
   To me did seem
   Apparelled in celestial light,
The glory and the freshness of a dream,

---

1. This may refer to the poem to his brother John, 'When to the attractions of a busy world', which contains a reference to *Silver How* in line 91. See p. 68.

It is not now as it hath been of yore; –
    Turn wheresoe'er I may,
      By night or day,
The things which I have seen I now can see no more.

II

    The Rainbow comes and goes,
    And lovely is the Rose,
    The Moon doth with delight
Look round her when the heavens are bare,
     Waters on a starry night
     Are beautiful and fair;
   The sunshine is a glorious birth;
   But yet I know, where'er I go :
That there hath past away a glory from the earth.

III

Now, while the birds thus sing a joyous song,
    And while the young lambs bound
     As to the tabor's sound,
To me alone there came a thought of grief :
And timely utterance gave that thought relief,
    And I again am strong :
The cataracts blow their trumpets from the steep;
No more shall grief of mine the seasons wrong;
I hear the Echoes through the mountains throng,
The Winds come to me from the fields of sleep,
    And all the earth is gay;
     Land and sea
   Give themselves up to jollity,
    And with the heart of May
   Doth every Beast keep holiday; –
    Thou Child of Joy,
Shout round me, let me hear thy shouts, thou happy
     Shepherd-boy !

Ye blessed Creatures, I have heard the call
   Ye to each other make; I see
The heavens laugh with you in your jubilee;
   My heart is at your festival,
   My head hath its coronal,
The fulness of your bliss, I feel – I feel it all.
   Oh evil day ! if I were sullen
   While Earth herself is adorning,
     This sweet May-morning,
   And the Children are culling
     On every side,
   In a thousand valleys far and wide,
   Fresh flowers; while the sun shines warm,
And the Babe leaps up on his Mother's arm : –
   I hear, I hear, with joy I hear !
   – But there's a Tree, of many, one,
A single Field which I have looked upon,
Both of them speak of something that is gone :
   The Pansy at my feet
   Doth the same tale repeat :
Whither is fled the visionary gleam?
Where is it now, the glory and the dream?

*We do not know how much Wordsworth had written before he
went to visit Coleridge the following day. The 'timely utterance'
of verse III seems to refer to 'The Rainbow' written the night
before, which he made the Motto for the whole Ode. But he prob-
ably wrote the IVth verse later in the summer after seeing the
first draft of Coleridge's own 'Dejection: an Ode', which at this
time took the form of a letter to Sara Hutchinson (see below, 21
April). The interaction of the two great Odes on each other is
a most fascinating study. The 'Immortality' Ode, which was
not finished until March 1804, is now seen as a declaration of
belief and an answer to Coleridge's despair.*

Ye blessed Creatures, I have heard the call
 Ye to each other make; I see
The heavens laugh with you in your jubilee;
 My hèart is at your festival,
 My head hath its coronal,
The fulness of your bliss, I feel – I feel it all.
 Oh evil day! if I were sullen
 While Earth herself is adorning,
 This sweet May-morning,
 And the Children are culling
 On every side,
 In a thousand valleys far and wide,
 Fresh flowers; while the sun shines warm,
And the Babe leaps up on his Mother's arm : –
 I hear, I hear, with joy I hear!
 – But there's a Tree, of many, one,
A single Field which I have looked upon,
Both of them speak of something that is gone:
 The Pansy at my feet
 Doth the same tale repeat:
Whither is fled the visionary gleam?
Where is it now, the glory and the dream?

We do not know how much Wordsworth had written before
went to visit Coleridge the following day. The 'timely utteran
of verse III seems to refer to 'The Rainbow' written the nig
before, which he made the Motto for the whole Ode. But he pr
ably wrote the IVth verse later in the summer after seeing
first draft of Coleridge's own 'Dejection: an Ode', which at t
time took the form of a letter to Sara Hutchinson (see below,
April). The interaction of the two great Odes on each other
a most fascinating study. The 'Immortality' Ode, which v
not finished until March 1804, is now seen as a declaration
belief and an answer to Coleridge's despair.

TO THE CUCKOO

O blithe New-comer! I have heard,
I hear thee and rejoice.
O Cuckoo! shall I call thee Bird,
Or but a wandering Voice?

While I am lying on the grass
Thy twofold shout I hear,
From hill to hill it seems to pass,
At once far off, and near.

Though babbling only to the Vale,
Of sunshine and of flowers,
Thou bringest unto me a tale
Of visionary hours.

Thrice welcome, darling of the Spring!
Even yet thou art to me
No bird, but an invisible thing,
A voice, a mystery.

The same whom in my school-boy days
I listened to; that Cry
Which made me look a thousand ways
In bush, and tree, and sky.

To seek thee did I often rove
Through woods and on the green;
And thou wert still a hope, a love;
Still longed for, never seen.

And I can listen to thee yet;
Can lie upon the plain
And listen, till I do beget
That golden time again.

O blessed Bird! the earth we pace
Again appears to be
An unsubstantial, faery place;
That is fit home for Thee!

I was ill and in bad spirits – After dinner I sate 2 hours in the orchard. William and I walked together after tea, first to the top of White Moss, then to Mr Olliff's. I left Wm. and while he was absent wrote out poems. I grew alarmed, and went to seek him – I met him at Mr Olliff's. He has been trying, without success, to alter a passage – in *Silver How* poem.[1] He had written a conclusion just before he went out. While I was getting into bed, he wrote *The Rainbow*.

My heart leaps up when I behold
    A rainbow in the sky:
So was it when my life began;
So it is now I am a man;
So be it when I shall grow old,
    Or let me die !
The Child is father of the Man;
    And I could wish my days to be
Bound each to each by natural piety.

[*March 27th,*] *Saturday.* A divine morning. At breakfast William wrote part of an ode.

ODE

Intimations of Immortality from Recollections of Early Childhood

I

There was a time when meadow, grove and stream,
The earth, and every common sight,
    To me did seem
    Apparelled in celestial light,
The glory and the freshness of a dream,

It is not now as it hath been of yore; –
    Turn wheresoe'er I may,
        By night or day,
The things which I have seen I now can see no more.

II

    The Rainbow comes and goes,
    And lovely is the Rose,
    The Moon doth with delight
Look round her when the heavens are bare,
    Waters on a starry night
    Are beautiful and fair;
    The sunshine is a glorious birth;
    But yet I know, where'er I go:
That there hath past away a glory from the earth.

III

Now, while the birds thus sing a joyous song,
    And while the young lambs bound
        As to the tabor's sound,
To me alone there came a thought of grief:
And timely utterance gave that thought relief,
    And I again am strong:
The cataracts blow their trumpets from the steep;
No more shall grief of mine the seasons wrong;
I hear the Echoes through the mountains throng,
The Winds come to me from the fields of sleep,
    And all the earth is gay;
        Land and sea
    Give themselves up to jollity,
        And with the heart of May
Doth every Beast keep holiday; –
        Thou Child of Joy,
Shout round me, let me hear thy shouts, thou happy
    Shepherd-boy !

1. This may refer to the poem to his brother John, 'When to the attractions of a busy world', which contains a reference to *Silver How* in line 91. See p. 68.

[*March 28th*,] *Sunday.* We went to Keswick. Arrived wet to skin. A letter from Mary. C. was not tired with walking to meet us. I lay down after dinner with a bad headach.

[*April*] 7th, *Wednesday.* Wm.'s birthday. Wm. went to Middleham. I walked 6 miles with him. It rained a little, but a fine day. Broth to supper, and went soon to bed.

[*April*] 12th, *Monday.* Had the mantua-maker. The ground covered with snow. Walked to T. Wilkinson's and sent for letters. The woman brought me one from William and Mary.

It was probably in this letter that William and Mary finally told Dorothy of their decision to get married. Although this cannot have been a surprise to her, the passage which follows gives us a glimpse of the intensity of her feeling when the moment of certainty came. For de Selincourt's penetrating analysis of these days, see my Introduction, p. 13.

It was a sharp, windy night. Thomas Wilkinson came with me to Barton, and questioned me like a catechizer all the way. Every question was like the snapping of a little thread about my heart – I was so full of thought of my half-read letter and other things. I was glad when he left me. Then I had time to look at the moon while I was thinking over my own thoughts. The moon travelled through the clouds, tinging them yellow as she passed along, with two stars near her, one larger than the other. These stars grew or diminished as they passed from, or went into, the clouds. At this time William, as I found the next day, was riding by himself between Middleham and Barnard Castle, having parted from Mary. I read over my letter when I got to the house. Mr and Mrs C. were playing at cards.

April 13th, *Tuesday.* I had slept ill and was not well and obliged to go to bed in the afternoon – Mrs C. waked me from sleep with a letter from Coleridge. After tea I went down to see the bank and walked along the Lakeside to the field where Mr Smith thought of building his house. The air was become still, the lake was of a bright slate colour, the hills darkening. The bays shot into the low fading shores. Sheep resting. All things quiet. When I returned Jane met me – *William* was come. The surprise shot through me. He looked well, but he was tired and went soon to bed after a dish of tea.

April 14th, Wednesday. William did not rise till dinner time. I walked with Mrs C. I was ill, out of spirits, disheartened. Wm. and I took a long walk in the rain.

[April] 15th, Thursday. It was a threatening, misty morning, but mild. We set off after dinner from Eusemere. Mrs Clarkson went a short way with us, but turned back. The wind was furious and we thought we must have returned. We first rested in the large boat-house, then under a furze bush opposite Mr Clarkson's. Saw the plough going into the field. The wind seized our breath. The Lake was rough. There was a boat by itself floating in the middle of the bay below Water Millock. We rested again in the Water Millock Lane. The hawthorns are black and green, the birches here and there greenish, but there is yet more of purple to be seen on the twigs. We got over into a field to avoid some cows – people working. A few primroses by the roadside – woodsorrel flower, the anemone, scentless violets, strawberries, and that starry yellow flower which Mrs C. calls pile wort. When we were in the woods beyond Gowbarrow Park we saw a few daffodils close to the water-side. We fancied that the lake had floated the seeds ashore, and that the little colony had so sprung up. But as we went along there were more and yet more; and at last, under the boughs of the trees, we saw that there was a long belt of them along the shore, about the breadth of a country turnpike road. I never saw daffodils so beautiful. They grew among the mossy stones about and about them; some rested their heads upon these stones as on a pillow for weariness; and the rest tossed and reeled and danced, and seemed as if they verily laughed with the wind, that blew upon them over the lake; they looked so gay, ever glancing, ever changing. This wind blew directly over the

lake to them. There was here and there a little knot, and a few stragglers a few yards higher up; but they were so few as not to disturb the simplicity, unity, and life of that one busy highway.

THE DAFFODILS

I wandered lonely as a cloud
That floats on high o'er vales and hills,
When all at once I saw a crowd,
A host, of golden daffodils;
Beside the lake, beneath the trees,
Fluttering and dancing in the breeze.

Continuous as the stars that shine
And twinkle on the milky way,
They stretched in never-ending line
Along the margin of a bay:
Ten thousand saw I at a glance,
Tossing their heads in sprightly dance.

The waves beside them danced; but they
Out-did the sparkling waves in glee:
A poet could not but be gay,
In such a jocund company;
I gazed – and gazed – but little thought
What wealth the show to me had brought:

For oft, when on my couch I lie
In vacant or in pensive mood,
They flash upon that inward eye
Which is the bliss of solitude;
And then my heart with pleasure fills,
And dances with the daffodils.

We rested again and again. The bays were stormy, and we heard the waves at different distances, and in the middle of the water, like the sea. Rain came on – we were wet when we reached Luff's, but we called in. Luckily all was chearless and gloomy, so we faced the storm – we *must* have been wet if we had waited – put on dry clothes at Dobson's. I was very kindly treated by a young woman, the landlady looked sour, but it is her way. She gave us a goodish supper, excellent ham and potatoes. We paid 7/- when we came away. William was sitting by a bright fire when I came downstairs. He soon made his way to the library, piled up in a corner of the window. He brought out a volume of Enfield's *Speaker*, another miscellany, and an odd volume of Congreve's plays. We had a glass of warm rum and water. We enjoyed ourselves, and wished for Mary. It rained and blew, when we went to bed.

N.B. Deer in Gowbarrow Park like skeletons.

April 16th, Friday [*Good Friday*]. When I undrew my curtains in the morning, I was much affected by the beauty of the prospect, and the change. The sun shone, the wind had passed away, the hills looked chearful, the river was very bright as it flowed into the lake. The church rises up behind a little knot of rocks, the steeple not so high as an ordinary three-story house. Trees in a row in the garden under the wall. After Wm. had shaved we set forward; the valley is at first broken by little rocky woody knolls that make retiring places, fairy valleys in the vale; the river winds along under these hills, travelling, not in a bustle but not slowly, to the lake. We saw a fisherman in the flat meadow on the other side of the water. He came towards us, and threw his line over the two-arched bridge. It is a bridge of a heavy construction, almost bending inwards in the middle, but it is grey, and there is a look of ancientry in the architecture of it that pleased me. As we go on the vale opens out more into one vale, with somewhat of a cradle bed. Cottages, with groups of trees, on the side of the hills. We passed a pair of twin Children, 2 years old. Sate on the next bridge which we crossed – a single arch. We rested again upon the turf, and looked at the same bridge. We observed arches in the water, occasioned by the large stones sending it down in two streams. A sheep came plunging through the river, stumbled up the bank, and passed close to us, it had been frightened by an insignificant little dog on the other side. Its fleece dropped a glittering shower under its belly. Primroses by the road-side, pile wort that shone like stars of gold in the sun, violets, strawberries, retired and half-buried among the grass. When we came to the foot of Brothers Water, I left William sitting on the bridge, and went along the path on the right side of the Lake through the wood. I was delighted with what I saw. The water under the boughs of the bare old trees, the simplicity of the mountains, and the exquisite beauty of the path. There was one grey cottage. I repeated *The Glow-worm*,[1] as I walked along. I hung over the gate, and thought I could have stayed for ever. When I returned, I found William writing a poem descriptive of the sights and sounds we saw and heard. There was the gentle flowing of the stream, the glittering, lively lake, green fields without a living creature to be seen on them, behind us, a flat pasture with 42 cattle feeding; to our left, the road leading to the hamlet. No smoke there, the sun shone on the bare roofs. The people were at work ploughing, harrowing, and sowing; lasses spreading dung, a dog's barking now and then, cocks crowing, birds twittering, the snow in patches at the top of the highest hills, yellow palms, purple and green twigs on the birches, ashes with their glittering spikes quite bare. The hawthorn a bright green, with black stems under the oak. The moss of the oak glossy. We then went on, passed two sisters at work (*they first passed us*), one with two pitchforks in her hand, the other had a spade. We had some talk with them. They laughed aloud after we were gone, perhaps half in wantonness, half boldness. William finished his poem before we got to the foot of Kirkstone. There we ate our dinner.

WRITTEN IN MARCH

While resting on the bridge at the foot of Brother's Water

> The Cock is crowing,
> The stream is flowing,
> The small birds twitter,
> The lake doth glitter,

---

1. See 20 April.

The green field sleeps in the sun;
   The oldest and youngest
   Are at work with the strongest;
   The cattle are grazing,
   Their heads never raising;
There are forty feeding like one !

   Like an army defeated
   The snow hath retreated,
   And now doth fare ill
   On the top of the bare hill;
The ploughboy is whooping – anon – anon.
   There's joy in the mountains;
   There's life in the fountains;
   Small clouds are sailing,
   Blue sky prevailing;
The rain is over and gone !

There were hundreds of cattle in the vale. The walk up Kirk-stone was very interesting. The becks among the rocks were all alive. Wm. showed me the little mossy streamlet which he had before loved when he saw its bright green track in the snow. The view above Ambleside very beautiful. There we sate and looked down on the green vale. We watched the crows at a little distance from us become white as silver as they flew in the sunshine, and when they went still further, they looked like shapes of water passing over the green fields. The whitening of Ambleside church is a great deduction from the beauty of it, seen from this point. We called at the Luffs, the Boddingtons there. Did not go in, and went round by the fields. I pulled off my stockings, intending to wade the beck, but I was obliged to put them on, and we climbed over the wall at the bridge. The post passed us. No letters ! Rydale Lake was in its own evening brightness : the islands and Points distinct. Jane Ashburner came up to us when we were sitting upon the wall. We rode in her cart to Tom Dawson's. All well. The garden looked pretty in the half-moonlight, half-daylight. As we went up the vale of Brother's Water more and more cattle feeding, 100 of them.

April 17th, Saturday. A mild warm rain. We sate in the garden all the morning. William dug a little. I transplanted a honeysuckle. The lake was still. The sheep on the island, reflected in the water, like the grey deer we saw in Gowbarrow Park. We walked after tea by moonlight. I had been in bed in the afternoon, and William had slept in his chair. We walked towards Rydale first, then backwards and forwards below Mr Olliff's. The village was beautiful in the moonlight. Helm Crag we observed very distinct. The dead hedge round Benson's field bound together at the top by an interlacing of ash sticks, which made a chain of silver when we faced the moon. A letter from C. and also from S.H. I saw a robin chacing a scarlet butterfly this morning.

[April] 18, *Sunday.* I lay in bed late, again a mild grey morning, with rising vapours. We sat in the orchard. William wrote the poem on *The Robin and the Butterfly.* I went to drink tea at Luff's, but as we did not dine till 6 o'clock it was late. It was mist and small rain all the way, but very pleasant. William met me at Rydale – Aggie accompanied me thither. We sate up late. He met me with the conclusion of the poem of the Robin. I read it to him in bed. We left out some lines.

THE REDBREAST CHASING THE BUTTERFLY

Art thou the bird whom Man loves best,
The pious bird with the scarlet breast,
  Our little English Robin;
The bird that comes about our doors
When Autumn-winds are sobbing?
Art thou the Peter of Norway Boors?
  Their Thomas in Finland,
  And Russia far inland?
The bird, that by some name or other
All men who know thee call their brother,
The darling of children and men?
Could Father Adam open his eyes
And see this sight beneath the skies,

He'd wish to close them again.
– If the Butterfly knew but his friend,
Hither his flight he would bend;
And find his way to me,
Under the branches of the tree:
In and out, he darts about;
Can this be the bird, to man so good,
That, after their bewildering,
Covered with leaves the little children,
  So painfully in the wood?
What ailed thee, Robin, that thou could'st pursue
  A beautiful creature,
That is gentle by nature?
Beneath the summer sky
From flower to flower let him fly;
'Tis all that he wishes to do.
The cheerer Thou of our in-door sadness,
He is the friend of our summer gladness:
What hinders, then, that ye should be
Playmates in the sunny weather,
And fly about in the air together!
His beautiful wings in crimson are drest,
A crimson as bright as thine own;
Would'st thou be happy in thy nest,
O pious Bird! whom man loves best,
Love him, or leave him alone!

[April] 19th, Monday. A mild rain, very warm. Wm. worked in the garden – I made pies and bread. After dinner the mist cleared away and sun shone. Wm. walked to Luff's – I was not very well and went to bed. Wm. came home pale and tired. I could not rest when I got to bed.

April 20th, Tuesday. A beautiful morning. The sun shone. William wrote a conclusion to the poem of the Butterfly – 'I've watched you now a full half-hour'. I was quite out of spirits, and went into the orchard. When I came in, he had finished the poem.

I've watched you now a full half-hour,
Self-poised upon that yellow flower;
And, little Butterfly ! indeed
I know not if you sleep or feed.
How motionless ! – not frozen seas
More motionless ! and then
What joy awaits you, when the breeze
Hath found you out among the trees,
And calls you forth again !

This plot of orchard-ground is ours;
My trees they are, my Sister's flowers;
Here rest your wings when they are weary;
Here lodge as in a sanctuary !
Come often to us, fear no wrong;
Sit near us on the bough !
We'll talk of sunshine and of song,
And summer days, when we were young;
Sweet childish days, that were as long
As twenty days are now.

We sate in the orchard after dinner – it was a beautiful after-
noon. The sun shone upon the level fields, and they grew greener
beneath the eye. Houses, villages, all chearful – people at work.
We sate in the orchard and repeated *The Glow-worm* and other
poems. Just when William came to a well or a trough, which
there is in Lord Darlington's park, he began to write that poem
of *The Glow-worm*, not being able to ride upon the long trot –
interrupted in going through the town of Staindrop, finished
it about 2 miles and a half beyond Staindrop. He did not feel
the jogging of the horse while he was writing; but, when he had
done, he felt the effect of it, and his fingers were cold with his
gloves. His horse fell with him on the other side of St Helen's,
Auckland. So much for *The Glow-worm*. It was written coming
from Middleham on Monday, 12th April, 1802.

Among all lovely things my Love had been;
Had noted well the stars, all flowers that grew
About her home; but she had never seen
A glow-worm, never one, and this I knew.

While riding near her home one stormy night
A single glow-worm did I chance to espy;
I gave a fervent welcome to the sight,
And from my horse I leapt; great joy had I.

Upon a leaf the glow-worm did I lay,
To bear it with me through the stormy night:
And, as before, it shone without dismay;
Albeit putting forth a fainter light.

When to the dwelling of my love I came,
I went into the orchard quietly;
And left the glow-worm, blessing it by name,
Laid safely by itself, beneath a tree.

The whole next day, I hoped, and hoped with fear;
At night the glow-worm shone beneath the tree;
I led my Lucy to the spot, 'Look here,'
Oh! joy it was for her, and joy for me!

*William included the whole of this poem in a letter to Coleridge,
written a few days earlier on 16 April, and told him that the
incident had happened to Dorothy and himself about seven years
ago. It was probably the intimate character of the poem which
stopped him publishing it in any of the complete editions of his
works.*

On Tuesday 20th, when we were sitting after tea, Coleridge
came to the door. I startled Wm. with my voice. C. came up
palish, but I afterwards found he looked well. William was not
well, and I was in low spirits.

April 21st, Wednesday. William and I sauntered a little in the garden. Coleridge came to us, and repeated the verses he wrote to Sara.

DEJECTION: AN ODE
A LETTER TO —

April 4, 1802   Sunday Evening.

Well ! if the Bard was weatherwise, who made
The grand old Ballad of Sir Patrick Spence,
This Night, so tranquil now, will not go hence
Unrous'd by winds, that ply a busier trade
Than that, which moulds yon clouds in lazy flakes,
   Or the dull sobbing Draft, that drones and rakes
Upon the strings of this Eolian Lute,
Which better far were mute.
For, lo ! the New Moon, winter-bright !
And overspread with phantom Light
(With swimming phantom Light o'erspread
But rimm'd and circled with a silver Thread)
I see the Old Moon in her Lap, foretelling
The coming-on of Rain and squally Blast-
O ! Sara ! that the Gust ev'n now were swelling,
And the slant Night-shower driving loud and fast !

A Grief without a pang, void, dark and drear,
A stifling, drowsy, unimpassion'd Grief
That finds no natural outlet, no Relief
In word, or sigh, or tear –
This, Sara ! well thou know'st,
Is that sore Evil, which I dread the most,
And oft'nest suffer ! In this heartless Mood,
To other thoughts by yonder Throstle woo'd,
That pipes within the Larch tree, not unseen,
(The Larch, which pushes out in tassels green
It's bundled Leafits) woo'd to mild Delights
By all the tender Sounds and gentle Sights
 Of this sweet Primrose-month – and vainly woo'd
O dearest Sara ! in this heartless Mood

All this long Eve, so balmy and serene,
Have I been gazing on the western Sky
And its peculiar Tint of Yellow Green –
And still I gaze – and with how blank an eye!
And those thin Clouds above, in flakes and bars,
That give away their Motion to the Stars;
Those Stars, that glide behind them or between,
Now sparkling, now bedimm'd, but always seen;
Yon crescent Moon, as fix'd as if it grew
In it's own cloudless, starless Lake of Blue –
A boat becalm'd! dear William's Sky Canoe!
– I see them all, so excellently fair!
I see, not feel, how beautiful they are.

My genial Spirits fail –
And what can these avail
To lift the smoth'ring Weight from off my Breast?
It were a vain Endeavor,
Tho' I should gaze for ever
On that Green Light that lingers in the West!
I may not hope from outward Forms to win
The Passions and the Life, whose Fountains are within!

These lifeless Shapes, around, below, Above,
    O what can they impart?
When even the gentle Thought, that thou, my Love!
Art gazing, now, like me,
And see'st the Heaven I see –
Sweet thought it is – yet feebly stirs my Heart!

    Feebly! O feebly! – Yet
(I well remember it)
In my first Dawn of Youth that Fancy stole
With many secret Yearnings on my Soul.
At eve, sky-gazing in 'ecstatic fit'
(Alas! for cloister'd in a city School
The Sky was all, I knew, of Beautiful)
At the barr'd window often did I sit,
And oft upon the leaded School-roof lay,

And to myself would say –
There does not live the Man so stripp'd of good affections
As not to love to see a Maiden's quiet Eyes
Uprais'd, and linking on sweet Dreams by dim Connections
To Moon, or Evening Star, or glorious western Skies –
While yet a Boy, this Thought would so pursue me,
That often it became a kind of Vision to me !

Sweet Thought ! and dear of old
To Hearts of finer Mould !
Ten thousand times by Friends and Lovers blest !
I spake with rash Despair,
And ere I was aware,
The Weight was somewhat lifted from my Breast !
O Sara ! in the weather-fended Wood,
Thy lov'd haunt ! where the Stock-doves coo at Noon
I guess, that thou hast stood
And watch'd you Crescent, and its ghost-like Moon.
And yet, far rather in my present Mood
I would, that thou'dst been sitting all this while
Upon the sod-built Seat of Camomile –
And tho' thy Robin may have ceas'd to sing,
Yet needs for my sake must thou love to hear
The Bee-hive murmuring near,
That ever-busy and most quiet Thing
Which I have heard at Midnight murmuring.

I feel my spirit moved.
And whereso'er thou be,
O Sister ! O Beloved !
Those dear mild Eyes, that see
Even now the Heaven, I see –
There is a Prayer in them ! It is for me –
And I, dear Sara, I am blessing thee !

It was as calm as this, that happy night
When Mary, thou, and I together were,
The low decaying Fire our only Light,
And listen'd to the Stillness of the Air !

O that affectionate and blameless Maid,
Dear Mary! on her Lap my head she lay'd –
Her Hand was on my Brow,
Even as my own is now;
And on my Cheek I felt the eye-lash play.
Such joy I had, that I may truly say,
My spirit was awe-stricken with the Excess
And trance-like Depth of its brief Happiness.
Ah fair Remembrances, that so revive
The Heart, and fill it with a living Power,
Where were they, Sara? – or did I not strive
To win them to me? – on the fretting Hour
Then when I wrote thee that complaining Scroll,
Which even to bodily Sickness bruis'd thy Soul!
And yet thou blam'st thyself alone! And yet
Forbidd'st me all Regret!

And must I not regret, that I distress'd
Thee, best belov'd, who lovest me the best?
My better mind had fled, I know not whither,
For O! was this an absent Friend's Employ
To send from far both Pain and Sorrow thither
Where still his Blessings should have call'd down Joy!
I read thy guileless Letter o'er again –
I hear thee of thy blameless Self complain –
And only this I learn – and this, alas! I know –
That thou art weak and pale with Sickness, Grief, and Pain –
And I, – I made thee so!
O for my own sake I regret perforce
Whatever turns thee, Sara! from the course
Of calm Well-being and a Heart at rest!
When thou, and with thee those, whom thou lov'st best,
Shall dwell together in one happy Home,
One House, the dear abiding Home of All,
I too will crown me with a Coronal –
Nor shall this Heart in idle Wishes roam
    Morbidly soft!
No! let me trust, that I shall wear away
In no inglorious Toils the manly Day,

And only now and then, and not too oft,
Some dear and memorable Eve will bless
Dreaming of all your Loves and Quietness.
Be happy, and I need thee not in sight.
Peace in thy Heart, and Quiet in thy Dwelling,
Health in thy Limbs, and in thine eyes the Light
Of Love and Hope and honourable Feeling –
Where e'er I am, I shall be well content !
Not near thee, haply shall be more content !
To all things I prefer the Permanent.
And better seems it, for a Heart, like mine,
Always to know, than sometimes to behold,
   Their Happiness and thine –
For Change doth trouble me with pangs untold !
To see thee, hear thee, feel thee – then to part
   Oh, it weighs down the heart !
To visit those I love, as I love thee,
Mary, and William, and dear Dorothy,
It is but a temptation to repine –
The transientness is Poison in the Wine,
Eats out the pith of Joy, and makes all Joy hollow,
All pleasure a dim Dream of Pain to follow !
My own peculiar Lot, my house-hold Life
It is, and will remain, Indifference or Strife.
While Ye are well and happy, 'twould but wrong you
If I should fondly yearn to be among you –
Wherefore, O wherefore ! should I wish to be
A wither'd branch upon a blossoming Tree?

But (let me say it ! for I vainly strive
To beat away the Thought), but if thou pin'd
Whate'er the Cause, in body or in mind,
I were the miserablest Man alive
To know it and be absent ! Thy Delights
Far off, or near, alike I may partake –
But O ! to mourn for thee, and to forsake
All power, all hope, of giving comfort to thee –
To know that thou art weak and worn with pain,
And not to hear thee, Sara ! not to view thee –

Not sit beside thy Bed,
Not press thy aching Head,
Not bring thee Health again –
At least to hope, to try –
By this Voice, which thou lov'st, and by this earnest Eye –
Nay, wherefore did I let it haunt my Mind
The dark distressful Dream!
I turn from it, and listen to the Wind
Which long has rav'd unnotic'd! What a Scream
Of agony, by Torture lengthen'd out
That Lute sent forth! O thou wild Storm without!
Jagg'd Rock, or mountain Pond, or blasted Tree,
Or Pine-Grove, whither Woodman never clomb,
Or lonely House, long held the Witches' Home,
Methinks were fitter Instruments for Thee,
Mad Lutanist! that in this month of Showers,
Of dark brown Gardens and of peeping Flowers,
Mak'st Devil's Yule with worse than wintry Song
The Blossoms, Buds, and timorous Leaves among!
Thou Actor, perfect in all tragic Sounds!
Thou mighty Poet, even to frenzy bold!
What tell'st thou now about?
'Tis of the Rushing of an Host in Rout
And many groans for men with smarting Wounds –
At once they groan with smart, and shudder with the cold!
'Tis hush'd! there is a Trance of deepest Silence,
Again! but all that Sound, as of a rushing Crowd,
And Groans and tremulous Shudderings, all are over.
And it has other Sounds, and all less deep, less loud!
A Tale of less Affright,
And tempered with Delight,
As William's self had made the tender Lay –
'Tis of a little Child
Upon a heathy Wild,
Not far from home, but it has lost its way –
And now moans low in utter grief and fear –
And now screams loud, and hopes to make it's Mother hear!

'Tis Midnight ! and small Thoughts have I of Sleep.
Full seldom may my Friend such Vigils keep –
O breathe She softly in her gentle Sleep !
Cover her, gentle sleep ! with wings of Healing.
And be this Tempest but a Mountain Birth !
May all the Stars hang bright above her Dwelling,
Silent, as though they watch'd the sleeping Earth !
Healthful and light, my Darling ! may'st thou rise
With clear and chearful Eyes –
And of the same good Tidings to me send !
For oh ! beloved Friend !
I am not the buoyant Thing I was of yore
When like an own Child, I to Joy belong'd :
For others mourning oft, myself oft sorely wrong'd,
Yet bearing all things then, as if I nothing bore !
Yes, dearest Sara, yes !
There was a time when tho' my path was rough,
The Joy within me dallied with Distress;
And all Misfortunes were but as the Stuff
Whence Fancy made me Dreams of Happiness :
For Hope grew round me, like the climbing Vine,
And Leaves and Fruitage, not my own, seem'd mine !
But now Ill Tidings bow me down to earth,
Nor care I that they rob me of my Mirth –
But Oh, each Visitation
Suspends what nature gave me at my Birth,
My shaping spirit of Imagination !

I speak not now of those habitual Ills
That wear out Life, when two unequal Minds
Meet in one House and two discordant Wills –
    This leaves me, where it finds,
Past Cure, and past Complaint, – a fate austere
Too fix'd and hopeless to partake of Fear !
But thou, dear Sara ! (dear indeed thou art,
My Comforter, a Heart within my Heart !)
Thou, and the Few, we love, tho' few ye be,
Make up a World of Hope and Fears for me.

And if Affliction, or distemp'ring Pain,
Or wayward Chance befall you, I complain
Not that I mourn – O Friends, most dear ! most true !
  Me thinks to weep with you
  Were better far than to rejoice alone –
But that my coarse domestic Life has known
No Habits of heart-nursing Sympathy,
No Griefs but such as dull and deaden me,
No mutual mild Enjoyment of it's own,
No Hopes of its own Vintage, None O ! none –
Whence when I mourn'd for you, my Heart might borrow
Fair form and living Motions for it's Sorrow.
For not to think of what I needs must feel,
But to be still and patient all I can;
And haply by abstruse Research to steal
From my own Nature, all the Natural man –
This was my sole Resource, my wisest plan !
And that, which suits a part, infects the whole,
And now is almost grown the Temper of my soul.
My little Children are a Joy, a Love,
  A good Gift from above!
But what is Bliss, that still calls up a Woe,
  And makes it doubly keen
Compelling me to feel, as well as know,
What a most blessed Lot mine might have been.
Those little Angel Children (woe is me !)
There have been hours when feeling how they bind
And pluck out the Wing-feathers of my Mind,
Turning my Error to Necessity,
I have half-wish'd they never had been born !
That seldom ! but sad Thoughts they always bring,
And like the Poet's Philomel, I sing
My Love-song, with my breast against a Thorn.

With no unthankful Spirit I confess,
This clinging Grief, too, in its turn, awakes
That Love, and Father's Joy; but O ! it makes
The Love the greater, and the Joy far less.
These Mountains too, these Vales, these Woods, these Lakes,

Scenes full of Beauty and of Loftiness
Where all my Life I fondly hop'd to live –
I were sunk low indeed, did they no solace give;
But oft I seem to feel, and evermore I fear,
They are not to me now the Things, which once they were.

O Sara ! we receive but what we give,
And in our life alone does Nature live
Our's is her Wedding Garment, our's her Shroud –
And would we aught behold of higher Worth
Than that inanimate cold World allow'd
To that poor loveless ever anxious Crown,
Ah ! from the Soul itself must issue forth
A light, a Glory, and a luminous Cloud
Enveloping the Earth !
And from the Soul itself must there be sent
A sweet and potent Voice, of it's own Birth,
Of all sweet Sounds, the Life and Element.
O pure Heart ! thou need'st not ask of me
What this strong music in the Soul may be,
What and wherein it doth exist,
This Light, this Glory, this fair luminous Mist,
This beautiful and beauty-making Power !
Joy, innocent Sara ! Joy, that ne'er was given
Save to the pure, and in their purest Hour,
Joy, Sara ! is the Spirit and the Power,
That wedding Nature to us gives in Dower
    A new Earth and new Heaven,
Undreamt of by the Sensual and the Proud !
Joy is that strong Voice, Joy that luminous Cloud –
    We, we ourselves rejoice !
And thence flows all that charms or ear or sight,
All melodies, the Echoes of that Voice,
All Colors a Suffusion of that Light.
Sister and Friend of my devoutest Choice
Thou being innocent and full of love,
And nested with the Darlings of thy Love,
And feeling in thy Soul, Heart, Lips, and Arms
Even what the conjugal and mother Dove,

That borrows genial Warmth from those, she warms,
Feels the thrill'd wings, blessedly outspread –
Thou free'd awhile from Cares and human Dread
By the Immenseness of the Good and Fair
    Which thou seest everywhere –
Thus, thus, should'st thou rejoice!
To thee would all things live from Pole to Pole;
Their Life the Eddying of thy living Soul –
O dear! O Innocent! O full of love!
A very Friend! A Sister of my Choice –
O dear, as Light and Impulse from above,
Thus may'st thou ever, evermore rejoice!

*This is the earliest version of the poem and is reprinted from
Wordsworthian and Other Studies by Ernest de Selincourt
(1947), pp. 67–76.*

I was affected with them, and was on the whole, not being well,
in miserable spirits. The sunshine, the green fields, and the
fair sky made me sadder; even the little happy, sporting lambs
seemed but sorrowful to me. The pile wort spread out on the
grass a thousand shining stars. The primroses were there, and
the remains of a few daffodils. The well, which we cleaned out
last night, is still but a little muddy pond, though full of water.
I went to bed after dinner, could not sleep, went to bed again.
Read Ferguson's[1] life and a poem or two – fell asleep for 5 minutes
and awoke better. We got tea, sate comfortably in the evening. I
went to bed early.

---

1. Robert Fergusson, a Scottish poet who wrote vivid descriptions
of Edinburgh life. His poems appeared in 1773 and were much
praised by Burns.

8

> 'But who is He, with modest looks,
> And clad in homely russet brown?
> He murmurs near the running brooks
> A music sweeter than their own.'

From A *Poet's Epitaph*

April 22nd, Thursday. A fine mild morning – we walked into Easedale. The sun shone. Coleridge talked of his plan of sowing the laburnum in the woods. The waters were high, for there had been a great quantity of rain in the night. I was tired and sate under the shade of a holly tree that grows upon a rock, I sate there and looked down the stream. I then went to the single holly behind that single rock in the field, and sate upon the grass till they came from the waterfall. I saw them there and heard Wm. flinging stones into the river, whose roaring was loud even where I was. When they returned, William was repeating the poem: 'I have thoughts that are fed by the sun'.

I

I have been here in the Moon-light,
I have been here in the Day,
I have been here in the Dark Night,
And the Stream was still roaring away.

II

These Chairs they have no words to utter,
No fire is in the gate to stir or flutter,
The ceiling and floor are mute as a stone,
My chamber is hush'd and still,
   And I am alone,
   Happy and alone.

Oh who would be afraid of life,
The passion the sorrow and the strife
  When he may be
  Shelter'd so easily?
May lie in peace on his bed
Happy as they who are dead.

        Half an hour afterwards
I have thoughts that are fed by the sun.
  The things which I see
  Are welcome to me,
  Welcome every one:
I do not wish to lie
  Dead, dead,
Dead without any company;
  Here alone on my bed,
With thoughts that art fed by the Sun,
And hopes that are welcome every one,
  Happy am I.

O Life, there is about thee
A deep, delicious peace,
I would not be without thee,
  Stay, oh stay!
Yet be thou ever as now,
Sweetness and breath with the quiet of death,
Be but thou ever as now,
  Peace, peace, peace.

It had been called to his mind by the dying away of the stunning of the waterfall when he came behind a stone.

This extraordinary and un-Wordsworthian fragment was found in MSS. M and was never published in the poet's lifetime.

When we got into the vale heavy rain came on. We saw a family of little children sheltering themselves under a wall before the rain came on; they sat in a row making a canopy for each other of their clothes. The servant lass was planting potatoes near them. Coleridge changed his clothes – we were all wet. Wilkinson came in while we were at dinner. Coleridge and I after dinner drank black currants and water.

April 23rd, 1802, Friday. It being a beautiful morning we set off at 11 o'clock, intending to stay out of doors all the morning. We went towards Rydale, and before we got to Tom Dawson's we determined to go under Nab Scar. Thither we went. The sun shone and we were lazy. Coleridge pitched upon several places to sit down upon, but we could not be all of one mind respecting sun and shade, so we pushed on to the foot of the Scar. It was very grand when we looked up, very stony, here and there a budding tree. William observed that the umbrella yew tree, that breasts the wind, had lost its character as a tree, and had become something like to solid wood. Coleridge and I pushed on before. We left William sitting on the stones, feasting with silence; and C. and I sat down upon a rock seat – a couch it might be under the bower of William's eglantine, Andrew's Broom. He was below us, and we could see him. He came to us, and repeated his poems, while we sate beside him upon the ground. He had made himself a seat in the crumbling ground.

THE WATERFALL AND THE EGLANTINE

I

'Begone, thou fond presumptuous Elf,'
Exclaimed an angry Voice,
'Nor dare to thrust thy foolish self
Between me and my choice!'
A small Cascade fresh swoln with snows
Thus threatened a poor Briar-rose,
That, all bespattered with his foam,
And dancing high and dancing low,
Was living, as a child might know,
In an unhappy home.

II

'Dost thou presume my course to block?
Off, off ! or, puny Thing !
I'll hurl thee headlong with the rock
To which thy fibres cling.'
The Flood was tyrannous and strong;
The patient Briar suffered long,
Nor did he utter groan or sigh,
Hoping the danger would be past;
But, seeing no relief, at last,
He ventured to reply.

III

'Ah !' said the Briar, 'blame me not;
Why should we dwell in strife?
We who in this sequestered spot
Once lived a happy life !
You stirred me on my rocky bed –
What pleasure through my veins you spread
The summer long, from day to day,
My leaves you freshened and bedewed;
Nor was it common gratitude
That did your cares repay.

IV

'When spring came on with bud and bell,
Among these rocks did I
Before you hang my wreaths to tell
That gentle days were nigh !
And in the sultry summer hours,
I sheltered you with leaves and flowers;
And in my leaves – now shed and gone,
The linnet lodged, and for us two
Chanted his pretty songs, when you
Had little voice or none.

'But now proud thoughts are in your breast –
What grief is mine you see,
Ah ! would you think, even yet how blest
Together we might be !
Though of both leaf and flower bereft,
Some ornaments to me are left –
Rich store of scarlet hips is mine,
With which I, in my humble way,
Would deck you many a winter day,
A happy Eglantine !'

What more he said I cannot tell,
The Torrent down the rocky dell
Came thundering loud and fast;
I listened, nor aught else could hear;
The Briar quaked – and much I fear
Those accents were his last.

THE OAK AND THE BROOM

A Pastoral

I

His simple truths did Andrew glean
Beside the babbling rills;
A careful student he had been
Among the woods and hills.
One winter's night, when through the trees
The wind was roaring, on his knees
His youngest born did Andrew hold :
And while the rest, a ruddy quire,
Were seated round their blazing fire,
This Tale the Shepherd told.

II

'I saw a crag, a lofty stone
As ever tempest beat !
Out of its head an Oak had grown,
A Broom out of its feet.
The time was March, a cheerful noon –
The thaw-wind, with the breath of June,
Breathed gently from the warm south-west:
When, in a voice sedate with age,
This Oak, a giant and a sage,
His neighbour thus addressed:

III

' "Eight weary weeks, through rock and clay,
Along this mountain's edge,
The Frost hath wrought both night and day,
Wedge driving after wedge.
Look up ! and think, above your head
What trouble, surely, will be bred;
Last night I heard a crash – 'tis true,
The splinters took another road –
I see them yonder – what a load
For such a Thing as you !

IV

' "You are preparing as before,
To deck your slender shape;
And yet, just three years back – no more –
You had a strange escape:
Down from yon cliff a fragment broke;
It thundered down, with fire and smoke,
And hitherward pursued its way;
This ponderous block was caught by me,
And o'er your head, as you may see,
'Tis hanging to this day !

V

' "If breeze or bird to this rough steep
Your kind's first seed did bear;
The breeze had better been asleep,
The bird caught in a snare:
For you and your green twigs decoy
The little witless shepherd-boy
To come and slumber in your bower;
And, trust me, on some sultry noon,
Both you and he, Heaven knows how soon!
Will perish in one hour.

VI

' "From me this friendly warning take" –
The Broom began to doze,
And thus, to keep herself awake,
Did gently interpose:
"My thanks for your discourse are due;
That more than what you say is true,
I know, and I have known it long;
Frail is the bond by which we hold
Our being, whether young or old,
Wise, foolish, weak or strong.

VII

' "Disasters, do the best we can,
Will reach both great and small;
And he is oft the wisest man,
Who is not wise at all.
For me, why should I wish to roam?
This spot is my paternal home,
It is my pleasant heritage;
My father many a happy year
Spread here his careless blossoms, here
Attained a good old age.

‘ “Even such as he may be my lot.
What cause have I to haunt
My heart with terrors? Am I not
In truth a favoured plant!
On me such bounty Summer pours,
That I am covered o’er with flowers;
And, when the Frost is in the sky,
My branches are so fresh and gay
That you might look at me and say,
This Plant can never die.

IX

‘ “The butterfly, all green and gold,
To me hath often flown,
Here in my blossoms to behold
Wings lovely as his own.
When grass is chill with rain or dew,
Beneath my shade, the mother-ewe
Lies with her infant lamb; I see
The love they to each other make,
And the sweet joy which they partake,
It is a joy to me.”

X

‘Her voice was blithe, her heart was light;
The Broom might have pursued
Her speech, until the stars of night
Their journey had renewed;
But in the branches of the oak
Two ravens now began to croak
Their nuptial song, a gladsome air;
And to her own green bower the breeze
That instant brought two stripling bees
To rest, or murmur there.

XI

'One night, my Children! from the north
There came a furious blast;
At break of day I ventured forth,
And near the cliff I passed.
The storm had fallen upon the Oak,
And struck him with a mighty stroke,
And whirled, and whirled him far away;
And, in one hospitable cleft,
The little careless Broom was left.'

Both these poems were composed and published in 1800.

After we had lingered long, looking into the vales, – Ambleside vale, with the copses, the village under the hill, and the green fields – Rydale, with a lake all alive and glittering, yet but little stirred by breezes, and our own dear Grasmere, first making a little round lake of nature's own, with never a house, never a green field, but the copses and the bare hills enclosing it, and the river flowing out of it. Above rose the Coniston Fells, in their own shape and colour – not man's hills, but all for themselves, the sky and the clouds, and a few wild creatures. C. went to search for something new. We saw him climbing up towards a rock. He called us, and we found him in a bower – the sweetest that was ever seen. The rock on one side is very high, and all covered with ivy, which hung loosely about, and bore bunches of brown berries. On the other side it was higher than my head. We looked down upon the Ambleside vale, that seemed to wind away from us, the village *lying* under the hill. The fir-tree island was reflected beautifully. We now first saw that the trees are planted in rows. About this bower there is mountain-ash, common-ash, yew-tree, ivy, holly, hawthorn, mosses and flowers, and a carpet of moss. Above, at the top of the rock, there is another spot – it is scarce a bower, a little parlour on[ly], not *enclosed* by walls, but shaped out for a resting-place by the rocks, and the ground rising about it. It had a sweet moss carpet. We resolved to go and plant flowers in both these places to-morrow.

We wished for Mary and Sara. Dined late. After dinner Wm. and I worked in the garden. C. read letter from Sara.

[April] 24th, *Saturday*. A very wet day. William called me out to see a waterfall behind the barberry tree. We walked in the evening to Rydale, Coleridge and I lingered behind. C. stopped up the little runner by the road side to make a lake. We all stood to look at Glow-worm Rock – a primrose that grew there, and just looked out on the road from its own sheltered bower.[1] The clouds moved, as William observed, in one regular body like a multitude in motion – a sky all clouds over, not one cloud.[2] On our return it broke a little out, and we saw here and there a star. One appeared but for a moment in a lake [of] pale blue sky.

April 25th, *Sunday*. After breakfast we set off with Coleridge towards Keswick. Wilkinson overtook us near the Potter's, and interrupted our discourse. C. got into a gig with Mr Beck, and drove away from us. A shower came on, but it was soon over. We spent the morning in the orchard – read the *Prothalamium* of Spenser; walked backwards and forwards. Mr Simpson drank tea with us. I was not well before tea. Mr S. sent us some quills by Molly Ashburner, and his brother's book. The Luffs called at the door.

[April] 26th, *Monday*. I copied Wm.'s poems for Coleridge. Letters from Peggy and Mary H. – wrote to Peggy and Coleridge. A terrible rain and wind all day – went to bed at 12 o'clock.

[April] 27th, *Tuesday*. A fine morning. Mrs Luff called. I walked with her to the boat-house. William met me at the top of the hill with his fishing-rod in his hand. I turned with him, and we sate on the hill looking to Rydale. I left him, intending to join him, but he came home, and said his lines would not stand

---

1. 'The Primrose of the Rock', 1831.
2. 'To the Clouds', 1808.

the pulling – he had several bites. He sate in the orchard,
I made bread. Miss Simpson called, I walked with her to Goan's.
When I came back I found that he and John Fisher had cleaned
out the well; John had sodded about the bee-stand. In the evening
Wm. began to write *The Tinker*. We had a letter and verses
from Coleridge.

April 28th, Wednesday. A fine sunny but coldish morning. I
copied *The Prioress's Tale*. Wm. was in the orchard. I went to
him; he worked away at his poem though he was ill and tired.
I happened to say that when I was a child I would not have
pulled a strawberry blossom. I left him, and wrote out *The
Manciple's Tale*.[1] At dinner time he came in with the poem of
Children gathering Flowers, but it was not quite finished, and it
kept him long off his dinner. It is now done.

   'Children gathering Flowers' was entitled 'Foresight'.

FORESIGHT

That is work of waste and ruin –
Do as Charles and I are doing !
Strawberry-blossoms, one and all,
We must spare them – here are many :
Look at it – the flower is small,
Small and low, though fair as any :
Do not touch it ! summers two
I am older, Anne, than you.

Pull the primrose, sister Anne !
Pull as many as you can.
– Here are daisies, take your fill;
Pansies, and the cuckoo-flower :
Of the lofty daffodil
Make your bed, or make your bower;
Fill your lap, and fill your bosom;
Only spare the strawberry-blossom !

---

1. See 2 December 1801.

Primroses, the Spring may love them –
Summer knows but little of them :
Violets, a barren kind,
Withered on the ground must lie;
Daisies leave no fruit behind
When the pretty flowerets die;
Pluck them, and another year
As many will be blowing here.

God has given a kindlier power
To the favoured strawberry-flower.
Hither soon as spring is fled
You and Charles and I will walk;
Lurking berries, ripe and red,
Then will hang on every stalk,
Each within its leafy bower;
And for that promise spare the flower !

He is working at *The Tinker*. He promised me he would get his tea, and do no more, but I have got mine an hour and a quarter, and he has scarcely begun his. I am not quite well. We have let the bright sun go down without walking. Now a heavy shower comes on, and I guess we shall not walk at all. I wrote a few lines to Coleridge. Then we walked backwards and forwards between our house and Olliff's. We talked about T. Hutchinson, and Bell Addison. William left me sitting on a stone. When we came in we corrected the Chaucers, but I could not finish them to-night. Went to bed.

[April] 29th, Thursday. A beautiful morning – the sun shone and all was pleasant. We sent off our parcel to Coleridge by the waggon. Mr Simpson heard the Cuckow to-day. Before we went out, after I had written down *The Tinker*, which William finished this morning, Luff called – he was very lame, limped into the kitchen. He came on a little pony.

Who leads a happy life
If it's not the merry Tinker,
Not too old to have a Wife;
Not too much a thinker?
Through the meadows, over stiles,
Where there are no measured miles,
Day by day he finds his way
Among the lonely houses;
Right before the Farmer's door
Down he sits; his brows he knits;
Then his hammer he rouzes;
Batter! Batter! Batter!
He begins to clatter;
And while the work is going on
Right good ale he bouzes;
And, when it is done, away he is gone;
    And, in his scarlet coat,
    With a merry note,
    He sings the sun to bed;
    And, without making a pother,
Finds some place or other
For his own careless head.
When in the woods the little fowls
Begin their merry-making,
Again the jolly Tinker bowls
Forth with small leave-taking:
Through the valley, up the hill;
He can't go wrong, go where he will:
      Tricks he has twenty,
      And pastimes in plenty;
  He's the terror of boys in the midst of their noise;

    When the market Maiden,
    Bringing home her lading,
    Hath pass'd him in a nook,
    With his outlandish look,
    And visage grim and sooty,

Bumming, bumming, bumming,
What is that that's coming?
Silly maid as ever was!
She thinks that she and all she has
Will be the Tinker's booty;
At the pretty Maiden's dread
The Tinker shakes his head,
  Laughing, laughing, laughing,
As if he would laugh himself dead.
And thus, with work or none,
The Tinker lives in fun,
With a light soul to cover him;
And sorrow and care blow over him,
Whether he's up or a-bed.

*'The Tinker' though in the Longman manuscripts of the poems
of 1800–7 was withdrawn from publication during Wordsworth's
lifetime.*

We then went to John's Grove, sate a while at first. Afterwards
William lay, and I lay, in the trench under the fence – he with
his eyes shut, and listening to the waterfalls and the birds.
There was not one waterfall above another – it was a sound of
waters in the air – the voice of the air. William heard me
breathing and rustling now and then, but we both lay still, and
unseen by one another; he thought that it would be as sweet
thus to lie so in the grave, to hear the *peaceful* sounds of the
earth, and just to know that our dear friends were near. The
lake was still; there was a boat out. Silver How reflected with
delicate purple and yellowish hues, as I have seen spar; lambs
on the island, and running races together by the half-dozen,
in the round field near us. The copses greenish, hawthorns green.
Came home to dinner, then went to Mr Simpson – we rested a
long time under a wall, sheep and lambs were in the field –
cottages smoking. As I lay down on the grass, I observed the
glittering silver line on the ridge of the backs of the sheep, owing
to their situation respecting the sun, which made them look
beautiful, but with something of strangeness, like animals of

another kind, as if belonging to a more splendid world. Met old
Mrs S. at the door – Mrs S. poorly. I got mullins and pansies. I
was sick and ill and obliged to come home soon. We went
to bed immediately – I slept upstairs. The air coldish, where it
was felt – somewhat frosty.

April 30th, Friday. We came into the orchard directly after
breakfast, and sate there. The lake was calm, the day cloudy.
We saw two fishermen by the lake side. William began to
write the poem of The Celandine. I wrote to Mary H. sitting on
the fur-gown. Walked backwards and forwards with William –
he repeated his poem to me, then he got to work again and
could not give over. He had not finished his dinner till 5
o'clock. After dinner we took up the fur gown into the Hollins
above. We found a sweet seat, and thither we will often go. We
spread the gown, put on each a cloak, and there we lay.
William fell asleep – he had a bad headache owing to his having
been disturbed the night before, with reading C.'s letter which
Fletcher had brought to the door. I did not sleep, but I lay
with half-shut eyes looking at the prospect as in a vision almost,
I was so resigned to it. Loughrigg Fell was the most distant
hill; then came the lake, slipping in between the copses, and
above the copse the round swelling field; nearer to me, a wild
intermixture of rocks, trees, and slacks of grassy ground.
When we turned the corner of our little shelter, we saw the
church and the whole vale. It is a blessed place. The birds were
about us on all sides – skobbies, robins, bull-finches. Crows
now and then flew over our heads, as we were warned by the
sound of the beating of the air above. We stayed till the light of
day was going, and the little birds had begun to settle their
singing. But there was a thrush not far off, that seemed to sing
louder and clearer than the thrushes had sung when it was
quite day. We came in at 8 o'clock, got tea, wrote to Cole-
ridge, and I wrote to Mrs Clarkson part of a letter. We went
to bed at 20 minutes past 11, with prayers that William might
sleep well.

May 1st, Saturday. Rose not till half past 8, a heavenly morning. As soon as breakfast was over, we went into the garden, and sowed the scarlet beans about the house. It was a clear sky, a heavenly morning.

I sowed the flowers, William helped me. We then went and sate in the orchard till dinner time. It was very hot. William wrote *The Celandine.*

TO THE SMALL CELANDINE

Pansies, lilies, kingcups, daisies,
Let them live upon their praises;
Long as there's a sun that sets,
Primroses will have their glory;
Long as there are violets,
They will have a place in story :
There's a flower that shall be mine,
'Tis the little Celandine.

Eyes of some men travel far
For the finding of a star;
Up and down the heavens they go,
Men that keep a mighty rout !
I'm as great as they, I trow,
Since the day I found thee out,
Little Flower ! – I'll make a stir,
Like a sage astronomer.

Modest, yet withal an Elf
Bold, and lavish as thyself;
Since we needs must first have met
I have seen thee, high and low,
Thirty years or more, and yet
'Twas a face I did not know;
Thou hast now, go where I may,
Fifty greetings in a day.

Ere a leaf is on a bush,
In the time before the thrush
Has a thought about her nest,

Thou wilt come with half a call,
Spreading out thy glossy breast
Like a careless Prodigal;
Telling tales about the sun,
When we've little warmth, or none.

Poets, vain men in their mood!
Travel with the multitude:
Never heed them; I aver
That they are all wanton wooers;
But the thrifty cottager,
Who stirs little out of doors,
Joys to spy thee near her home;
Spring is coming, Thou art come!
Comfort have thou of thy merit,
Kindly, unassuming Spirit!
Careless of thy neighbourhood,
Thou dost show thy pleasant face
On the moor, and in the wood,
In the lane; – there's not a place,
Howsoever mean it be,
But 'tis good enough for thee.

Ill befall the yellow flowers,
Children of the flaring hours!
Buttercups, that will be seen,
Whether we will see or no;
Others, too, of lofty mien;
They have done as worldlings do,
Taken praise that should be thine,
Little, humble Celandine!

Prophet of delight and mirth,
Ill-requited upon earth;
Herald of a mighty band,
Of a joyous train ensuing,
Serving at my heart's command,
Tasks that are no tasks renewing,
I will sing, as doth behove,
Hymns in praise of what I love!

Written at Town-end, Grasmere. It is remarkable that this flower, coming out so early in the spring as it does, and so bright and beautiful, and in such profusion, should not have been noticed earlier in English verse. What adds much to the interest that attends it is its habit of shutting itself up and opening out according to the degree of light and temperature of the air.

We planned a shed, for the sun was too much for us. After dinner we went again to our old resting-place in the Hollins under the rock. We first lay under a holly, where we saw nothing but the holly tree, and a budding elm [?], and the sky above our heads. But that holly tree had a beauty about it more than its own, knowing as we did where we were. When the sun had got low enough, we went to the rock shade. Oh, the overwhelming beauty of the vale below, greener than green! Two ravens flew high, high in the sky, and the sun shone upon their bellies and their wings, long after there was none of his light to be seen but a little space on the top of Loughrigg Fell. We went down to tea at 8 o'clock, had lost the poem, and returned after tea. The landscape was fading; sheep and lambs quiet among the rocks. We walked towards King's and backwards and forwards. The sky was perfectly cloudless. N.B. Is it often so? Three solitary stars in the middle of the blue vault, one or two on the points of the high hills. Wm. wrote *The Celandine*, 2nd part, tonight. Heard the cuckow to-day, this first of May.

TO THE SAME FLOWER

Pleasures newly found are sweet,
When they lie about our feet;
February last, my heart
First at sight of thee was glad;
All unheard of as thou art,
Thou must needs, I think, have had,
Celandine! and long ago,
Praise of which I nothing know.

228

I have not a doubt but he,
Whosoe'er the man might be,
Who the first with pointed rays
(Workman worthy to be sainted)
Set the sign-board in a blaze,
When the rising sun he painted,
Took the fancy from a glance,
At thy glittering countenance.

Soon as gentle breezes bring
News of winter's vanishing,
And the children build their bowers,
Sticking 'kerchief-plots of mould
All about with full-blown flowers,
Thick as sheep in shepherd's fold!
With the proudest thou art there,
Mantling in the tiny square.

Often have I sighed to measure
By myself a lonely pleasure,
Sighed to think, I read a book
Only read, perhaps, by me;
Yet I long could overlook
Thy bright coronet and Thee,
And thy arch and wily ways,
And thy store of other praise.

Blithe of heart, from week to week
Thou dost play at hide-and-seek;
While the patient primrose sits
Like a beggar in the cold,
Thou, a flower of wiser wits,
Slipp'st into thy sheltering hold;
Liveliest of the vernal train
When ye all are out again.

Drawn by what peculiar spell,
By what charm of sight or smell,
Does the dim-eyed curious Bee,
Labouring for her waxen cells,

Fondly settle upon Thee
Prized above all buds and bells
Opening daily at thy side,
By the season multiplied?

Thou art not beyond the moon,
But a thing 'beneath our shoon':
Let the bold Discoverer thrid
In his bark the polar sea;
Rear who will a pyramid;
Praise it is enough for me,
If there be but three or four
Who will love my little Flower.

9

'With him there often walked in friendly guise,
Or lay upon the moss by brook or tree,
A noticeable Man with large gray eyes . . .'

From 'stanzas about C. and himself'

May 4th, Tuesday. William had slept pretty well and though he
went to bed nervous, and jaded in the extreme, he rose refreshed.
I wrote *The Leech Gatherer*[1] for him, which he had begun the
night before, and of which he wrote several stanzas in bed this
morning. It was very hot; we called at Mr Simpson's door as we
passed, but did not go in. We rested several times by the way,
read, and repeated *The Leech Gatherer*. We were almost melted
before we were at the top of the hill. We saw Coleridge on the
Wytheburn side of the water; he crossed the beck to us. Mr
Simpson was fishing there. William and I ate a luncheon, then
went on towards the waterfall. It is a glorious wild solitude under
that lofty purple crag. It stood upright by itself. Its own self,
and its shadow below, one mass — all else was sunshine. We
went on further. A bird at the top of the crags was flying round
and round, and looked in thinness and transparency, shape and
motion like a moth. We climbed the hill, but looked in vain for
a shade, except at the foot of the great waterfall, and there we
did not like to stay on account of the loose stones above our
heads. We came down, and rested upon a moss-covered rock,
rising out of the bed of the river. There we lay, ate our dinner,
and stayed there till about 4 o'clock or later. William and C.
repeated and read verses. I drank a little brandy and water, and
was in Heaven. The stag's horn is very beautiful and fresh,
springing upon the fells. Mountain ashes, green. We drank tea
at a farm house. The woman had not a pleasant countenance,
but was civil enough. She had a pretty boy, a year old, whom

---

1. 'Resolution and Independence' in its first form. It was not com-
pleted in its final form until 4 July, where it can be found.

she suckled. We parted from Coleridge at Sara's crag, after having looked at the letters which C. carved in the morning. I kissed them all. William deepened the T with C.'s pen-knife. We sate afterwards on the wall, seeing the sun go down, and the reflections in the still water. C. looked well, and parted from us chearfully, hopping up upon the side stones.

Suppressed passage from 'The Waggoner'.

Rock of Names!
Light is the strain, but not unjust
To Thee, and thy memorial-trust
That once seemed only to express
Love that was love in idleness;
Tokens, as year hath followed year
How changed, alas, in character !
For they were graven on thy smooth breast
By hands of those my soul loved best;
Meek women, men as true and brave
As ever went to a hopeful grave :
Their hands and mine, when side by side
With kindred zeal and mutual pride,
We worked until the Initials took
Shapes that defied a scornful look. –
Long as for us a genial feeling
Survives, or one in need of healing,
The power, dear Rock, around thee cast,
Thy monumental power, shall last
For me and mine! O thought of pain,
That would impair it or profane !
Take all in kindness then, as said
With a staid heart but playful head;
And fail not Thou, loved Rock ! to keep
Thy charge when we are laid asleep.

The Rock of Names is usually referred to as 'Sara's Rock' in the Journal and was a great haunt of all of them. The initials carved there were those of the names Dorothy scribbled down opposite

15 May 1802 and may have been in the same formation. She attached a strange importance to this practice.

On the Rays we met a woman with two little girls, one in her arms, the other, about four years old, walking by her side, a pretty little thing, but half-starved. She had on a pair of slippers that had belonged to some gentleman's child, down at the heels, but it was not easy to keep them on, but, poor thing! young as she was, she walked carefully with them; alas, too young for such cares and such travels. The mother, when we accosted her, told us that her husband had left her, and gone off with another woman, and how she '*pursued*' them. Then her fury kindled, and her eyes rolled about. She changed again to tears. She was a Cockermouth woman, thirty years of age – a child at Cockermouth when I was. I was moved, and gave her a shilling – I believe 6d. more than I ought to have given. We had the crescent moon with the 'auld moon in her arms'.[1] We rested often, always upon the bridges. Reached home at about ten o'clock. The Lloyds had been here in our absence. We went soon to bed. I repeated verses to William while he was in bed; he was soothed, and I left him. 'This is the spot' over and over again.

May 5th, Wednesday. A very fine morning, rather cooler than yesterday. We planted ¾ of the bower. I made bread. We sate in the orchard. The thrush sang all day, as he always sings. I wrote to the Hutchinsons, and to Coleridge – packed off *Thalaba*.[2] William had kept off work till near bed-time, when we returned from our walk. Then he began again, and went to bed very nervous. We walked in the twilight, and walked till night came on. The moon had the old moon in her arms, but not so plain to be seen as the night before. When we went to bed it was a boat without the circle. I read *The Lover's Complaint* to Wm. in bed, and left him composed.

---

1. From the 'Ballad of Sir Patrick Spens', quoted as heading to Coleridge's 'Dejection'.
2. Poem by Robert Southey.

May 6th, Thursday. A sweet morning. We have put the finishing touch to our bower, and here we are sitting in the orchard. It is one o'clock. We are sitting upon a seat under the wall, which I found my brother building up, when I came to him with his apple. He had intended that it should have been done before I came. It is a nice, cool, shady spot. The small birds are singing, lambs bleating, cuckow calling, the thrush sings by fits. Thomas Ashburner's axe is going quietly (without passion) in the orchard, hens are cackling, flies humming, the women talking together at their doors, plumb and pear trees are in blossom – apple trees greenish – the opposite woods green, the crows are cawing. We have heard ravens. The ash trees are in blossom, birds flying all about us. The stitchwort is coming out, there is one budding lychnis, the primroses are passing their prime, celandine, violets, and wood sorrel for ever more, little geraniums and pansies on the wall. We walked in the evening to Tail End, to enquire about hurdles for the orchard shed and about Mr Luff's flower. The flower dead ! no hurdles. I went on to look at the falling wood; Wm. also, when he had been at Benson's, went with me. They have left a good many small oak trees but we dare not hope that they are all to remain. The ladies are come to Mr Gell's cottage. We saw them as we went, and their light when we returned. When we came in we found a Magazine, and Review, and a letter from Coleridge with verses to Hartley, and Sara H. We read the review, etc. The moon was a perfect boat, a silver boat, when we were out in the evening. The birch tree is all over green in *small* leaf, more light and elegant than when it is full out. It bent to the breezes, as if for the love of its own delightful motions. Sloe-thorns and hawthorns in the hedges.

May 7th, Friday. William had slept uncommonly well, so, feeling himself strong, he fell to work at *The Leech Gatherer*; he wrote hard at it till dinner time, then gave over, tired to death – he had finished the poem.[1] I was making Derwent's frocks. After

---

1. That is, the first version of the poem which was sent to Sara Hutchinson. The revised version is the only one we have and is printed beneath 4 July, the day it was finished.

dinner we sate in the orchard. It was a thick, hazy, dull air. The thrush sang almost continually; the little birds were more than usually busy with their voices. The sparrows are now full fledged. The nest is so full that they lie upon one another, they sit quietly in their nest with closed mouths. I walked to Rydale after tea, which we drank by the kitchen fire. The evening very dull – a terrible kind of threatening brightness at sunset above Easedale. The sloe-thorn beautiful in the hedges, and in the wild spots higher up among the hawthorns. No letters. William met me. He had been digging in my absence, and cleaning the well. We walked up beyond Lewthwaites. A very dull sky; coolish; crescent moon now and then. I had a letter brought me from Mrs Clarkson while we were walking in the orchard. I observed the sorrel leaves opening at about 9 o'clock. William went to bed tired with thinking about a poem.

May 8th, Saturday Morning. We sowed the scarlet beans in the orchard, and read *Henry V.* there. William lay on his back on the seat. I wept 'For names, sounds, faiths, delights and duties lost – taken from a poem upon Cowley's wish to retire to the Plantations. Read in the Review. I finished Derwent's frocks. After dinner William added a step to the orchard steps.

May 9th, Saturday Morning. The air considerably colder to-day but the sun shone all day. William worked at *The Leech Gatherer* almost incessantly from morning till tea-time. I copied *The Leech Gatherer* and other poems for Coleridge. I was oppressed and sick at heart, for he wearied himself to death. After tea he wrote two stanzas in the manner of Thomson's *Castle of Indolence,* and was tired out. Bad news of Coleridge.

May 10th, Monday. A fine clear morning, but coldish. William is still at work, though it is past ten o'clock – he will be tired out, I am sure. My heart fails in me. He worked a little at odd things, but after dinner he gave over. An affecting letter from Mary H. We sate in the orchard before dinner. Old Joyce spent the day. I wrote to Mary H. Mrs Jameson and Miss Simpson called just when William was going to bed at 8 o'clock. I wrote to Coleridge, sent off reviews and poems. Went to bed at 12 o'clock. William did not sleep till 3 o'clock.

May 11th, Tuesday. A cool air. William finished the stanzas about C. and himself.

STANZAS

Written in my pocket-copy of Thomson's
'Castle of Indolence'

Within our happy Castle there dwelt One
Whom without blame I may not overlook;
For never sun on living creature shone
Who more devout enjoyment with us took:
Here on his hours he hung as on a book,
On his own time here would he float away,
As doth a fly upon a summer brook;
But go to-morrow, or belike to-day,
Seek for him, – he is fled; and whither none can say.

Thus often would he leave our peaceful home,
And find elsewhere his business or delight;
Out of our Valley's limits did he roam:
Full many a time, upon a stormy night,
His voice came to us from the neighbouring height:
Oft could we see him driving full in view
At mid-day when the sun was shining bright;
What ill was on him, what he had to do,
A mighty wonder bred among our quiet crew.

Ah! piteous sight it was to see this Man
When he came back to us, a withered flower, –
Or like a sinful creature, pale and wan.
Down would he sit; and without strength or power

Look at the common grass from hour to hour:
And oftentimes, how long I fear to say,
Where apple-trees in blossom made a bower,
Retired in that sunshiny shade he lay;
And, like a naked Indian, slept himself away.

Great wonder to our gentle tribe it was
Whenever from our Valley he withdrew:
For happier soul no living creature has
Than he had, being here the long day through.
Some thought he was a lover, and did woo:
Some thought far worse of him, and judged him wrong:
But verse was what he had been wedded to:
And his own mind did like a tempest strong
Come to him thus, and drove the weary Wight along.

With him there often walked in friendly guise,
Or lay upon the moss by brook or tree,
A noticeable Man with large gray eyes,
And a pale face that seemed undoubtedly
As if a blooming face it ought to be;
Heavy his low-hung lip did oft appear,
Deprest by weight of using phantasy;
Profound his forehead was, though not severe;
Yet some did think that he had little business here:

Sweet heaven forfend ! his was a lawful right;
Noisy he was, and gamesome as a boy;
His limbs would toss about him with delight
Like branches when strong winds the trees annoy.
Nor lacked his calmer hours device or toy
To banish listlessness and irksome care;
He would have taught you how you might employ
Yourself; and many did to him repair, —
And certes not in vain; he had inventions rare.

Expedients, too, of simplest sort he tried:
Long blades of grass, plucked round him as he lay,
Made, to his ear attentively applied,
A pipe on which the wind would deftly play;

Glasses he had, that little things display,
The beetle panoplied in gems and gold,
A mailèd angel on a battle-day;
The mysteries that cups of flowers enfold,
And all the gorgeous sights which fairies do behold.

He would entice that other Man to hear
His music, and to view his imagery:
And, sooth, these two were each to the other dear:
No livelier love in such a place could be:
There did they dwell – from earthly labour free,
As happy spirits as were ever seen;
If but a bird, to keep them company,
Or butterfly sate down, they were, I ween,
As pleased as if the same had been a Maiden-queen.

The first four verses refer to Wordsworth, and the next three to Coleridge. Matthew Arnold originally allotted them the other way round, but as he later admitted, the evidence is against him and Hartley Coleridge has called the description of his father 'the liveliest that has been written about him'.

Miss Simpson came in to tea, which was lucky enough, for it interrupted his labours. I walked with her to Rydale. The evening cool; the moon only now and then to be seen; the Lake purple as we went; primroses still in abundance. William did not meet me. He completely finished his poems, I finished Derwent's frocks. We went to bed at 12 o'clock. Wm. pretty well – he looked very well – he complains that he gets cold in his chest.

May 12th, Wednesday. A sunshiny, but coldish morning. We walked into Easedale and returned by George Rawnson's and the lane. We brought some heckberry blossom, crab blossom, the anemone nemorosa, marsh marigold, speedwell, – that beautiful blue one, the colour of the blue-stone or glass used in jewellery – with its beautiful pearl-like chives. Anemones are in abundance, and still the dear dear primroses, violets in beds, pansies in abundance, and the little celandine. I pulled a bunch of the taller celandine. Butterflies of all colours. I often see some small ones of a pale purple lilac, or emperor's eye colour, something of the colour of that large geranium which grows by the lake side. Wm. observed the beauty of Geordy Green's house. We see it from our Orchard. Wm. pulled ivy with beautiful berries – I put it over the chimney-piece. Sate in the orchard the hour before dinner, coldish. We have now dined. My head aches – William is sleeping in the window. In the evening we were sitting at the table, writing, when we were rouzed by Coleridge's voice below. He had walked; looked palish, but was not much tired. We sate up till one o'clock, all together; then William went to bed, and I sate with C. in the sitting-room (where he slept) till a ¼ past 2 o'clock. Wrote to M.H.

May 13th, Thursday. The day was very cold, with snow showers. Coleridge had intended going in the morning to Keswick, but the cold and showers hindered him. We went with him after tea as far as the plantations by the roadside descending to Wytheburn. He did not look very well when we parted from him. We sate an hour at Mrs Simpson's.

May 14th, Friday. A very cold morning – hail and snow showers all day. We went to Brother's wood, intending to get plants, and to go along the shore of the lake to the foot. We did go a part of the way, but there was no pleasure in stepping along that difficult sauntering road in this ungenial weather. We turned again, and walked backwards and forwards in Brother's wood. William teased himself with seeking an epithet for the cuckow.[1] I sate a while upon my last summer seat, the mossy stone. William's, unemployed, beside me, and the space between, where Coleridge has so often lain. The oak trees are just putting forth yellow knots of leaves. The ashes with their

---

1. See 26 March 1802, p. 187.

flowers passing away, and leaves coming out. The blue hyacinth is not quite full blown; gowans are coming out, marsh marigolds in full glory; the little star plant, a star without a flower. We took home a great load of gowans, and planted them in the cold about the orchard. After dinner, I worked bread, then came and mended stockings beside William; he fell asleep. After tea I walked to Rydale for letters. It was a strange night. The hills were covered over with a slight covering of hail or snow, just so as to give them a hoary winter look with the black rocks. The woods looked miserable, the coppices green as grass, which looked quite unnatural, and they seemed half shrivelled up, as if they shrank from the air. O, thought I! what a beautiful thing God has made winter to be, by stripping the trees, and letting us see their shapes and forms. What a freedom does it seem to give to the storms! There were several new flowers out, but I had no pleasure in looking at them. I walked as fast as I could back again with my letter from S.H. which I skimmed over at Tommy Fleming's. Met Wm. at the top of White Moss. We walked a little beyond Olliff's. Near 10 when we came in. Wm. and Molly had dug the ground and planted potatoes in my absence. We wrote to Coleridge; sent off a letter to Annette, bread and frocks to the C.'s. Went to bed at ½ past 11. William very nervous. After he was in bed, haunted with altering *The Rainbow.*

May 15th, Saturday Morning. It is now ½ past 10, and he is not up. Miss Simpson called when I was in bed. I have been in the garden. It looks fresh and neat in spite of the frost. Molly tells me they had thick ice on a jug at their door last night. A very cold and chearless morning. I sate mending stockings all the morning. I read in Shakespeare. William lay very late because he slept ill last night. It snows this morning just like Christmas. We had a melancholy letter from Coleridge just at bed-time. It distressed me very much, and I resolved upon going to Keswick the next day.

The following is written on the blotting-paper opposite this date:

S. T. Coleridge.
Dorothy Wordsworth.   William Wordsworth.
Mary Hutchinson.   Sara Hutchinson.
William.   Coleridge.   Mary.
Dorothy.   Sara.
16th May
1802
John Wordsworth

May 21st, Friday. A very warm gentle morning, a little rain. William wrote two sonnets on Buonaparte, after I had read Milton's sonnets to him.

We only know of one such sonnet written at this date.

> I grieved for Buonaparte, with a vain
> And an unthinking grief! The tenderest mood
> Of that Man's mind – what can it be? what food
> Fed his first hopes? what knowledge could *he* gain?
> 'Tis not in battles that from youth we train
> The Governor who must be wise and good,
> And temper with the sternness of the brain
> Thoughts motherly, and meek as womanhood.
> Wisdom doth live with children round her knees:
> Books, leisure, perfect freedom, and the talk
> Man holds with week-day man in the hourly walk
> Of the mind's business: these are the degrees
> By which true Sway doth mount; this is the stalk
> True Power doth grow on; and her rights are these.

In the evening he went with Mr Simpson with Borwick's boat to gather ling in Bainriggs. I planted about the well, was much heated, and I think I caught cold.

May 22nd, Saturday. A very hot morning. A hot wind, as if coming from a sand desert. We met Coleridge. He was sitting under Sara's rock when we reached him. He turned with us. We sate a long time under the wall of a sheep-fold. Had some interesting melancholy talk about his private affairs. We drank tea at a farmhouse. The woman was very kind. There was a woman with 3 children travelling from Workington to Manchester. The woman served them liberally. Afterwards she said that she never suffered any to go away without a trifle 'sec as we have'. The woman at whose house we drank tea the last time was rich and senseless – she said 'she never served any but their own poor'. C. came home with us. We sate some time in the orchard. Then they came in to supper – mutton chops and potatoes. Letters from S. and M.H.

[May 23rd,] Sunday. I sate with C. in the orchard all the morning. I was ill in the afternoon, took laudanum. We walked in Bainriggs after tea. Saw the juniper – umbrella shaped. C. went to S. and M. Points, joined us on White Moss.

'Mary and Sara Points' were such a feature of the daily walks at Grasmere, that it seems right to print the poem Wordsworth wrote to commemorate them. It was not composed until 1845, ten years after Sara Hutchinson's death, and was one of the last poems he wrote.

> Forth from a jutting ridge, around whose base
> Winds our deep Vale, two heath-clad Rocks ascend
> In fellowship, the loftiest of the pair
> Rising to no ambitious height; yet both,
> O'er lake and stream, mountain and flowery mead,
> Unfolding prospects fair as human eyes
> Ever beheld. Up-led with mutual help,
> To one or other brow of those twin Peaks
> Were two adventurous Sisters wont to climb,
> And took no note of the hour while thence they gazed,
> The blooming heath their couch, gazed, side by side,
> In speechless admiration. I, a witness
> And frequent sharer of their calm delight
> With thankful heart, to either Eminence
> Gave the baptismal name each Sister bore.
> Now they are parted, far as Death's cold hand

Hath power to part the Spirits of those who love
As they did love. Ye kindred Pinnacles –
That, while the generations of mankind
Follow each other to their hiding-place
In time's abyss, are privileged to endure
Beautiful in yourselves, and richly graced
With like command of beauty – grant your aid
For MARY's humble, SARAH's silent claim,
That their pure joy in nature may survive
From age to age in blended memory.

May 24th, Monday. A very hot morning. We were ready to go off with Coleridge, but foolishly sauntered, and Miss Taylor and Miss Stanley called. William and Coleridge and I went afterwards to the top of the Rays.

I had sent off a letter to Mary by C. I wrote again, and to C. Then went to bed. William slept not till 5 o'clock.

[May] 28th, Friday. I was much better than yesterday, though poorly. William tired himself with hammering at a passage. After dinner he was better and I greatly better. We sate in the orchard. The sky cloudy, the air sweet and cool. The young bullfinches, in their party-coloured raiment, bustle about among the blossoms, and poize themselves like wire-dancers or tumblers, shaking the twigs and dashing off the blossoms. There is yet one primrose in the orchard. The stitchwort is fading. The wild columbines are coming into beauty, the vetches are in abundance, blossoming and seeding. That pretty little wavy-looking dial-like yellow flower, the speedwell, and some others, whose names I do not yet know. The wild columbines are coming into beauty – some of the gowans fading. In the garden we have lilies, and many other flowers. The scarlet beans are up in crowds. It is now between 8 and nine o'clock. It has rained sweetly for two hours and a half; the air is very mild. The heckberry blossoms are dropping off fast, almost gone – barberries are in beauty – snow-balls coming forward – May roses blossoming.

[May] 29th, Saturday. I was much better – I made bread and a wee rhubarb tart and batter pudding for William. We sate in the orchard after dinner. William finished his poem on going for Mary. I wrote it out.

A FAREWELL

Farewell, thou little Nook of mountain-ground,
Thou rocky corner in the lowest stair
Of that magnificent temple which doth bound
One side of our whole vale with grandeur rare;
Sweet garden-orchard, eminently fair,
The loveliest spot that man hath ever found,
Farewell ! – we leave thee to Heaven's peaceful care,
Thee, and the Cottage which thou dost surround.

Our boat is safely anchored by the shore,
And there will safely ride when we are gone;
The flowering shrubs that deck our humble door
Will prosper, though untended and alone :
Fields, goods, and far-off chattels we have none :
These narrow bounds contain our private store
Of things earth makes, and sun doth shine upon;
Here are they in our sight – we have no more.

Sunshine and shower be with you, bud and bell !
For two months now in vain we shall be sought;
We leave you here in solitude to dwell
With these our latest gifts of tender thought;
Thou, like the morning, in thy saffron coat,
Bright gowan, and marsh-marigold, farewell !
Whom from the borders of the Lake we brought,
And placed together near our rocky Well.

We go for One to whom ye will be dear;
And she will prize this Bower, this Indian shed,
Our own contrivance, Building without peer !
– A gentle Maid, whose heart is lowly bred,
Whose pleasures are in wild fields gathered,

With joyousness, and with a thoughtful cheer,
Will come to you; to you herself will wed;
And love the blessed life that we lead here.

Dear Spot ! which we have watched with tender heed,
Bringing thee chosen plants and blossoms blown
Among the distant mountains, flower and weed,
Which thou hast taken to thee as thy own,
Making all kindness registered and known;
Thou for our sakes, though Nature's child indeed,
Fair in thyself and beautiful alone,
Hast taken gifts which thou dost little need.

And O most constant, yet most fickle Place,
Thou hast thy wayward moods, as thou dost show
To them who look not daily on thy face;
Who, being loved, in love no bounds dost know
And say'st, when we forsake thee, 'Let them go !'
Thou easy-hearted Thing, with thy wild race
Of weeds and flowers, till we return be slow,
And travel with the year at a soft pace.

Help us to tell Her tales of years gone by,
And this sweet spring, the best loved and best;
Joy will be flown in its mortality;
Something must stay to tell us of the rest.
Here, thronged with primroses, the steep rocks' breast
Glittered at evening like a starry sky;
And in this bush our sparrow built her nest,
Of which I sang one song that will not die.

O happy Garden ! whose seclusion deep
Hath been so friendly to industrious hours;
And to soft slumbers, that did gently steep
Our spirits, carrying with them dreams of flowers,
And wild notes warbled among leafy bowers;
Two burning months let summer overleap,
And, coming back with Her who will be ours,
Into thy bosom we again shall creep.

I wrote to Mary H., having received a letter from her in the evening. A sweet day. We nailed up the honeysuckles, and hoed the scarlet beans.

May 30th, Sunday. I wrote to Mrs Clarkson. It was a clear but cold day. The Simpsons called in the evening. I had been obliged to go to bed before tea, and was unwell all day. Gooseberries, a present from Peggy Hodgson. I wrote to my Aunt Cookson.

[*May*] *31st, Monday.* I was much better. We sat out all day. Mary Jameson dined. I wrote out the poem on 'Our Departure', which he seemed to have finished. In the evening Miss Simpson brought us a letter from M.H., and a complimentary and critical letter to W. from John Wilson of Glasgow, post-paid. I went a little way with Miss S. My tooth broke today. They will soon be gone. Let that pass, I shall be beloved – I want no more.

10

'Help us to tell Her tales of years gone by,
    And this sweet spring, the best beloved and best;'
From 'poem on going for Mary' – A *Farewell*

[*June* 1st,] *Tuesday.* A very sweet day, but a sad want of rain.
We went into the orchard before dinner, after I had written
to M.H. Then on to Mr Olliff's intakes. We found some torn
birds nests. The columbine was growing upon the rocks; here
and there a solitary plant, sheltered and shaded by the tufts and
bowers of trees. It is a graceful slender creature, a female seeking
retirement, and growing freest and most graceful where it is
most alone. I observed that the more shaded plants were always
the tallest. A short note and gooseberries from Coleridge.

June 2nd, *Wednesday.* In the morning we observed that the
scarlet beans were drooping in the leaves in great numbers,
owing, we guess, to an insect. We sate awhile in the orchard –
then we went to the old carpenter's about the hurdles. Yester-
day an old man called, a grey-headed man, above 70 years of
age. He said he had been a soldier, that his wife and children
had died in Jamaica. He had a beggar's wallet over his shoulders;
a coat of shreds and patches, altogether of a drab colour; he
was tall, and though his body was bent, he had the look of one
used to have been upright. I talked a while, and then gave him
a piece of cold bacon and a penny. Said he, 'You're a fine woman !'
I could not help smiling; I suppose he meant, 'You're a kind
woman'. Afterwards a woman called, travelling to Glasgow. After
dinner we went into Frank's field, crawled up the little glen, and
planned a seat, then went to Mr Olliff's Hollins and sate there –
found a beautiful shell-like purple fungus in Frank's field. After
tea we walked to Butterlip How, and backwards and forwards
there. All the young oak tree leaves are dry as powder. A cold
south wind, portending rain. I ought to have said that on Tues-

day evening, namely June 1st, we walked upon the turf near John's Grove. It was a lovely night. The clouds of the western sky reflected a saffron light upon the upper end of the lake. All was still. We went to look at Rydale. There was an Alpine, fire-like red upon the tops of the mountains. This was gone when we came in view of the lake. But we saw the Lake in a new and most beautiful point of view, between two little rocks, and behind a small ridge that had concealed it from us. This White Moss, a place made for all kinds of beautiful works of art, and nature, woods and valleys, fairy valleys and fairy tarns, miniature mountains, alps above alps. Little John Dawson came in from the woods with a stick over his shoulder.

June 3rd, 1802, Thursday. A very fine rain. I lay in bed till ten o'clock. William much better than yesterday. We walked into Easedale – sheltered in a cow-house – came home wet. The cuckow sang, and we watched the little birds as we sate at the door of the cow-house. The oak copses are brown, as in autumn, with the late frosts – scattered over with green trees, birches or hazels. The ashes are coming into full leaf, some of them injured. We came home quite wet. We have been reading the life and some of the writings of poor Logan[1] since dinner. 'And everlasting longings for the lost.' It is an affecting line. There are many affecting lines and passages in his poem. William is now sleeping, with the window open, lying on the window seat. The thrush is singing. There are, I do believe, a thousand buds on the honeysuckle tree, all small and far from blowing, save one that is retired behind the twigs close to the wall, and as snug as a bird's nest. John's rose tree is very beautiful, blended with the honeysuckle.

On Tuesday evening when we were among the rocks we saw in the woods what seemed to be a man resting or looking about him – he had a piece of wood near him. William was on before

---

1. John Logan (1747–88), a Scottish poet. Dorothy is quoting from 'Ode written on a Visit to the Country in Autumn'. Logan was thought to be the author of the poem 'To the Cuckoo' which influenced Wordsworth's own poem on the subject.

me when we returned and as I was going up to him I found that this supposed man was John Dawson. I spoke to him and I suppose he thought I asked him what my Brother had said to him before, for he replied: 'William asks me how my head is'. Poor fellow – he says it is worse and worse, and he walks as if he were afraid of putting his body in motion.

Yesterday morning William walked as far as the Swan with Aggy Fisher. She was going to attend upon Goan's dying infant. She said, 'There are many heavier crosses than the death of an infant'; and went on, 'There was a woman in this vale who buried 4 grown-up children in one year, and I have heard her say, when many years were gone by, that she had more pleasure in thinking of those 4 than of her living children, for as children get up and have families of their own, their duty to their parents "*wears out and weakens*". She could trip lightly by the graves of those who died when they were young with a light step, as she went to church on a Sunday.'

We walked while dinner was getting ready up into Mr King's Hollins. I was weak and made my way down alone, for Wm. took a difficult way. After dinner we walked upon the turf path – a showery afternoon. A very affecting letter came from M.H., while I was sitting in the window reading Milton's *Penseroso* to William. I answered this letter before I went to bed.

June 4th, Friday. It was a very sweet morning. There had been much rain in the night. Dined late. In the evening we walked on our favourite path. Then we came in and sate in the orchard. The evening was dark and warm – a tranquil night. I left William in the orchard. I read *Mother Hubbard's Tale*[1] before I went to bed.

[*June*] *5th, Saturday*. A fine showery morning. I made both pies and bread; but we first walked into Easedale, and sate under the oak trees, upon the mossy stones. There were one or two slight showers. The gowans were flourishing along the banks of the

---

1. Poem by Spenser.

stream. The strawberry flower (Geum) hanging over the brook – all things soft and green. In the afternoon William sate in the orchard. I went there, was tired, and fell asleep. Mr Simpson drank tea, Mrs Smith called with her daughter. We began the letter to John Wilson.

This was in answer to the letter they had received from him on 31 May. Wordsworth's reply (helped by Dorothy) is written on the same lines as his Preface. It gives further insight into the moral purpose behind his poems and is especially illuminating about the 'Idiot Boy'. It is well worth reading in his Early Letters, p. 292.

June 6th, Sunday. A showery morning. We were writing the letter to John Wilson when Ellen came. Molly at Goan's child's funeral. After dinner I walked into John Fisher's intake with Ellen. She brought us letters from Coleridge, Mrs Clarkson, and Sara Hutchinson. William went out in the evening and sate in the orchard, it was a showery day. In the evening there was one of the heaviest showers I ever remember.

June 7th, Monday. I wrote to Mary H. this morning, sent the C. Indolence poem. Copied the letter to John Wilson, and wrote to my brother Richard and Mrs Coleridge. In the evening I walked with Ellen to Butterlip How and to George Mackareth's for the horse. It was a very sweet evening; there was the cuckow and the little birds; the copses still injured, but the trees in general looked most soft and beautiful in tufts. William was walking when we came in – he had slept miserably for 2 nights past, so we all went to bed soon. I went with Ellen in the morning to Rydale Falls. Letters from Annette, Mary H. and Cook.

June 8th, Tuesday. Ellen and I rode to Windermere. We had a fine sunny day, neither hot nor cold. I mounted the horse at the quarry. We had no difficulties or delays but at the gates. I was enchanted with some of the views. From the High Ray the view is very delightful, rich, and festive, water and wood, houses, groves, hedgerows, green fields, and mountains; white houses, large and small. We passed 2 or 3 nice-looking statesmen's houses. Mr Curwen's shrubberies looked pitiful enough under the native trees. We put up our horses, ate our dinner by the water-side, and walked up to the Station. Then we went to the Island, walked round it, and crossed the lake with our horse in the ferry. The shrubs have been cut away in some parts of the island. I observed to the boatman that I did not think it improved. He replied: 'We think it is, for one could hardly see the house before.' It seems to me to be, however, no better than it was. They have made no natural glades; it is merely a lawn with a few miserable young trees, standing as if they were half-starved. There are no sheep, no cattle upon these lawns. It is neither one thing or another – neither *natural*, nor wholly cultivated and artificial, which it was before. And that great house! Mercy upon us! if it *could* be concealed, it *would* be well for all who are not pained to see the pleasantest of earthly spots deformed by man. But it *cannot* be covered. Even the tallest of our old oak trees would not reach to the top of it. When we went into the boat, there were two men standing at the landing-place. One seemed to be about 60, a man with a jolly red face; he looked as if he might have lived many years in Mr Curwen's house. He wore a blue jacket and trowsers, as the people who live close by Windermere, particularly at the places of chief resort, in affectation, I suppose. He looked significantly at our boatman just as we were rowing off, and said, 'Thomas, mind you take off the directions off that cask. You know what I mean. It will serve as a blind for them, *you* know. It was a blind business, both for you, and the coachman, and me and all of us. Mind you take off the directions. A wink's as good as a nod with some folks'; and then he turned round, looking at his companions with such an air of self-satisfaction, and deep insight into unknown things! I could hardly help laughing outright at him. Laburnums blossom freely at the island, and in the shrubberies on the shore – they are blighted everywhere else. Roses of various sorts now out. The brooms were in full glory everywhere, 'veins of gold' among the copses.[1] The hawthorns in the valley fading away – beautiful upon the hills. We reached home at 3 o'clock. After tea William went out and walked and wrote that poem, 'The sun has long been set', etc. He first went up to G. Mackareth's with the horse, afterwards he walked on our own path and wrote the lines; he called me into the orchard, and there repeated them to me – he then stayed there till 11 o'clock.

> The sun has long been set,
>   The stars are out by two and threes,
> The little birds are piping yet
>   Among the bushes and trees;
> There's a cuckoo, and one or two thrushes,
> And a far-off wind that rushes,
> And a sound of water that gushes,
> And the cuckoo's sovereign cry
> Fills all the hollow of the sky.
>   Who would 'go parading'
> In London, 'and masquerading',
> On such a night of June
> With that beautiful soft half-moon,
> And all these innocent blisses?
> On such a night as this is!

The poem was published in 1807 and not again until 1835. Wordsworth in a note to Isabella Fenwick said it was then 'reprinted at the Request of My Sister in whose presence the lines were thrown off'.

June 9th, Wednesday. Wm. slept ill. A soaking all day rain. We should have gone to Mr Simpson's to tea but we walked up after tea. Lloyds called. The hawthorns on the mountain sides like orchards in blossom. Brought rhubarb down. It rains hard. Ambleside fair. I wrote to Christr. and M.H.

---

1. See p. 43 n., 16 June 1800.

June 10th, Thursday. I wrote to Mrs Clarkson and Luff – went with Ellen to Rydale. Coleridge came in with a sack full of books, etc., and a branch of mountain ash. He had been attacked by a cow. He came over by Grisdale. A furious wind. Mr Simpson drank tea. William very poorly – we went to bed latish – I slept in sitting room.

June 11th, Friday. A wet day. William had slept very ill. Wm. and C. walked out. I went to bed after dinner, not well. I was tired with making beds, cooking etc., Molly being very ill.

June 12th, Saturday. A rainy morning. C. set off before dinner. We went with him to the Rays, but it rained, so we went no further. Sheltered under a wall. He would be sadly wet, for a furious shower came on just when we parted. We got no dinner, but gooseberry pie to our tea. I baked both pies and bread, and walked with William, first on our own path, but it was too wet there, next over the rocks to the road, and backward and forward, and last of all up to Mr King's. Miss Simpson and Robert had called. Letters from Sara and Annette.

June 13th, Sunday. A fine morning. Sunshiny and bright, but with rainy clouds. William had slept better but not well, he has been altering the poem to Mary this morning, he is now washing his feet. I wrote out poems for our journey and I wrote a letter to my Uncle Cookson. Mr Simpson came when we were in the orchard in the morning, and brought us a beautiful drawing which he had done. In the evening we walked, first on our own path – there we walked a good while. It was a silent night. The stars were out by ones and twos, but no cuckow, no little birds, the air was not warm, and we have observed that since Tuesday, 8th, when William wrote, 'The sun has long been set', that we have had no birds singing after the evening is fairly set in. We walked to our new view of Rydale, but it put on a sullen face. There was an owl hooting in Bainriggs. Its first halloo was so like a human shout that I was

253

surprized, when it made its second call tremulous and length-ened out, to find that the shout had come from an owl. The full moon (not quite full) was among a company of steady island clouds, and the sky bluer about it than the natural sky blue. William observed that the full moon, above a dark fir grove, is a fine image of the descent of a superior being. There was a shower which drove us into John's Grove before we had quitted our favourite path. We walked upon John's path before we went to view Rydale. We went to bed immediately upon our return home.

June 14th, Monday. I was very unwell – went to bed before I drank my tea – was sick and afterwards almost asleep when William brought me a letter from Mary, which he read to me sitting by the bed-side. Wm. wrote to Mary and Sara about *The Leech Gatherer*, I wrote to both of them in one and to Annette, to Coleridge also.

William's letter to Mary and Sara.

My dear Sara,

I am exceedingly sorry that the latter part of the Leechgatherer has displeased you, the more so because I cannot take to myself (that being the case) much pleasure or satisfaction in having pleased you in the former part. I will explain to you in prose my feeling in writing that poem and then you will be better able to judge whether the fault be mine or yours or partly both. I describe myself as having been exalted to the highest pitch of delight by the joyousness and beauty of Nature; and then as depressed, even in the midst of those beautiful objects, to the lowest dejection and despair. A young Poet in the midst of the happiness of Nature is described as overwhelmed by the thought of the miserable reverses which have befallen the happiest of all men, viz. Poets. I think of this till I am so deeply impressed with it, that I consider the manner in which I was rescued from my dejection and despair almost as an interposition of Providence.

Now whether it was by peculiar grace, A leading from above – A person reading this Poem with feelings like mine will have been awed and controuled, expecting almost something spiritual or supernatural. What is brought forward? 'A lonely place, a Pond', 'by which an old man was, far from all house or home': not stood, not sat, but was – the figure presented in the most naked simplicity possible. This feeling of spirituality or supernatural-ness is again referred to as being strong in my mind in this passage. How came he here? thought I, or what can he be doing! I then describe him, whether ill or well is not for me to judge with perfect confidence; but this I can confidently affirm, that though I believe God has given me a strong imagination, I cannot conceive a figure more impressive than that of an old Man like this, the survivor of a Wife and ten children, travelling along among the mountains and all lonely places, carrying with him his own fortitude, and the necessities which an unjust state of society has entailed upon him. You say and Mary (that is you can say no more than that) the poem is very well after the intro-duction of the old man, this is not true, if it is not more than very well it is very bad – there is no intermediate state. You speak of his speech as tedious: everything is tedious when one does not read with the feelings of the Author. The Thorn is tedious to hundreds; and so is The Idiot Boy to hundreds. It is in the character of the old man to tell his story, which an impatient reader must necessarily feel as tedious. But, Good God, Such a figure, in such a place; a pious, self-respecting, miserably infirm and [   ] Old Man tell such a tale!

My dear Sara, it is not a matter of indifference whether you are pleased with this figure and his employment; it may be compara-tively so, whether you are pleased or not with this Poem; but it is of the utmost importance that you should have had pleasure from contemplating the fortitude, independence, persevering spirit, and the general moral dignity of this old man's character. Your feelings about the Mother, and the Boys with the Butter-fly, were not indifferent: it was an affair of whole continents of moral sympathy. I will talk more with you on this when we meet – at present, farewell and Heaven for ever bless you.

Dorothy writes:

Dear Sara,

When you happen to be displeased with what you may suppose to be the tendency or moral of any poem which William writes, ask yourself whether you have hit upon the real tendency and true moral, and above all never think that he writes for no reason but merely because a thing happened – and when you feel any poem of his to be tedious, ask yourself in what spirit it was written – whether merely to tell the tale and be through with it, or to illustrate a particular character or truth.

It is clear from Wordsworth's letter that the version of the poem sent to Sara was considerably different from the final one. It is the only evidence there is since the page containing 'The Leech-Gatherer' has been torn out of Sara's notebook in which the 1801–2 poems were transcribed. But obviously there had been much more description of the old man, his family, and his hardships on the lines of the original encounter of 3 October 1800 and it was this which Sara found tedious. But though William defends himself here, he took Sara's criticism to heart, cut out the stanza on the old man's difficulties, and inserted what is now the ninth stanza and perhaps the finest one of all.

I was better after tea – I walked with Wm. when I had put up my parcel, on our own path. We were driven away by the horses that go on the commons; then we went to look at Rydale, walked a little in the fir grove, went again to the top of the hill, and came home. A mild and sweet night. William stayed behind me. I threw him the cloak out of the window. The moon overcast. He sate a few minutes in the orchard, came in sleepy, and hurried to bed. I carried him his bread and butter.

[June] 15th, Tuesday. A sweet grey, mild morning. The birds sing soft and low. William has not slept all night. It wants only 10 minutes of 10, and he is in bed yet. After William rose we went and sate in the orchard till dinner time. We walked a long time in the evening upon our favourite path; the owls hooted, the night hawk sang to itself incessantly, but there were no little birds, no thrushes. I left William writing a few lines about the night-hawk and other images of the evening, and went to seek for letters.

He was probably writing the opening lines of 'The Waggoner' which are printed below in their final version. But we know from a note to Isabella Fenwick that what he wrote that evening was as follows:

> At last this loitering day of June
> This long long day is going out.
> The Night-hawk is singing his frog-like tune,
> Twirling his watchman's rattle about –

'but from unwillingness to startle the reader at the outside by so bold a mode of expression, the passage was altered as it now stands.'   W. 1836.

> 'Tis spent – this burning day of June!
> Soft darkness o'er its latest gleams is stealing;
> The buzzing dor-hawk, round and round, is wheeling, –
> That solitary bird
> Is all that can be heard
> In silence deeper far than that of deepest noon!
>   Confiding Glow-worms, 'tis a night
> Propitious to your earth-born light!
> But, where the scattered stars are seen
> In hazy straits the clouds between,
> Each, in his station twinkling not,
> Seems changed into a pallid spot.
> The mountains against heaven's grave weight
> Rise up, and grow to wondrous height.
> The air, as in a lion's den,
> Is close and hot; – and now and then
> Comes a tired and sultry breeze
> With a haunting and a panting,
> Like the stifling of disease;
> But the dews allay the heat,
> And the silence makes it sweet.

We walked backwards and forwards a little, after I returned to William, and then up as far as Mr King's. Came in. There was a basket of lettuces, a letter from M.H. about the delay of mine, and telling of one she had sent by the other post, one from Wade, and one from Sara to C. William did not read them. M.H. growing fat.

June 16th, Wednesday. We walked towards Rydale for letters – met Frank Batey with the expected one from Mary. We went up into Rydale woods and read it there. We sate near an old wall, which fenced a hazel grove, which Wm. said was exactly like the filbert grove at Middleham. It is a beautiful spot, a sloping or rather steep piece of ground, with hazels growing 'tall and erect' in clumps at distances, almost seeming regular, as if they had been planted. We returned to dinner. I wrote to Mary after dinner, while William sate in the orchard. Old Mr Simpson drank tea with us. When Mr S. was gone I read my letter to William, speaking to Mary about having a cat. I spoke of the little birds keeping us company, and William told me that that very morning a bird had perched upon his leg. He had been lying very still, and had watched this little creature, it had come under the bench where he was sitting, and then flew up to his leg; he thoughtlessly stirred himself to look further at it, and it flew on to the apple tree above him. It was a little young creature, that had just left its nest, equally unacquainted with man, and unaccustomed to struggle against storms and winds. While it was upon the apple tree the wind blew about the stiff boughs, and the bird seemed bemazed, and not strong enough to strive with it. The swallows come to the sitting-room window as if wishing to build, but I am afraid they will not have courage for it, but I believe they will build in my room window. They twitter and make a bustle and a little chearful song, hanging against the panes of glass, with their soft white bellies close to the glass, and their forked fish-like tails. They swim round and round, and again they come. It was a sweet evening. We first walked to the top of the hill to look at Rydale, then to Butterlip How. I do not now see the brownness that was in the coppices. The lower hawthorn blossoms passed away. Those on the hills are a faint white. The wild guelder-rose is coming out, and the wild roses. I have seen no honey-suckles yet, except our own one nestling, and a tree of the yellow kind at Mrs Townley's the day I went with Ellen to Windermere. Foxgloves are now frequent, the first I saw was that day with Ellen and the first ripe strawberries. William went to bed immediately.

[June] 17th, Thursday. William had slept well. I took castor oil and lay in bed till 12 o'clock. William injured himself with working a little. When I got up we sate in the orchard – a sweet mild day. Miss Hudson called – I went with her to the top of the hill. When I came home I found William at work attempting to alter a stanza in the poem on our going for Mary, which I convinced him did not need altering.

At the end of Wordsworth's letter to Sara Hutchinson written on 14 June (see p. 254) he discusses the alterations he has made to 'the poem on our going for Mary', printed in its final form on p. 244. By this time he has already inserted what are now the fifth and sixth verses of the poem, those beginning 'Dear Spot, which we have watched with tender heed' and 'And O most constant, yet most fickle Place'. In the letter he confessed that he is never certain how far his alterations are successful, but as we see from this entry he still is not satisfied with this poem and continues to try and rework it.

We sate in the house after dinner. In the evening walked on our favourite path. A short letter from Coleridge. William added a little to the Ode he is writing.[1]

June 18th, Friday. When we were sitting after breakfast – William about to shave – Luff came in. It was a sweet morning – he had rode over the Fells. He brought news about Lord Lowther's intention to pay all debts, etc., and a letter from Mr Clarkson.

---

1. See p. 188

The Wordsworths' father had been in the service of Sir James Lowther, later Lord Lonsdale, and had died in 1784 with a large amount of money still owed to him. For many years Lord Lonsdale refused to pay more than a fraction of this debt and it was not until his death on 24 May of this year that his heir decided to pay off the debts on the Lowther estate. Although the Wordsworths did not receive the money for another three years, this meant that they were at least assured of a small income for the rest of their lives.

He saw our garden, was astonished at the scarlet beans, etc., etc. When he was gone, we wrote to Coleridge, M.H., and my brother Richard about the affair. William determined to go to Eusemere on Monday. In the afternoon we walked to Rydale with our letters – found no letters there. A sweet evening. I had a woful headache, and was ill in stomach from agitation of mind – went to bed at nine o'clock, but did not sleep till late.

[June] 19th, Saturday. The swallows were very busy under my window this morning. I slept pretty well, but William has got no sleep. It is after 11 and he is still in bed. A fine morning. Coleridge, when he was last here, told us that for many years, there being no Quaker meeting held at Keswick, a single old Quaker woman used to go regularly alone every Sunday to attend the meeting-house, and there used to sit and perform her worship, alone in that beautiful place among those fir trees, in that spacious vale, under the great mountain Skiddaw ! ! ! Poor old Willy – we never pass by his grave close to the Churchyard gate without thinking of him and having his figure brought back to our minds. He formerly was an ostler at Hawkshead having spent a little estate. In his old age he was boarded or as they say *let* by the parish. A boy of the house that hired him was riding one morning pretty briskly beside John Fisher's – 'Hullo ! has aught particular happened?' said John to the boy – 'Nay, naught at aw, nobbut auld Willy's dead.' He was going to order the passing bell to be tolled. On Thursday morning Miss Hudson of Workington called. She said, 'O ! I love flowers ! I sow flowers in the parks several miles from home.

260

and my mother and I visit them, and watch them how they grow.' This may show that botanists may be often deceived when they find rare flowers growing far from houses. This was a very ordinary young woman, such as in any town in the North of England one my find a score. I sate up a while after William – he then called me down to him. (I was writing to Mary H.) I read Churchill's *Rosciad*.[1] Returned again to my writing, and did not go to bed till he called to me. The shutters were closed, but I heard the birds singing. There was our own thrush, shouting with an impatient shout – so it sounded to me. The morning was still, the twittering of the little birds was very gloomy. The owls had hooted a 1/4 of an hour before, now the cocks were crowing. It was near daylight, I put out my candle, and went to bed. In a little time I thought I heard William snoring, so I composed myself to sleep. Charles Lloyd called. [?] at my sweet Brother.

June 20th, *Sunday*. He had slept better than I could have expected, but he was far from well all day; we were in the orchard a great part of the morning. After tea we walked upon our own path for a long time. We talked sweetly together about the disposal of our riches. We lay upon the sloping turf. Earth and sky were so lovely that they melted our very hearts. The sky to the north was of a chastened yet rich yellow, fading into pale blue, and streaked and scattered over with steady islands of purple, melting away into shades of pink. It made my heart almost feel like a vision to me. We afterwards took our cloaks and sate in the orchard. Mr and Miss Simpson called. We told them of our expected good fortune.[2] We were astonished and somewhat hurt to see how coldly Mr Simpson received it – Miss S. seemed very glad. We went into the house when they left us, and Wm. went to bed. I sat up about an hour. He then called me to talk to him – he could not fall asleep. I wrote to Montagu.

---

1. A satire by Charles Churchill on contemporary actors, published in 1761.
2. See p. 260.

[*June*] 21*st, Monday*. William was obliged to be in bed late, he had slept so miserably. It was a very fine morning, but as we did not leave home till 12 o'clock it was very hot. I parted from my Beloved in the green lane above the Blacksmith's, then went to dinner at Mr Simpson's – we walked afterwards in the garden. Betty Towers and her son and daughter came to tea. The little lad is 4 years old, almost as little a thing as Hartley, and as sharp too, they say, but I saw nothing of this, being a stranger, except in his bonny eyes, which had such a sweet brightness in them when any thing was said to him that made him ashamed and draw his chin into his neck, while he sent his eyes upwards to look at you. His Mother is a delicate woman. She said she thought that both she and her husband were so tender in their health that they must be obliged to sell their land. Speaking of old Jim Jackson she said: 'They might have looked up with the best in Grasmere, if they had but been careful' – 'They began with a clear estate, and had never had but one child, he to be sure is a half-wit' – 'How did they get through with their money?' – 'Why in eating and drinking. The wife would make tea 4 or 5 times in a day and sec' folks for sugar ! Then she would have nea Teapot, but she would take the water out of a brass pan on the fire and pour it on to the tea in a quart pot. This all for herself, for she boiled the tea leaves always for her husband and their son.'

I brought plants home, sunflowers, and planted them.

Aggy Fisher was talking with me on Monday morning, 21st of June, about her son. She went on – Old Mary Watson was at Goan's there when the child died. I had never seen her before since her son was drowned last summer, 'we were all in trouble and trouble opens folks' hearts'. She began to tell about her daughter that's married to Leonard Holmes, how now that sickness is come upon him they are breaking down and failing in the world. Debts are coming in every day, and he can do nothing, and they fret and jar together. One day he came riding over to Grasmere – I wondered what was the matter, and I resolved to speak to him when he came back. He was as pale as a ghost, and he did not suffer the horse to gang quicker than a snail could crawl. He had come over in a trick of passion to auld Mary to tell her she might take her own again, her daughter and the bairns. Mary replied nobly (said Aggy) that she would not part man and wife, but that all should come together, and she would keep them while she had anything. Old Mary went to see them at Ambleside afterwards, and he begged her pardon. Aggy observed that they would never have known this sorrow, if it had pleased God to take him off suddenly.

June 23rd, Wednesday. I slept till ½ past 3 o'clock – called Molly before 4, and had got myself dressed and breakfasted before 5, but it rained and I went to bed again. It is now 20 minutes past 10 – a sunshiny morning. I walked to the top of the hill and sate under a wall near John's Grove, facing the sun. I read a scene or two in *As You Like It.* I met Charles Lloyd, and old Mr Lloyd was upstairs – Mrs Ll. had been to meet me. I wrote a line to Wm. by the Lloyds. Coleridge and Leslie came just as I had lain down after dinner. C. brought me W.'s letter. He had got well to Eusemere. C. and I accompanied Leslie to the boat-house. It was a sullen, coldish evening, no sunshine; but after we had parted from Leslie a light came out suddenly that repaid us for all. It fell only upon one hill, and the island, but it arrayed the grass and trees in gem-like brightness. I cooked C. his supper. We sate up till one o'clock.

June 24th, Thursday. I went with C. half-way up the Rays. It was a cool morning. I dined at Mr Simpson's and helped Aggy Fleming to quilt a petticoat. Miss Simpson came with me after tea round by the White Bridge. I ground paint when I reached home, and was tired. Wm. came in just when Molly had left me. It was a mild rainy evening – he was cool and fresh and smelt sweetly – his clothes were wet. We sate together talking till the first dawning of day – a happy time. He was pale and not much tired. He thought I looked well too.

June 25th, Friday. Wm. had not fallen asleep till after 3 o'clock, but he slept tolerably. Miss Simpson came to colour the rooms.

I began with whitewashing the ceiling. I worked with them (William was very busy) till dinner time, but after dinner I went to bed and fell asleep. When I rose I went just before tea into the garden. I looked up at my swallow's nest, and it was gone. It had fallen down. Poor little creatures, they could not themselves be more distressed than I was. I went upstairs to look at the ruins. They lay in a large heap upon the window ledge; these swallows had been ten days employed in building this nest, and it seemed to be almost finished. I had watched them early in the morning, in the day many and many a time, and in the evenings when it was almost dark. I had seen them sitting together side by side in their unfinished nest, both morning and night. When they first came about the window they used to hang against the panes, with their white bellies and their forked tails, looking like fish; but then they fluttered and sang their own little twittering song. As soon as the nest was broad enough, a sort of ledge for them, they sate both mornings and evenings, but they did not pass the night there. I watched them one morning, when William was at Eusemere, for more than an hour. Every now and then there was a feeling motion in their wings, a sort of tremulousness, and they sang a low song to one another.

A page has been torn out of the M.S. here. Among other things it must have told that the swallows had started rebuilding their nest.

[*June 29th, Tuesday*] ... that they would not call here. I was going to tea. It is an uncertain day, sunshine, showers, and wind. It is now 8 o'clock; I will go and see if my swallows are on their nest. Yes! there they are, side by side, both looking down into the garden. I have been out on purpose to see their faces. I knew by looking at the window that they were there. Young George Mackareth is come down from London. Molly says: 'I did not get him asked if he had got his la'al green purse yet'. When he went away he went round to see aw't neighbours and some gave him 6d., some a shilling, and I have heard his Mother say "t la'al green purse was never out of his hand'. I wrote to M.H., my brother Christr. and Miss Griffiths, then went to bed in the sitting room. C. and Wm. came in at about half past eleven. They talked till after twelve.

June 30th, Wednesday. William slept ill, his head terribly bad. We walked part of the way up the Rays with Coleridge, a threatening windy coldish day. We did not go with C. far up the Rays, but sate down a few minutes together before we parted. I was not very well – I was inclined to go to bed when we reached home, but Wm. persuaded me to have tea instead. We met an old man between the [?] shed and Lewthwaite's. He wore a rusty but untorn hat, an excellent blue coat, waistcoat, and breeches, and good mottled worsted stockings. His beard was very thick and grey, of a fortnight's growth we guessed, it was a regular beard, like grey plush. His bundle contained Sheffield ware. William said to him, after he had asked him what his business was, 'You are a very old man?' 'Aye, I am 83.' I joined in, 'Have you any children?' 'Children? Yes, plenty. I have children and grand-children, and great grand-children. I have a great grand-daughter, a fine lass, 13 years old.' I then said, 'What, they take care of you?' He replied, half offended, 'Thank God, I can take care of myself.' He said he had been a servant of the Marquis of Granby – 'O he was a good man, he's in heaven – I hope he is'. He then told us how he shot himself at Bath, that he was with him in Germany, and travelled with him everywhere. 'He was a famous boxer, sir.' And then he told us a story of his fighting with his farmer. 'He used always to call me hard and sharp.' Then every now and then he broke out, 'He was a good man! When we were travelling he never asked at the public-houses, as it might be there' (pointing to the 'Swan'), 'what we were to pay, but he would put his hand into his pocket and give them what he liked; and when he came out of the house he would say, Now, they would have charged me a shilling or tenpence. God help them, poor creatures!!' I asked him again about his children, how many he had. Says he, 'I cannot tell you' (I suppose he confounded children and grand-children together); 'I have one daughter that keeps a boarding-school at Skipton in Craven. She teaches flowering and marking. And another that keeps a boarding-school at Ingleton. I brought up my family under the Marquis.' He was familiar with all parts of Yorkshire. He asked us where we lived. 'At Grasmere.' 'The bonniest dale in all England!' says the old man. I bought a pair of scissors of him, and we sate together by the road-side. When we parted I tried to lift his bundle, and it was almost more than I could do.

July 2nd, Friday. A very rainy morning. There was a gleam of fair weather, and we thought of walking into Easedale. Molly began to prepare the linen for putting out, but it rained worse than ever. In the evening we walked up to the view of Rydale, and afterwards towards Mr King's. I left William, and wrote a short letter to M.H. and to Coleridge, and transcribed the alterations in *The Leech Gatherer*.

July 4th, Sunday. Cold and rain and very dark. I was sick and ill, had been made sleepless by letters. I lay in bed till 4 o'clock. When I rose, I was very far from well, but I grew better after tea. William walked out a little, I did not. We sate by the window together. It came on a terribly wet night. Wm. finished *The Leech Gatherer* today.

RESOLUTION AND INDEPENDENCE

I

There was a roaring in the wind all night;
The rain came heavily and fell in floods;
But now the sun is rising calm and bright;
The birds are singing in the distant woods;
Over his own sweet voice the Stock-dove broods;
The Jay makes answer as the Magpie chatters;
And all the air is filled with pleasant noise of waters.

II

All things that love the sun are out of doors;
The sky rejoices in the morning's birth;
The grass is bright with rain-drops; on the moors
The hare is running races in her mirth;
And with her feet she from the plashy earth
Raises a mist, that, glittering in the sun,
Runs with her all the way, wherever she doth run.

III

I was a Traveller then upon the moor,
I saw the hare that raced about with joy;
I heard the woods and distant waters roar;
Or heard them not, as happy as a boy:
The pleasant season did my heart employ:
My old remembrances went from me wholly:
And all the ways of men, so vain and melancholy.

IV

But, as it sometimes chanceth, from the might
Of joy in minds that can no further go,
As high as we have mounted in delight
In our dejection do we sink as low;
To me that morning did it happen so;
And fears and fancies thick upon me came;
Dim sadness – and blind thoughts, I knew not, nor
    could name.

V

I heard the sky-lark warbling in the sky;
And I bethought me of the playful hare:
Even such a happy Child of earth am I;
Even as these blissful creatures do I fare;
Far from the world I walk, and from all care;
But there may come another day to me –
Solitude, pain of heart, distress, and poverty.

VI

My whole life I have lived in pleasant thought,
As if life's business were a summer mood;
As if all needful things would come unsought
To genial faith, still rich in genial good;
But how can He expect that others should
Build for him, sow for him, and at his call
Love him, who for himself will take no heed at all?

VII

I thought of Chatterton, the marvellous Boy,
The sleepless Soul that perished in his pride;
Of Him who walked in glory and in joy
Following his plough, along the mountainside:
By our own spirits are we deified:
We Poets in our youth begin in gladness;
But thereof come in the end despondency and madness.

VIII

Now, whether it were by peculiar grace,
A leading from above, a something given,
Yet it befell, that, in this lonely place,
When I with these untoward thoughts had striven,
Beside a pool bare to the eye of heaven
I saw a Man before me unawares;
The oldest man he seemed that ever wore grey hairs.

IX

As a huge stone is sometimes seen to lie
Couched on the bald top of an eminence;
Wonder to all who do the same espy:
By what means it could thither come, and whence;
So that it seems a thing endued with sense:
Like a sea-beast crawled forth, that on a shelf
Of rock or sand reposeth, there to sun itself;

X

Such seemed this Man, not all alive nor dead,
Nor all asleep – in his extreme old age:
His body was bent double, feet and head
Coming together in life's pilgrimage;
As if some dire constraint of pain, or rage
Of sickness felt by him in times long past,
A more than human weight upon his frame had cast.

Himself he propped, limbs, body, and pale face,
Upon a long grey staff of shaven wood:
And, still as I drew near with gentle pace,
Upon the margin of that moorish flood
Motionless as a cloud the old Man stood,
That heareth not the loud winds when they call
And moveth all together, if it moves at all.

At length, himself unsettling, he the pond
Stirred with his staff, and fixedly did look
Upon the muddy water, which he conned,
As if he had been reading in a book:
And now a stranger's privilege I took;
And, drawing to his side, to him did say,
'This morning gives us promise of a glorious day.'

A gentle answer did the old Man make,
In courteous speech which forth he slowly drew:
And him with further words I thus bespake,
'What occupation do you there pursue?
This is a lonesome place for one like you.'
Ere he replied, a flash of mild surprise
Broke from the sable orbs of his yet-vivid eyes,

XIV

His words came feebly, from a feeble chest,
But each in solemn order followed each,
With something of a lofty utterance drest –
Choice words and measured phrase, above the reach
Of ordinary men; a stately speech;
Such as grave Livers do in Scotland use,
Religious men, who give to God and man their dues.

XV

He told, that to these waters he had come
To gather leeches, being old and poor;
Employment hazardous and wearisome !
And he had many hardships to endure :
From pond to pond he roamed, from moor to moor;
Housing, with God's good help, by choice or chance,
And in this way he gained an honest maintenance.

XVI

The old Man still stood talking by my side;
But now his voice to me was like a stream
Scarce heard; nor word from word could I divide;
And the whole body of the Man did seem
Like one whom I had met with in a dream;
Or like a man from some far region sent,
To give me human strength, by apt admonishment.

XVII

My former thoughts returned : the fear that kills;
And hope that is unwilling to be fed;
Cold, pain, and labour, and all fleshly ills;
And mighty Poets in their misery dead.
– Perplexed, and longing to be comforted,
My question eagerly did I renew,
'How is it that you live, and what is it you do?'

XVIII

He with a smile did then his words repeat;
And said, that, gathering leeches, far and wide
He travelled; stirring thus about his feet
The waters of the pool where they abide.
'Once I could meet with them on every side;
But they have dwindled long by slow decay;
Yet still I persevere, and find them where I may.'

XIX

While he was talking thus, the lonely place,
The old Man's shape, and speech – all troubled me:
In my mind's eye I seemed to see him pace
About the weary moors continually,
Wandering about alone and silently.
While I these thoughts within myself pursued,
He, having made a pause, the same discourse renewed.

XX

And soon with this he other matter blended,
Cheerfully uttered, with demeanour kind,
But stately in the main; and when he ended,
I could have laughed myself to scorn to find
In that decrepit Man so firm a mind.
'God,' said I, 'be my help and stay secure;
I'll think of the Leech-gatherer on the lonely moor!'

July 5th, Monday. A very sweet morning. William stayed some time in the orchard. I went to him there – it was a beautiful morning. I copied out The L.-G. for Coleridge, and for us. Wrote to Annette, – Mrs Clarkson, M.H., and Coleridge. It came on a heavy rain, and we could not go to Dove Nest as we had intended, though we had sent Molly for the horse, and it was come. The roses in the garden are fretted and battered and quite spoiled, the honey suckle, though in its glory, is sadly teazed. The peas are beaten down. The scarlet beans want sticking. The garden is overrun with weeds.

[July] 7th, Wednesday. A very fine day. William had slept ill, so he lay in bed till 11 o'clock. I wrote to John, ironed the linen, packed up. Lay in the orchard all the afternoon. In the morning Wm. nailed up the trees while I was ironing. We lay sweetly in the orchard. The well is beautiful. The orchard full of foxgloves. The honeysuckle beautiful – plenty of roses, but they are battered. Wrote to Molly Ritson [?] and Coleridge. Walked on the White Moss. Glow-worms. Well for them children are in bed when they shine.

[July] 8th, Thursday. A rainy morning. I paid Thomas Ashburner and Frank Baty. When I was coming home, a post-chaise passed with a little girl behind in a patched, ragged red cloak [?]. We sat in tranquillity together by the fire in the morning. In the afternoon, after we had talked a little, William fell asleep. I read the *Winter's Tale*; then I went to bed, but did not sleep. The swallows stole in and out of their nest, and sate there, *whiles* quite still, *whiles* they sung low for two minutes or more at a time just like a muffled robin. William was looking at *The Pedlar* when I got up. He arranged it, and after tea I wrote it out – 280 lines. In the meantime the evening being fine he carried his coat to the tailor's, and went to George Mackareth's to engage the horse. He came in to me at about ½ past nine pressing me to go out; he had got letters which we were to read out of doors – I was rather unwilling, fearing I could not see to read the letters, but I saw well enough. One was from M.H., a very tender affecting letter, another from Sara to C., from C. to us, and from my Br. Rd. The moon was behind. William hurried me out in hopes that I should see her. We walked first to the top of the hill to see Rydale. It was dark and dull, but our own vale was very solemn – the shape of Helm Crag was quite distinct, though black. We walked backwards and forwards on the White Moss path; there was a sky-like white brightness on the lake. The Wyke cottage light at the foot of Silver How. Glow-worms out, but not so numerous as last night. O, beautiful place! Dear Mary, William. The horse is come – Friday morning – so I must give over. William is eating his broth. I must prepare to go. The swallows, I must leave them, the well, the garden, the roses, all. Dear creatures!! they sang last night after I was in bed – seemed to be singing to one another, just before they settled to rest for the night. Well, I must go. Farewell.

II

'What wonder if a Poet now and then,
Among the many movements of his mind,
Felt for thee [England] as a lover or a child.'

On Friday morning, July 9th, William and I set forward to Keswick on our road to Gallow Hill. We had a pleasant ride, though the day was showery. It rained heavily when Nelly Mackareth took the horse from us, at the Blacksmith's. Coleridge met us at Sara's Rock. He had inquired about us before of Nelly Mackareth and we had been told by a handsome man, an inhabitant of Wytheburn, with whom he had been talking (and who seemed, by the bye, much pleased with his companion), that C. was waiting for us. We reached Keswick against tea-time. We called at Calvert's on the Saturday evening. On Sunday I was poorly and the day was wet, so we could not move from Keswick, but on Monday 12th July 1802 we went to Eusemere. Coleridge walked with us 6 or 7 miles. He was not well, and we had a melancholy parting after having sate together in silence by the road-side. We turned aside to explore the country near Hutton-John, and had a new and delightful walk. The valley, which is subject to the decaying mansion that stands at its head, seems to join its testimony to that of the house to the falling away of the family greatness. The hedges are in bad condition, the land wants draining, and is overrun with brackens, yet there is a something everywhere that tells of its former possessors. The trees are left scattered about as if intended to be like a park, and these are very interesting, standing as they do upon the sides of the steep hills that slope down to the bed of the river, a little stony-bedded stream that spreads out to a considerable breadth at the village of Dacre. A little above Dacre we came into the right road to Mr Clarkson's, after having walked through woods and fields, never exactly knowing whether we were right or wrong. We learnt, however, that we had saved half-a-mile. We sate down by the river-side to rest, and saw some swallows flying about and about under the bridge, and two little schoolboys were loitering among the scars seeking after their nests. We reached Mr Clarkson's at about eight o'clock after a sauntering walk, having lingered and loitered and sate down together that we might be alone. Mr and Mrs C. were just come from Luff's.

We spent Tuesday, the 13th of July, at Eusemere; and on Wednesday morning, the 14th, we walked to Emont Bridge, and mounted the coach between Bird's Nest and Hartshorn Tree. Mr Clarkson's bitch followed us so far. A soldier and his young wife wanted to be taken up by that Coachman, but there was no room. We had a chearful ride though cold till we got on to Stain-moor, and then a heavy shower came on, but we buttoned our-selves up both together in the Guard's coat, and we liked the hills and the rain the better for bringing us so close to one another – I never rode more snugly. At last however it grew so very rainy that I was obliged to go into the coach at Bowes. Lough of Pen-rith was there and very impertinent – I was right glad to get out again to my own dear Brother at Greta Bridge; the sun shone chearfully, and a glorious ride we had over Gaterly Moor. Every building was bathed in golden light. The trees were more bright than earthly trees, and we saw round us miles beyond miles – Darlington spire, etc. etc. We reached Leeming Lane at about 9 o'clock: supped comfortably, and enjoyed our fire.

On Thursday morning, at a little before seven, being the 15th July, we got into a post-chaise and went to Thirsk to breakfast. We were well treated, but when the landlady understood that we were going to *walk* off, and leave our luggage behind, she threw out some saucy words in our hearing. The day was very hot, and we rested often and long before we reached the foot of the Hambledon Hills, and while we were climbing them, still oftener. We had a sandwich in our pockets which we finished when we had climbed part of the hill, and we were almost over-powered with thirst, when I heard the trickling of a little stream of water. I was before William, and I stopped till he came up to me. We sate a long time by this water, and climbed the hill slowly. I was footsore, the sun shone hot, the little Scotch cattle panted and tossed fretfully about. The view was hazy, and we could see nothing from the top of the hill but an indistinct wide-spreading country, full of trees, but the buildings, towns, and houses were lost. We stopped to examine that curious stone, then walked along the flat common. It was now cooler, but I was still footsore and could not walk quick, so I left William sitting two or three times, and when he followed me he took a sheep for me, and then me for a sheep. I rested opposite the Sign of the Sportsman and was questioned by the Landlady. Arrived very hungry at Rivaux. Nothing to eat at the Millers, as we expected, but at an exquisitely neat farmhouse we got some boiled milk and bread; this strengthened us, and I went down to look at the ruins. Thrushes were singing, cattle feeding among green-grown hillocks about the ruins. These hillocks were scattered over with *grovelets* of wild roses and other shrubs, and covered with wild flowers. I could have stayed in this solemn quiet spot till evening, without a thought of moving, but William was waiting for me, so in a quarter of an hour I went away. We walked upon Mr Duncombe's terrace and looked down upon the Abbey. It stands in a larger valley among a brotherhood of valleys, of different length and breadth, – all woody, and running up into the hills in all directions. We reached Helmsly just at dusk. We had a beautiful view of the castle from the top of the hill, slept at a very nice inn, and were well treated – bright bellows and floors as smooth as ice. On Friday morning, 16th July, we walked to Kirby. Met people coming to Helmsly fair. Were misdirected, and walked a mile out of our way – met a double horse at Kirby. A beautiful view above Pickering – Sinnington village very beautiful. Met Mary and Sara seven miles from G.H. Sheltered from the rain; beautiful glen, spoiled by the large house – sweet church and churchyard. Arrived at Gallow Hill at 7 o'clock.

July 16th, Friday Evening. The weather bad, almost all the time. Sara, Tom, and I rode up Bedale. Wm., Mary, Sara, and I went to Scarborough, and we walked in the Abbey pasture, and to Wykeham; and on Monday, the 26th, we went off with Mary in a post-chaise. We had an interesting ride over the Wolds, though it rained all the way. Single thorn bushes were scattered about on the turf, sheep-sheds here and there, and now and then a little hut. Swelling grounds, and sometimes a single tree or a clump of trees. Mary was very sick, and every time we stopped to open a gate she felt the motion of her whole body – indeed I was sick too, and perhaps the smooth gliding of the chaise over the turf made us worse. We passed through one or two little villages, embosomed in tall trees. After we had parted from Mary, there were gleams of sunshine, but with showers. We saw Beverley in a heavy rain, and yet were much pleased with the beauty of the town. Saw the Minster – a pretty, clean building, but injured very much with Grecian architecture. The country between Beverley and Hull very rich, but miserably flat – brick houses, windmills, houses again – dull and endless. Hull a frightful, dirty, brick-housey, tradesmanlike, rich, vulgar place; yet the river, though the shores are so low that they can hardly be seen, looked beautiful with the evening lights upon it, and boats moving about. We walked a long time, and returned to our dull day-room but quiet evening one, quiet and our own, to supper.

July 27th, Tuesday. Market day. Streets dirty, very rainy, did not leave Hull till 4 o'clock, and left Barton at about six; rained all the way almost. A beautiful village at the foot of a hill with trees. A gentleman's house converted into a lady's boarding-school. We had a woman in bad health in the coach and took in a lady and her daughter – supper at Lincoln, duck and peas, and cream cheese – paid 2/–. We left Lincoln on Wednesday morning, 28th July, at six o'clock. It rained heavily, and we could see nothing but the antientry of some of the buildings as we passed along. The night before, however, we had seen enough to make us regret this. The minster stands at the edge of a hill overlooking an immense plain. The country very flat as we went along – the day mended. We went to see the outside of the Minster while the passengers were dining at Peterborough; the West End very grand. The little girl, who was a great scholar and plainly her Mother's favourite, though she had a large family at home, had bought 'The Farmer's Boy'.[1] She said it was written by a man without education and was very wonderful.

On Thursday morning, 29th, we arrived in London. Wm. left

---

1. Poem by Robert Bloomfield, 1800.

me at the Inn. I went to bed, etc. etc. After various troubles and disasters, we left London on Saturday morning at ½-past 5 or 6, the 31st of July. (I have forgot which.) We mounted the Dover Coach at Charing Cross. It was a beautiful morning. The city, St Paul's, with the river and a multitude of little boats, made a most beautiful sight as we crossed Westminster Bridge. The houses were not overhung by their cloud of smoke, and they were spread out endlessly, yet the sun shone so brightly, with such a fierce light, that there was even something like the purity of one of nature's own grand spectacles.

COMPOSED UPON WESTMINSTER BRIDGE

Earth has not anything to show more fair:
Dull would he be of soul who could pass by
A sight so touching in its majesty:
This City now doth, like a garment, wear
The beauty of the morning; silent, bare,
Ships, towers, domes, theatres, and temples lie
Open unto the fields, and to the sky;
All bright and glittering in the smokeless air.
Never did sun more beautifully steep
In his first splendour, valley, rock, or hill;
Ne'er saw I, never felt, a calm so deep!
The river glideth at his own sweet will:
Dear God! the very houses seem asleep;
And all that mighty heart is lying still!

The sonnet was always dated 3 September by Wordsworth. It was clearly inspired by this occasion but it is possible that he completed it when he returned to London in September.

We rode on chearfully, now with the Paris diligence before us, now behind. We walked up the steep hills, a beautiful prospect everywhere, till we even reached Dover. At first the rich, populous, wide-spreading, woody country about London, then the River Thames, ships sailing, chalk cliffs, trees, little villages. Afterwards Canterbury, situated on a plain, rich and woody, but the City and Cathedral disappointed me. Hop grounds on each side of the road some miles from Canterbury, then we came to a common, the race ground, an elevated plain, villages among trees in the bed of a valley at our right, and, rising above this valley, green hills scattered over with wood, neat gentlemen's houses. One white house, almost hid with green trees, which we longed for, and the parson's house, as neat a place as could be, which would just have suited Coleridge. No doubt we might have found one for Tom Hutchinson and Sara, and a good farm too. We halted at a half-way house – fruit carts under the shade of trees, seats for guests, a tempting place to the weary traveller. Still, as we went along, the country was beautiful, hilly, with cottages lurking under the hills, and their little plots of hop ground like vineyards. It was a bad hop year. A woman on the top of the coach said to me, 'It is a sad thing for the poor people, for the hop-gathering is the women's harvest; there is employment about the hops both for women and children.'

We saw the castle of Dover, and the sea beyond, 4 or 5 miles before we reached D. We looked at it through a long vale, the castle being upon an eminence, as it seemed, at the end of this vale, which opened to the sea. The country now became less fertile, but near Dover it seemed more rich again. Many buildings stand on the flat fields, sheltered with tall trees. There is one old chapel that might have been there just in the same state in which it now is when this vale was as retired, and as little known to travellers as our own Cumberland mountain wilds 30 years ago. There was also a very old building on the other side of the road, which had a strange effect among the many new ones that are springing up everywhere. It seemed odd that it could have kept itself pure in its ancientry among so many upstarts. It was near dark when we reached Dover. We were told that the packet was about to sail, so we went down to the custom-house in half-an-hour – had our luggage examined, etc. etc., and then we drank tea with the Honourable Mr Knox and his tutor. We arrived at Calais at 4 o'clock on Sunday morning, the 1st of August. We stayed in the vessel till ½ past 7, then William went for letters, at about ½ past 8 or 9 we found out Annette and C. chez Madame Avril dans la Rue de la Tête d'or. We lodged opposite two ladies, in tolerably decent-sized rooms, but badly furnished and with large store of bad smells and dirt in the yard, and all about. The weather was very hot. We walked by the sea-shore almost every evening with Annette and Caroline, or Wm. and I alone. I had a bad cold, and could not bathe at first, but William did. It was a pretty sight to see, as we walked upon the sands when the tide was low, perhaps a hundred people bathing about a quarter of a mile distant from us, and we had delightful walks after the heat of the day was passed away – seeing far off in the west the coast of England like a cloud crested with Dover Castle, which was but like the summit of the cloud – the evening star and the glory of the sky.

COMPOSED BY THE SEA-SIDE, NEAR CALAIS, AUGUST 1802

Fair Star of evening, Splendour of the west,
Star of my Country ! – on the horizon's brink
Thou hangest, stopping, as might seem, to sink
On England's bosom; yet well pleased to rest,
Meanwhile and be to her a glorious crest
Conspicuous to the Nations. Thou, I think,
Should'st be my Country's emblem; and should'st wink,
Bright Star ! with laughter on her banners, drest
In thy fresh beauty. There ! that dusky spot
Beneath thee, that is England; there she lies.
Blessings be on you both; one hope, one lot,
One life, one glory ! – I, with many a fear
For my dear Country, many heartfelt sighs,
Among men who do not love her, linger here.

The reflections in the water were more beautiful than the sky itself, purple waves brighter than precious stones, for ever melting away upon the sands. The fort, a wooden building, at the entrance of the harbour at Calais, when the evening twilight was coming on, and we could not see anything of the building but its shape, which was far more distinct than in perfect daylight, seemed to be reared upon pillars of ebony, between which pillars the sea was seen in the most beautiful colours that can be conceived. Nothing in romance was ever half so beautiful. Now came in view, as the evening star sank down, and the colours of the west faded away, the two lights of England, lighted up by Englishmen in our country, to warn vessels off rocks or sands. These we used to see from the pier, when we could see no other distant objects but the clouds, the sky, and the sea itself: All was dark behind. The town of Calais seemed deserted of the light of heaven, but there was always light and life and joy upon the sea.

One night, though, I shall never forget – the day had been very hot, and William and I walked alone together upon the pier. The sea was gloomy, for there was a blackness over all the sky, except when it was overspread with lightning, which often revealed to us a distant vessel. Near us the waves roared and broke against the pier, and they were interfused with greenish fiery light. The more distant sea always black and gloomy. It was also beautiful, on the calm hot night, to see the little boats row out of harbour with wings of fire, and the sail boats with the fiery track which they cut as they went along, and which closed up after them with a hundred thousand sparkles, balls, shooting and streams of glow-worm light. Caroline was delighted.

> It is a beauteous evening, calm and free,
> The holy time is quiet as a Nun
> Breathless with adoration; the broad sun
> Is sinking down in its tranquillity;
> The gentleness of heaven broods o'er the Sea :
> Listen ! the mighty Being is awake,
> And doth with his eternal motion make
> A sound like thunder – everlastingly.
> Dear Child ! dear Girl ! that walkest with me here,
> If thou appear untouched by solemn thought,
> Thy nature is not therefore less divine :
> Thou liest in Abraham's bosom all the year;
> And worship'st at the Temple's inner shrine,
> God being with thee when we know it not.

On Sunday, the 29th of August, we left Calais at twelve o'clock in the morning and landed at Dover at one on Monday the 30th.

I was sick all the way. It was very pleasant to me, when we were in harbour at Dover, to breathe the fresh air, and to look up and see the stars among the ropes of the vessel.

COMPOSED IN THE VALLEY NEAR DOVER,
ON DAY OF LANDING

Here, on our native soil, we breathe once more.
The cock that crows, the smoke that curls, that sound
Of bells; those boys who in yon meadow-ground
In white-sleeved shirts are playing; and the roar
Of the waves breaking on the chalky shore : –
All, all are English. Oft have I looked round
With joy in Kent's green vales; but never found
Myself so satisfied in heart before.
Europe is yet in bonds; but let that pass,
Thought for another moment. Thou art free,
My Country ! and 'tis joy enough and pride
For one hour's perfect bliss, to tread the grass
Of England once again, and hear and see,
With such a dear Companion at my side.

The next day was very hot. We both bathed, and sate upon the Dover Cliffs, and looked upon France with many a melancholy and tender thought. We could see the shores almost as plain as if it were but an English lake.

NEAR DOVER, SEPTEMBER 1802

Inland, within a hollow vale, I stood;
And saw, while sea was calm and air was clear,
The coast of France – the coast of France how near !
Drawn almost into frightful neighbourhood.
I shrunk; for verily the barrier flood
Was like a lake, or river bright and fair,
A span of water; yet what power is there !
What mightiness for evil and for good !

Even so doth God protect us if we be
Virtuous and wise. Winds blow, and waters roll,
Strength to the brave, and Power, and Deity;
Yet in themselves are nothing ! One decree
Spake laws to *them*, and said that by the soul
Only, the Nations shall be great and free.

We mounted the coach at ½ past 4, and arrived in London at
6, the 30th August. It was misty, and we could see nothing. We
stayed in London till Wednesday the 22nd of September, and
arrived at Gallow Hill on Friday.

12

'Nor wilt thou then forget
That after many wanderings, many years
Of absence, these steep woods and lofty cliffs,
And this green pastoral landscape, were to me
More dear, both for themselves and for thy sake!'

[*Friday,*] *Septembtr 24th*. Mary first met us in the avenue. She looked so fat and well that we were made very happy by the sight of her; then came Sara, and last of all Joanna. Tom was forking corn, standing upon the corn cart. We dressed ourselves immediately and got tea – the garden looked gay with asters and sweet peas. Jack and George came on Friday evening, 1st October. On Saturday, 2nd, we rode to Hackness, William, Jack, George, and Sara single – I behind Tom. On Sunday 3rd, Mary and Sara were busy packing.

On Monday, 4th October 1802, my brother William was married to Mary Hutchinson. I slept a good deal of the night, and rose fresh and well in the morning. At a little after 8 o'clock I saw them go down the avenue towards the church. William had parted from me upstairs. When they were absent my dear little Sara prepared the breakfast. I kept myself as quiet as I could, but when I saw the two men running up the walk, coming to tell us it was over, I could stand it no longer, and threw myself on the bed, where I lay in stillness, neither hearing or seeing anything till Sara came upstairs to me, and said, 'They are coming'. This forced me from the bed where I lay, and I moved, I knew not how, straight forward, faster than my strength could carry me, till I met my beloved William, and fell upon his bosom. He and John Hutchinson led me to the house, and there I stayed to welcome my dear Mary. As soon as we had breakfasted, we departed. It rained when we set off. Poor Mary was much agitated, when she parted from her brothers and sisters, and her home. Nothing particular occurred till we reached Kirby. We had sunshine and showers, pleasant talk, love and chearfulness. We were obliged to stay two hours at K. while the horses were feeding. We wrote a few lines to Sara, and then walked out; the sun shone, and we went to the churchyard after we had put a letter into the post-office for the York Herald. We sauntered about, and read the gravestones. There was one to the memory of five children, who had all died within five years, and the longest lived had only lived four years. There was another stone erected to the memory of an unfortunate woman (as we supposed, by a stranger). The verses engraved upon it expressed that she had been neglected by her relations, and counselled the readers of those words to look within, and recollect their own frailties. We left Kirby at about half-past two. There is not much variety of prospect from K. to Helmsley, but the country is very pleasant, being rich and woody, and Helmsley itself stands very sweetly at the foot of the rising grounds of Duncombe Park, which is scattered over with tall woods; and, lifting itself above the common buildings of the town, stands Helmsley Castle, now a ruin, formerly inhabited by the gay Duke of Buckingham. Every foot of the road was, of itself, interesting to us, for we had travelled along it on foot, Wm. and I, when we went to fetch our dear Mary, and had sate upon the turf by the roadside more than once. Before we reached Helmsley, our driver told us that he could not take us any further, so we stopped at the same inn where we had slept before. My heart danced at the sight of its cleanly outside, bright yellow walls, casements overshadowed with jasmine, and its low, double gavel-ended front. We were not shown into the same parlour where Wm. and I were; it was a small room with a drawing over the chimney piece which the woman told us had been bought at a sale. Mary and I warmed ourselves at the kitchen fire. We then walked into the garden, and looked over a gate, up to the old ruin which stands at the top of a mount, and round about it the moats are grown up into soft green cradles, hollows surrounded with green grassy hillocks, and there are overshadowed by old trees, chiefly ashes. I prevailed upon William to go up with me to the ruins. We left Mary sitting by the kitchen fire. The sun shone, it was warm and very pleasant. One part of the castle seems to be inhabited. There was a man mowing nettles in the open space which had most likely once been the castle-court. There is one gateway exceedingly beautiful. Children were playing upon the sloping ground. We came home by the street. After about an hour's delay we set forward again, had an excellent driver, who opened the gates so dexterously that the horses never stopped. Mary was very much delighted with the view of the castle from the point where we had seen it before. I was pleased to see again the little path which we had walked upon, the gate I had climbed over, and the road down which we had seen the two little boys drag a log of wood, and a team of horses struggle under the weight of a great load of timber. We had felt compassion for the poor horses that were under the governance of oppressive and ill-judging drivers, and for the poor boys, who seemed of an age to have been able to have dragged the log of wood merely out of the love of their own activity, but from poverty and bad food they panted for weakness, and were obliged to fetch their father from the town to help them. Duncombe House looks well from the road – a large building, though I believe only two-thirds of the original design are completed. We rode down a very steep hill to Rivaux valley, with woods all round us. We stopped upon the bridge to look at the Abbey, and again when we had crossed it. Dear Mary had never seen a ruined abbey before except Whitby. We recognised the cottages, houses, and the little valleys as we went along. We walked up a long hill, the road carrying us up the cleft or valley with woody hills on each side of us. When we went to G. H. I had walked down the valley alone. William followed me.

It was not dark evening when we passed the little publick house, but before we had crossed the Hambledon Hill, and reached the point overlooking Yorkshire, it was quite dark. We had not wanted, however, fair prospects before us, as we drove along the flat plain of the high hill. Far far off us, in the western sky, we saw shapes of castles, ruins among groves, a great spreading wood, rocks, and single trees, a minster with its tower unusually distinct, minarets in another quarter, and a round Grecian Temple also; the colours of the sky of a bright grey, and the forms of a sober grey, with a dome. As we descended the hill there was no distinct view, but of a great space; only near us we saw the wild and (as the people say) bottomless tarn in the hollow at the side of the hill. It seemed to be made visible to us only by its own light, for all the hill about us was dark.

Dark and more dark the shades of evening fell;
The wished-for point was reached – but at an hour
When little could be gained from that rich dower
Of prospect, whereof many thousands tell.
Yet did the glowing west with marvellous power
Salute us; there stood Indian citadel,
Temple of Greece, and minster with its tower
Substantially expressed – a place for bell
Or clock to toll from ! Many a tempting isle,
With groves that never were imagined, lay
'Mid seas how steadfast ! objects all for the eye
Of silent rapture; but we felt the while
We should forget them; they are of the sky,
And from our earthly memory fade away.

*Although Wordsworth says he wrote this one the day of his mar-
riage, it is so like this passage in the Journal that he may have
written the sonnet after reading Dorothy's account much later.
Equally Dorothy would not have written in her Journal until she
arrived at Grasmere and may have been echoing William's poem.*

Before we reached Thirsk we saw a light before us, which we at
first thought was the moon, the lime-kilns; but when we drove
into the market-place it proved a large bonfire, with lads dancing
round it, which is a sight I dearly love. The inn was like an illu-
minated house – every room full. We asked the cause, and were
told by the girl that it was 'Mr John Bell's birthday, that he had
heired his estate !' The landlady was very civil. She did not recog-
nise the despised foot-travellers. We rode nicely in the dark, and
reached Leeming Lane at eleven o'clock. I am always sorry to get
out of a chaise when it is night. The people of the house were
going to bed and we were not very well treated, though we got
a hot supper. We breakfasted next morning and set off at about
½ past 8 o'clock. It was a chearful, sunny morning. We soon
turned out of Leeming Lane and passed a nice village with a
beautiful church. We had a few showers, but when we came to
the green fields of Wensley, the sun shone upon them all, and the

Ure in its many windings glittered as it flowed along under the green slopes of Middleham and Middleham Castle. Mary looked about her for her friend Mr Place, and thought she had him sure on the contrary side of the vale from that on which we afterwards found that he lived. We went to a new built house at Leyburn, the same village where William and I had dined with George Hutchinson on our road to Grasmere 2 years and ¾ ago, but not the same house. The landlady was very civil, giving us cake and wine, but the horses being out we were detained at least two hours, and did not set off till 2 o'clock. We paid for 35 miles, i.e. to Sedbergh, but the landlady did not encourage us to hope to get beyond Hawes. A shower came on just after we left the inn – while the rain beat against the windows we ate our dinners, which M. and W. heartily enjoyed – I was not quite well. When we passed through the village of Wensley my heart was melted away with dear recollections – the bridge, the little waterspout, the steep hill, the church. They are among the most vivid of my own inner visions, for they were the first objects that I saw after we were left to ourselves, and had turned our whole hearts to Grasmere as a home in which we were to rest. The vale looked most beautiful each way. To the left the bright silver stream inlaid the flat and very green meadows, winding like a serpent. To the right we did not see it so far, it was lost among trees and little hills. I could not help observing, as we went along, how much more varied the prospects of Wensley Dale are in the summer time than I could have thought possible in the winter. This seemed to be in great measure owing to the trees being in leaf, and forming groves and screens, and thence little openings upon recesses and concealed retreats, which in winter only made a part of the one great vale. The *beauty* of the summer time here as much excels that of the winter, as the variety, owing to the excessive greenness of the fields, and the trees in leaf half concealing, and, where they do not conceal, softening the hard bareness of the limey white roofs. One of our horses seemed to grow a little restive as we went through the first village, a long village on the side of a hill. It grew worse and worse, and at last we durst not go on any longer. We walked a while, and then the post boy was obliged to take the horse out, and go back for another. We seated ourselves again snugly in the post-chaise. The wind struggled about us and rattled the window, and gave a gentle motion to the chaise, but we were warm and at our ease within. Our station was at the top of a hill, opposite Bolton Castle, the Ure flowing beneath. William has since wrote a sonnet on this our imprisonment. 'Hard was thy durance, Queen! compared with ours.' Poor Mary!

In a note to Isabella Fenwick, Wordsworth explains how he wrote this sonnet to beguile the time and contrast the Queen's confinement with their own, but, he adds, 'it was not thought worthy of being preserved'.

Wm. fell asleep, lying upon my breast, and I upon Mary. I lay motionless for a long time, but I was at last obliged to move. I became very sick and continued so for some time after the boy brought the horse to us. Mary had been a little sick but it soon went off. We had a sweet ride till we came to a publick-house on the side of a hill, where we alighted and walked down to see the waterfalls.

Throughout this passage there are echoes of Wordsworth's first letter to Coleridge on arriving at Grasmere which is printed at the beginning of this book. Poor Dorothy cannot help a wistful note creeping in as she remembers their first happy journey there 'after we were left to ourselves and had turned our whole hearts to Grasmere . . .'.

The sun was not set, and the woods and fields were spread over with the yellow light of evening, which made their greenness a thousand times more green. There was too much water in the river for the beauty of the falls, and even the banks were less interesting than in winter. Nature had entirely got the better in her struggles against the giants who first cast the mould of these works; for, indeed, it is a place that did not in winter remind one of God, but one could not help feeling as if there had been the agency of some 'mortal instruments', which Nature had been struggling against without making a perfect conquest. There was something so wild and new in this feeling, knowing, as we did in the inner man, that God alone had laid his hand upon it, that I could not help regretting the want of it; besides, it is a pleasure to a real lover of Nature to give winter all the glory he can, for summer will make its own way and speak its own praises. We saw the pathway which William and I took at the close of evening, the path leading to the rabbit warren where we lost ourselves. The farm, with its holly hedges, was lost among the green hills and hedgerows in general, but we found it out, and were glad to look at it again. When William had left us to seek the water falls, Mary and I were frightened by a cow.

At our return to the inn, we found new horses and a new driver, and we went on nicely to Hawes, where we arrived before it was quite dark. Mary and I got tea and William had a partridge and mutton chops and tarts for his supper. Mary sate down with him. We also had a shilling's worth of negus, and Mary made me some broth, for all which supper we were only charged 2/−. I could not sit up long, I vomited and took the broth and then slept sweetly. We rose at six o'clock – a rainy morning. We had a good breakfast and then departed. There was a very pretty view about a mile from Hawes, where we crossed a bridge; bare and very green fields with cattle, a glittering stream, cottages, a few ill-grown trees, and high hills. The sun shone now. Before we got upon the bare hills, there was a hunting lodge on our right, exactly like Greta Hill, with fir plantations about it. We were very fortunate in the day, gleams of sunshine, passing clouds, that travelled with their shadows below them. Mary was much pleased with Garsdale. It was a dear place to William and me. We noted well the publick-house (Garsdale Hall) where we had baited, and drunk our pint of ale, and afterwards the mountain which had been adorned by Jupiter in his glory when we were here before. It was mid-day when we reached Sedbergh, and market day. We were in the same room where we had spent the evening together in our road to Grasmere. We had a pleasant ride to Kendal, where we arrived at about 2 o'clock. The day favoured us. M. and I went to see the house where dear Sara had lived, then we went to seek Mr Bonsfield's shop, but we found him not. He had sold all his goods the day before. We then went to the Pot-woman's, and bought 2 jugs and a dish, and some paper at Pennington's. When we came to the Inn William was almost ready for us. The afternoon was not chearful but it did not rain till we came near Windermere. I am always glad to see Stavely; it is a place I dearly love to think of – the first mountain village that I came to with

Wm. when we first began our pilgrimage together. Here we drank a bason of milk at a publick house, and here I washed my feet in the brook, and put on a pair of silk stockings by Wm.'s advice. Nothing particular occurred till we reached Ings chapel. The door was open, and we went in. It is a neat little place, with a marble floor and marble communion table, with a painting over it of the last supper, and Moses and Aaron on each side. The woman told us that 'they had painted them as near as they could by the dress- es as they are described in the Bible', and gay enough they are. The marble had been sent by Richard Bateman[1] from Leghorn. The woman told us that a man had been at her house a few days before, who told her he had helped to bring it down the Red Sea, and she had believed him gladly! It rained very hard when we reached Windermere. We sate in the rain at Wilcock's to change horses and arrived at Grasmere at about 6 o'clock on Wednesday evening, the 6th of October 1802. Molly was overjoyed to see us, for my part I cannot describe what I felt, and our dear Mary's feelings would I daresay not be easy to speak of. We went by candle light into the garden, and were astonished at the growth of the brooms, Portugal laurels, etc. etc. etc. The next day, Thurs- day, we unpacked the boxes. On Friday, 8th, we baked bread and Mary and I walked, first upon the hill-side, and then in John's Grove, then in view of Rydale, the first walk that I had taken with my sister.

[October] 11th, Monday. A beautiful day. We walked to the Easedale hills to hunt waterfalls.

A favourite pastime of theirs and the final line of 'Louisa'. Wordsworth almost certainly had Dorothy in mind in this poem. It seems to describe her perfectly. It was written at the same time as 'Dear Child of Nature' which was published on 11 February 1802.

1. The story of Richard Bateman comes into 'Michael', lines 258–70 (see p. 96). He was in fact called Robert, as is shown by a tablet in the chapel at Ings.

After accompanying her on a mountain excursion

I met Louisa in the shade,
And, having seen that lovely Maid,
Why should I fear to say
That, nymph-like, she is fleet and strong,
And down the rocks can leap along
Like rivulets in May?

She loves her fire, her cottage-home;
Yet o'er the moorland will she roam
In weather rough and bleak;
And, when against the wind she strains,
Oh ! might I kiss the mountain rains
That sparkle on her cheek.

Take all that's mine 'beneath the moon',
If I with her but half a noon
May sit beneath the walls
Of some old cave, or mossy nook,
When up she winds along the brook
To hunt the waterfalls.

William and Mary left me sitting on a stone on the solitary mountains, and went to Easedale tarn. I grew chilly and followed them. This approach to the tarn is very beautiful. We expected to have found C. at home, but he did not come till after dinner. He was well, but did not look so.

October 12, Tuesday. We walked with C. to Rydale.

[October] 13th, *Wednesday.* Set forwards with him towards Keswick, and he prevailed us to go on. We consented, Mrs C. not being at home. The day was delightful. We drank tea at John Stanley's. Wrote to Annette.

[October] 23rd, Saturday. Mary was baking. I walked with Wm. to see Langdale, Rydale and the foot of Grasmere. We had a heavenly walk, but I came home in the toothache and have since that day been confined upstairs till now, namely, Saturday, 30th October, 1802.

October 30th, Saturday. William is gone to Keswick. Mary went with him to the top of the Rays. She is returned, and is now sitting near me by the fire. It is a breathless, grey day, that leaves the golden woods of autumn quiet in their own tranquillity, stately and beautiful in their decaying; the lake is a perfect mirror.

William met Stoddart at the bridge at the foot of Legberthwaite dale. He returned with him and they surprized us by their arrival at four o'clock in the afternoon. Stoddart and W. dined. I went to bed, and after tea S. read Chaucer to us.

October 31st, Sunday. John Monkhouse called. William and S. went to K[eswick]. Mary and I walked to the top of the hill and looked at Rydale. I was much affected when I stood upon the second bar of Sara's gate. The lake was perfectly still, the sun shone on hill and vale, the distant birch trees looked like large golden flowers. Nothing else in colour was distinct and separate, but all the beautiful colours seemed to be melted into one another, and joined together in one mass, so that there were no differences, though an endless variety, when one tried to find it out. The fields were of one sober yellow brown. After dinner we both lay on the floor – Mary slept. I could not for I was thinking of so many things. We sate nicely together after tea looking over old letters. Molly was gone up to Mr Simpson's to see Mrs S. who was very ill.

[November] 7th, Sunday. Fine weather. Letters from Coleridge that he was gone to London. Sara at Penrith. I wrote to Mrs Clarkson. Wm. began to translate Ariosto.[1]

---

1. Wordsworth translated two books of Ariosto's *Orlando Furioso*, of which only stanzas 5 to 14 of the first Canto remain.

[November] 8th, Monday. A beautiful day. William got to work again at Ariosto, and so continued all the morning, though the day was so delightful that it made my very heart linger to be out of doors, and see and feel the beauty of the autumn in freedom. The trees on the opposite side of the lake are of a yellow brown, but there are one or two trees opposite our windows (an ash tree, for instance) quite green, as in spring. The fields are of their winter colour, but the island is as green as ever it was. Mary has been baking today, she is now sitting in the parlour. William is writing out his stanzas from Ariosto. We have a nice fire – the evening is quiet. Poor Coleridge ! Sara is at Keswick, I hope. William has been ill in his stomach, but he is better tonight. I have read one canto of Ariosto today.

December 24th, Christmas Eve. William is now sitting by me, at ½ past 10 o'clock. I have been beside him ever since tea running the heel of a stocking, repeating some of his sonnets to him, listening to his own repeating, reading some of Milton's and the *Allegro* and *Penseroso*. It is a quiet keen frost. Mary is in the parlour below attending to the baking of cakes, and Jenny Fletcher's pies. Sara is in bed in the toothache, and so we are [?]. My beloved William is turning over the leaves of Charlotte Smith's sonnets, but he keeps his hand to his poor chest, pushing aside his breastplate. Mary is well and I am well, and Molly is as blithe as last year at this time. Coleridge came this morning with Wedgwood. We all turned out of Wm.'s bedroom one by one, to meet him. He looked well. We had to tell him of the birth of his little girl, born yesterday morning at 6 o'clock. Wm. went with them to Wytheburn in the chaise, and M. and I met W. on the Rays. It was not an unpleasant morning to the feeling ! far from it. The sun shone now and then, and there was no wind, but all things looked chearless and distinct ; no meltings of sky into mountains, the mountains like stone work wrought up with huge hammers. Last Sunday was as mild a day as I ever remember. We all set off together to walk. I went to Rydale and Wm. returned with me. M. and S. went round the lakes. There were flowers of various kinds – the topmost bell of a foxglove, geraniums, daisies, a buttercup in the water (but this I saw two or three days before), small yellow flowers (I do not know their name) in the turf, a large bunch of strawberry blossoms. Wm. sate a while with me, then went to meet M. and S. Last Saturday I dined at Mr Simpson's, also a beautiful mild day. Monday was a frosty day and it has been frost ever since. It is to-day Christmas Day, Saturday 25th December 1802. I am thirty-one years of age. It is a dull, frosty day.

Again I have neglected to write my Journal – New Year's Day is passed, Old Christmas day and I have recorded nothing. It is today *Tuesday*, January 11th. On Christmas day I dressed myself ready to go [to] Keswick in a returned chaise, but did not go. On Thursday, 30th December, I went to K. William rode before me to the foot of the hill nearest K. There we parted close to a little watercourse, which was then noisy with water, but on my return a dry channel. We ate some potted beef on horseback and sweet cake. We stopped our horse close to the hedge, opposite a turf of primroses, three flowers in full blossom and a bud. They reared themselves up among the green moss. We debated long whether we should pluck [them], and at last left them to live out their day, which I was right glad of at my return the Sunday following; for there they remained, uninjured either by cold or wet. I stayed at K. over New Year's Day, and returned on Sunday, the 2nd January. Wm. Mackareth fetched me – (M. and S. walked as far as John Stanley's) – Wm. was alarmed at my long delay, and came to within three miles of Keswick. He mounted before me. It had been a sweet mild day and was a pleasant evening. C. stayed with us till Tuesday, January 4th. Wm. and I walked up to George M.'s to endeavour to get the horse, then walked with him to Ambleside. We parted with him at the turning of the lane, he going on horseback to the top of Kirkstone. On Thursday 6th C. returned, and on Friday, the 7th, he and Sara went to Keswick. W. accompanied them to the foot of Wytheburn. I to Mrs Simpson's, and dined, and called on Aggy Fleming sick in bed. It was a gentle day, and when Wm. and I returned home just before sunset, it was a heavenly evening. A soft sky was among the hills, and a summer sunshine above, blending with this sky, for it was more like sky than clouds. The turf looked warm and soft.

Jan[uary] 8th, Saturday. Wm. and I walked to Rydale – no letters. Still as mild as spring – a beautiful moonlight evening and a quiet night, but before morning the wind rose, and it became dreadfully cold. We were not well, Mary and I.

[January] 9th, Sunday. Mary lay long in bed and did not walk. Wm. and I walked in Brother's Wood. I was astonished with the beauty of the place for I had never been here since my return home – never since before I went away in June ! ! Wrote to Miss Lamb.

January 10th, 1803, Monday. I lay in bed to have a drench of sleep till one o'clock. Worked all day – petticoats – Mrs C'.s wrists. Ran Wm.'s woollen stockings, for he put them on today for the first time. We walked to Rydale and brought letters from Sara, Annette and [?] – furiously cold.

January 11th, Tuesday. A very cold day. Wm. promised me he would rise as soon as I had carried him his breakfast, but he lay in bed till between 12 and 1. We talked of walking, but the blackness of the cold made us slow to put forward, and we did not walk at all. Mary read the Prologue to Chaucer's tales to me in the morning. William was working at his poem to C. Letter from Keswick and from Taylor on Wm.'s marriage. C. poorly, in bad spirits. Canaries. Before tea I sate 2 hours in the parlour. Read part of The Knight's Tale with exquisite delight. Since tea Mary has been down stairs copying out Italian poems for Stuart. William has been working beside me, and here ends this imperfect summary. I will take a nice Calais Book, and will for the future write regularly and, if I can, legibly; so much for this my resolution on Tuesday night, January 11th, 1803. Now I am going to take tapioca for my supper, and Mary an egg, William some cold mutton – his poor chest is tired.

Jan[uary] 12th, Wednesday. Very cold, and cold all the week.

[*January*] 16th, *Sunday*. Intensely cold. Wm. had a fancy for some ginger bread. I put on Molly's cloak and my Spenser, and we walked towards Matthew Newton's. I went into the house. The blind man and his wife and sister were sitting by the fire, all dressed very clean in their Sunday clothes, the sister reading. They took their little stock of gingerbread out of the cupboard, and I bought 6 pennyworth. They were so grateful when I paid them for it that I could not find it in my heart to tell them we were going to make gingerbread ourselves. I had asked them if they had no thick – 'No,' answered Matthew, 'there was none on Friday, but we'll *endeavour* to get some.' The next day the woman came just when we were baking and we bought 2 pennyworth.

Here, in spite of Dorothy's good resolutions, the Journal finally breaks off. She seems to have been losing heart in it for some weeks. Perhaps because she now shares William with someone else, the impulse to write only for him dies away. In the years that followed, she must often have drawn strength from all he had written about her, such as this final passage from 'Lines composed a few miles above Tintern Abbey' :

> Nor perchance,
> If I were not thus taught, should I the more
> Suffer my genial spirits to decay :
> For thou art with me here upon the banks
> Of this fair river; thou my dearest Friend,
> My dear, dear Friend; and in thy voice I catch
> The language of my former heart, and read
> My former pleasures in the shooting lights
> Of thy wild eyes. Oh ! yet a little while
> May I behold in thee what I was once,
> My dear, dear Sister ! and this prayer I make,
> Knowing that Nature never did betray
> The heart that loved her; 'tis her privilege,
> Through all the years of this our life, to lead
> From joy to joy : for she can so inform
> The mind that is within us, so impress
> With quietness and beauty, and so feed
> With lofty thoughts, that neither evil tongues,

Rash judgements, nor the sneers of selfish men,
 Nor greetings where no kindness is, nor all
The dreary intercourse of daily life,
Shall e'er prevail against us, or disturb
Our cheerful faith, that all which we behold
Is full of blessings. Therefore let the moon
Shine on thee in thy solitary walk;
And let the misty mountain-winds be free
To blow against thee : and, in after years,
When these wild ecstasies shall be matured
Into a sober pleasure; when thy mind
Shall be a mansion for all lovely forms,
Thy memory be as a dwelling-place
For all sweet sounds and harmonies; oh ! then,
If solitude, or fear, or pain, or grief,
Should be thy portion, with what healing thoughts
 Of tender joy wilt thou remember me,
And these my exhortations ! Nor, perchance –
If I should be where I no more can hear
Thy voice, nor catch from thy wild eyes these gleams
Of past existence – wilt thou then forget
That on the banks of this delightful stream
We stood together; and that I, so long
A worshipper of Nature, hither came
Unwearied in that service: rather say
With warmer love – oh ! with far deeper zeal
 Of holier love. Nor wilt thou then forget
That after many wanderings, many years
Of absence, these steep woods and lofty cliffs,
And this green pastoral landscape were to me
More dear, both for themselves and for thy sake !

INDEX OF POEMS

INDEX OF FIRST LINES

MORE ABOUT PENGUINS
AND PELICANS

Penguinews, which appears every month, contains details of all the new books issued by Penguins as they are published. From time to time it is supplemented by our stocklist which includes around 5,000 titles.

A specimen copy of *Penguinews* will be sent to you free on request. Please write to Dept EP, Penguin Books Ltd, Harmondsworth, Middlesex, for your copy.

In the U.S.A.: For a complete list of books available from Penguins in the United States write to Dept CS, Penguin Books, 625 Madison Avenue, New York, New York 10022.

In Canada: For a complete list of books available from Penguins in Canada write to Penguin Books Canada Ltd, 2801 John Street, Markham, Ontario L3R 1B4.